KU-242-020

Oregon Trail

Oregon Trail

By INGVARD HENRY EIDE

Foreword by Ernest S. Osgood

RAND McNALLY & COMPANY
Chicago / New York / San Francisco

DEDICATED

To the Oregon Emigrants

Book Design by MARIO PAGLIAI

Copyright © 1972 by RAND MCNALLY & COMPANY

All rights reserved

Library of Congress Catalog Card Number: 72-4230

Printed in the UNITED STATES OF AMERICA
by RAND MCNALLY & COMPANY

ISBN: 528-81811-2

First printing 1973

ILLUSTRATION CREDITS

American Museum of Natural History, N.Y.C.: 46, 73; Aurora Colony, Oregon: 40, 217, 218; Champoeg Park Museum: 219 (bottom); Die Oeffentliche Kunstsammlung Basel als Eigentümerin: 89, 136 (bottom); R. J. Felling, M.D., Weston, Mo.: 65; Fort Leavenworth Museum: 19, 21, 26, 29, 30, 37; Paul Henderson: 56 (top, right); Idaho State Historical Society, Boise: 171; Kansas State Historical Society, Topeka: 31, 49, 52, 62 (top), 81; R. O. Klotz: 56 (bottom, right); M. Knoedler & Co., Inc., N.Y.C.: 184; Charles W. Martin, Omaha: 67; John F. Merriam, San Francisco, Calif.: 86; Nyle Miller (Kansas State Historical Society, Topeka): 52; Missouri Historical Society: 23, 39; Mr. and Mrs. J. Maxwell Moran, Paoli, Pa.: 70, 153; Newark Museum, Newark, N.J.: 85; Oregon Historical Society, Portland: 16, 190, 201, 202, 204 (bottom), 212, 214, 216; Donald Reynolds, Courtesy St. Joseph Museum: 61; St. Louis Art Museum, gift of Mr. J. Lionberger Davis, St. Louis: 83; State Historical Society of Wisconsin: 45, 108, 147

PHOTOGRAPHS NOT IDENTIFIED

Jacket: Devil's Gate (Wyoming); p. 1: Evening, Near Fort Bridger (Wyoming); p. 2-3: Wildcat Range (Scotts Bluff County, Nebraska); p. 4: Emigrant Carvings, Register Rocks (Guernsey, Wyoming); p. 5: Bear River Country (Idaho); p. 6-7: Uinta Mountains, Near Fort Bridger; p. 9: Wind River Range (Sublette County, Wyoming); p. 12: High Noon on Green River (Sweetwater County, Wyoming)

ACKNOWLEDGMENTS

Grateful appreciation must be tendered to the many spirited local and national historians who made possible this story of the Oregon Trail. The acquisition of historical notes and diaries, guidance along the Oregon Trail, and the physical and moral support expressed wherever and whenever there was need reveal the interest and the historiography of many people. Among those who sincerely cooperated and gave so much time to assist me are Helen and Paul Henderson, Bridgeport, Neb., who were with me uncounted hours on the trail in Wyoming and Nebraska; Ernest S. Osgood; the library staff of the Montana State University, Missoula; Mrs. Clifford M. Sather, Champoeg State Park, Portland, Ore.; Mrs. Ira J. Seitz, D.A.R., Roseburg, Ore.; H. Cranston Fossburg, U.S. Forest Service (ret.), Parkdale, Ore.; Charles W. Martin, Omaha, Neb.; Mrs. E. L. Myers, Portland, Ore.; Sharon Nesbit, Troutdale, Ore.; Charles Osborne, Hastings, Neb.; Matthew Cullen, chief librarian, Oregon Historical Society, Portland; Lawrence Smitton, Pendleton, Ore.; Dr. Merle Wells, Idaho State Historical Society, Boise; Mildred C. Cox, curator, Fort Leavenworth Museum, Kansas; Gene Wuester, Beattie, Kan.; Whitman Mission, National Park Service, Walla Walla, Wash.; Katherine Halverson, Wyoming State Archives and Historical Dept., Cheyenne; John Dalquist, Fort Bridger, Wyo.; Charles Dahlen, Rock Springs, Wyo.; Lyle Hildebrand, Douglas, Wyo.; Nyle Miller, Kansas State Historical Society, Topeka; Burlington Northern, Portland, Ore.; Randall A. Wagner, Wyoming Recreation Commission, Cheyenne. Special thanks to my typist, Margaret McGee, Missoula, Mont.

Contents

THE DISCOVERY OF the New World, coincident with the Renaissance and the Reformation, marked the beginning of a new era in the history of Western civilization. The compass that guided Columbus westward beyond the rim of the known world pointed the way to empire for the Atlantic nations of Europe. On an October night, nearly five centuries ago, the Admiral of the Ocean Sea descried a "light once or twice, and it was like a wax candle, rising and falling." That dim spark, beyond the darkened ocean, was destined to grow in brilliance until it illumined two great continents that reached for ten thousand miles from the polar north to Cape Horn. More than a century later, Captain John Smith exclaimed, " . . . only here and there . . . we have touched . . . the edges of those large dominions which do stretch themselves . . . God doth know how many thousand miles." This New World of sixteen million square miles might be a barrier to Cathay and the Indies, but to the Europeans and their descendants it was a challenge to explore, conquer, settle, and exploit. Every mile of coastline charted, every Indian trail followed, every river traced to its headwaters, every pass surmounted by future landfarers extended the ways of the seafarers.

Three centuries later, another of that proud company who had pushed back the darkness of the unknown sensed that his exploration was but a continuation of the drive across the ocean and into the strange new land. Thousands of miles from the spot where Columbus saw that little light "rising and falling" and far up the great river of the West, the Missouri, Meriwether Lewis wrote in his *Journal* on April 7, 1805, "Our . . . little fleet altho' not as rispectable as those of Columbus or Capt Cook was viewed by us with as much pleasure as those deservedly famed adventurers ever beheld theirs . . . we are now about to penetrate a country at least two thousand miles in width, on which the foot of civilized man had never trodden."

The untrodden land. The words of Lewis are those of all our frontiersmen from the Atlantic beachheads westward. What great treasures would they find? What hardships and dangers lay ahead as they faced their inveterate enemy, the hostile and terrifying wilderness? Even such a hardy pioneer as Daniel Boone is said to have described it as " . . . wild and horrid . . . . It is impossible to behold it without terror." Long after Lewis's day, the terms Wilderness or Desert meant any region not yet settled by civilized man.

Foreword

In another mood one of the earliest frontiersmen, the French Huguenot Jean Ribaut, could write in 1563, "... it is a thinge inspeakable, the comodities that be sene there and shalbe founde more and more in this incomprehensible lande, never as yet broken with plowe irons, bringing fourthe all thinges according to his first nature, whereof the eternall God endued yt."

In Madrid, Paris, and London, statesmen laid their plans for the conquest of "those large dominions" that for Captain Smith stretched God alone knew how far. Over the next two centuries, the great game of empire was played in the chancelleries of the nations facing the Atlantic. The counters on this vast chessboard were the armies and navies of the contending powers; the explorers; the missionaries, eager for heathen souls; the fur traders, eager for tremendous profits; the seekers for gold and treasure; the speculators who acquired great tracts of wild land by corrupting governments at home and in the colonies; and the landless folk who dreamed of a piece of land of their own and were willing to risk their lives to get it. Even the Indians were pitted against each other and then were pushed aside by the white man equipped with an advanced technology and bent on conquest. There were the clash of great armies on the plains of Europe, of navies on the seven seas, and the savage conflict in the forests of North America. France was driven from the game, and the great arch of empire that extended from the rock of Quebec to the mouth of the Mississippi crumbled. Beyond the river, no one knew how far, a region already defined as Louisiana was lost. The spoils of war went to the two remaining powers, England and Spain.

They had hardly renewed their game when by a rude bridge that arched a stream, so small that it would go unnoticed in a land of great rivers, shots were fired. After the guns of Yorktown were silenced and a treaty of peace signed, England had lost her thirteen colonies and all the land south of the Great Lakes and east of the Mississippi. A new nation, the young, vigorous, acquisitive, ruthlessly expansionist United States — with two centuries of clearing and settling the land, of forest warfare, and of nation building behind it — sat in on the game.

Across the great river, Spain, now in possession of French Louisiana, was already showing signs of weak-

ness. Spanish officials installed in St. Louis looked apprehensively across to the Illinois shore at the swarms of frontier-hardened Kentuckians and Tennesseans.

Then abruptly France rejoined the game. Napoleon, soon to become the master of Europe, forced Spain to cede all of Louisiana to him for a small principality in Italy and attempted to reestablish the French Empire in North America. This was, however, only an interlude. The probable renewal of war in Europe and the decimation of his army by disease and revolt in Santo Domingo were reasons enough for him to abandon the contest as suddenly as he had joined it. Our minister in Paris received the astonishing offer to buy all of Louisiana, its western and northern boundaries undetermined.

The price was agreed upon, a treaty signed, and in March 1804 the French tricolor was run down the staff on the plaza at St. Louis and the Stars and Stripes raised. In that moment in our history, it was clear that the United States would become a continental nation. Jefferson, who had anxiously awaited every dispatch from Paris, could now rejoice in the ratification of the purchase treaty and could feel assured that his dream would be realized: the building of a great nation that he was convinced would become a citadel of freedom in a disordered world. Lewis and Clark had witnessed the ceremony at St. Louis, and soon they set out on their voyage up the Missouri River.

On their return nearly three years later, farms were spreading rapidly along the banks of the river down which they hurried on their way home. Missouri became a state in 1821. There at its borders on the verge of the plains the frontier paused. At the little town of Independence, founded in 1827, gathered the landfarers, looking out on an "incomprehensible lande" that awakened memories of the ocean across which the seafarers voyaged centuries ago. There is the smell of salt air in their journals. Independence was "the general port of embarcation for every part of the great western and northern prairie ocean." There the Santa Fe caravans, the Rocky Mountain traders, the fur brigades, and the emigrants bound for Oregon gathered. From the rendezvous at Council Grove, the prairie schooners were "fairly launched" and set out across a country often as "level as the sea" and where "the compass was the surest as well as the principal guide." It was even suggested that every party should be organized under "some system of maritime law" and that the leader be given the same authority "as a captain of a ship on the high seas." One stretch along the North Platte, where the cliffs rise abruptly above the sandbars of the river, was called "the coasts of Nebraska," a name given it perhaps by some early traveler far from his boyhood home.

Beyond the plains was the stupendous barrier of the Rockies and beyond that the Pacific, an ocean twice as large as the familiar Atlantic. Three centuries had passed since that day when Balboa and his men " . . . . stared at the Pacific . . . with a wild surmise — silent, upon a peak in Darien." Before the close of the eighteenth century the whole coast of what the Elizabethan Hakluyt called "the backside" of North America had been explored, and the names of Juan de Fuca, Drake, Bering, Cook, and Vancouver were on the map. A Yankee out of Boston, Captain Robert Gray, had discovered the mouth of the Columbia, naming it after the ship he commanded.

The exploitation of the resources along the northwest coast was well under way. Seagoing fur traders — Spanish, French, English, Russian, and American — were eager to exchange their cheap European goods for the otter and seal pelts gathered by the coastal Indians. With their ships loaded to the gunnels, they headed across the Pacific to Chinese ports and enormous profits. Oregon, remote and only vaguely defined, had emerged above the western horizon.

South of the Oregon country, which the diplomats had decided would be "jointly occupied" by England and the United States, sprawled the Spanish dominions. The early years of the nineteenth century had witnessed the shattering of this the greatest empire in the New World. On its ruins emerged new nations in Central and South America, among them Mexico. Below the Rio Grande a government weakened by constant disorder meant only one thing to the frontiersman, for whom national boundaries were purely speculative; the Mexican provinces of Texas and California were ripe for the taking.

The politicians in Washington might debate endlessly over what was meant by the words "joint occupation," but the Oregon-bound emigrant had no such doubts. He and those who followed were jointly in league with a watchful Providence, who had willed that the blessings of American democracy should spread across the earth. The halls of Congress might ring with denunciations of the Mexican War, but it was merely "Manifest Destiny" at work. Americans have no copyright on that slogan, for it is the substance of every imperial dream.

These were spacious days in a big new land through which the emigrant trains rolled westward, days as exciting as those for the seafarers who had ventured forth and "encircled the great globe itself." There were the same sense of space, the same urge to bring the distant near, the same wonder over "a thinge inspeakable," and the same awareness of the dangers that lay ahead, of the risks that must be taken, and of the prizes to be won.

Theirs was the final onset. The wagon wheels rolling toward Oregon and California were geared to the same thrust that three centuries before had propelled the seafarers westward.

The wise ones back home insisted that it was sheer madness for thousands to risk their lives in crossing such a desert, for the explorers Zebulon Pike and Stephen H. Long had reported that these "Steppes of Tartary" were uninhabitable for civilized man. God had willed that they should remain the home of the savage Indian and the wild beasts, who might occupy them forever, unmolested and unmolesting. Across the maps of that day, the legend "The Great American Desert" was printed in capital letters that stretched all the way from the Rio Grande to the Red River of the North. Perhaps it was not all wasteland, but the men and women on their way across it did not tarry to find out. No company of emigrants, huddled between decks as their ship fought its way across the stormy Atlantic, ever longed for the journey's end more than did those bound for the valleys of the Willamette and the Sacramento.

Other men knew that Pike and Long did not have the last word. Lewis and Clark had led the way. There followed a great company of mountain men, the seekers of fur, who broke out new trails across the deserts and through the mountains. Jedediah Smith, Thomas Fitzpatrick, the Sublettes, Kit Carson, Jim Bridger, and many others knew the secrets of this land and often served as guides for the emigrant companies.

It took something more than a loosely organized band of individualists, impatient of any discipline, to establish homes in the wasteland through which the emigrants hurried. The Mormons, driven out of Illinois by frontier mobs, found a refuge in this wilderness. Under the leadership of Brigham Young, they set up their New Zion in the valley of the Great Salt Lake. They never doubted that the Providence who had brought them through so many trials would bless them with peace and plenty. So the Community of Saints brought water down from the surrounding mountains by irrigation canals onto the thirsty land and demonstrated that men might live and prosper in the land of sagebrush and short grass. Even that tough old plainsman Jim Bridger, who had advised these zealots to abandon their harebrained scheme, had to conclude that their success was as likely a miracle as he would ever see.

The notion of the Great American Desert might linger in the minds of most Americans, but the time was not far distant when the Texas cattlemen would begin their drive of longhorns northward. Their herds were the first to utilize Uncle Sam's great pasture, where millions of buffalo had grazed for centuries. Farther east, the frontier farmer was inching out onto the plains, there to discover that new methods of agriculture could be applied to produce crops of wheat, flax, soybeans, and alfalfa in the semiarid West.

From the very first, the folks back home, whether in London or Paris, Boston or Detroit, were eager to learn what each successive frontier was like. Journals, descriptive accounts, official reports, propaganda poured from the presses. A London broadside crying out "Joyefull Newes from Virginia" was no more beguiling or deceptive than a western railroad pamphlet promising "Farms For Thousands" in semiarid Dakota. For three centuries incipient Marco Polos rushed across the ocean, invaded the wilderness, hurried back to civilization to write about what they saw or thought they saw. They are still at it.

Then there were the artists, for with all this growing interest there was the insistent demand for pictures. As early as 1563, the Huguenot Le Moyne was at work along the coast of Florida, depicting the scenery and the native inhabitants. John White of Virginia, a few years later, was painting the beautiful watercolors that after all the years glow with life. The engraved reproductions of the pictures of both these artists circulated widely throughout Europe. Their successors followed the frontier as it moved westward along the Indian trails and up the rivers to their headwaters in the Appalachian Mountains. By the 1840s the mountain "wilderness" had been portrayed all the way from New Hampshire to the Carolinas. Soon the Middle West was swarming with trained artists and ambitious amateurs, who found plenty of subjects on that maturing frontier.

Beyond the Missouri, far more exciting scenery and subjects awaited the artists. Here they gathered at the jumping-off place, Independence, to continue as had their predecessors to record the course of empire as westward it took its way. They might board the American Fur Company steamboat on its annual trip up the Missouri to Fort Union or join the packtrain of fur traders bound for a rendezvous in the mountains. It was a strange and unfamiliar world that confronted Catlin, Miller, Bodmer, John Mix Stanley — a landscape that expanded with every mile, space that burdened the eye and challenged the skill of the artist. There was nothing small, nothing tame. There was the elemental, primeval power of the millions of buffalo that darkened the plains; there was the savage splendor of the plains Indian, horse and rider bearing the strange insignia of a wild chivalry; and there was the mountain man, the lone trapper, no less a part of this new wilderness of plains and mountains. The artists strove to capture these wonders. Some of their pictures, particularly those of Miller, Bodmer, and John Mix Stanley, were artistic triumphs; some were merely grandiose and melodramatic failures. Nevertheless all of them preserved for future generations what Bernard De Voto has called "a symbol of the ultimate West." The Indian, the trapper, the buffalo hunter, the cavalry trooper, the prospector, the cowboy are the "Wild West" — an incantation invoked by every writer of westerns, every filmsmith, every dude rancher, and every chamber of commerce west of the ninety-eighth meridian. Even Madison Avenue has found that its spell can sell cigarettes and automobiles. There are dude ranches in Ohio and Virginia.

While California and the Southwest were being conquered by force of arms and Oregon by settlement and diplomacy, inventors and tinkerers were busy perfecting a new instrument, the camera. There was no limit to its use in recording the American scene, the land and its people. Picture taking had advanced far enough by 1860 so that Matthew Brady could move the camera out of the studio and onto the battlefields of the Civil War. Burdened with bulky and awkward equipment, he recorded that tragic story in pictures that are a part of the documentary history of the conflict.

The United States survived the Civil War; industry and capital were ready to supply the last frontier with more tools of conquest. Photographers such as William Henry Jackson and F. Jay Haynes were already on the roads west. The painters Frederic Remington and Charlie Russell, successors to Catlin and Bodmer, were soon turning out pictures that would fix forever in the American mind the image of the Indian and the cowboy. Although the camera provided a new artistic medium, its use demanded all the pioneer virtues of strength, endurance, and courage. It was no easy task to climb mountains and descend into deep canyons loaded down with heavy cameras and a tent that would serve as a darkroom wherein the wet plates might be quickly developed. The magnificent pictures of Jackson and Haynes, taken under the most difficult conditions, testify to their devotion.

The frontier is gone, but the land is still there, the great protagonist in every act of the drama of our westering. Four-lane highways, barbed wire, and high tension lines may vex it, bulldozers may scarify it, industry may foul its air and waters, dams may flood its canyons, and nuclear missile sites may mock it, but there it will be long after the exploiters have met the fate they have brought upon themselves.

Suddenly, and possibly too late, the American people have become aware of how much has been lost and how little remains of what Ribaut four centuries ago had called "this incomprehensible lande." On the plains and in the mountains along the Oregon Trail, there are places where a man with a camera may record, for perhaps the last time, what the emigrants saw and wrote about. Ingvard Henry Eide has set about this task, bringing to it great skill and historical imagination. His photographs deserve a place beside those of all the others who with brush and camera strove to picture this incomparable land. His is another record of America in the days of its lusty youth ere the evil days had come and the years had drawn nigh when men would say, "I have no pleasure in them."

— *Ernest S. Osgood*
Wooster, Ohio

Oregon Chronology

1540—Coronado of Spain explores from Mexico into Wichita Indian land (Kansas). **1541**—De Soto reaches mid-continent (Oklahoma) from Florida. **1543**—Cabrillo explores coast north of Mexico for Spain. **1576**—Frobisher of England seeks Northwest Passage.

1579—Capt. Francis Drake claims San Francisco and "New Albion" to the north for Queen Elizabeth. **1609-10**—Santa Fe is founded. **1670**—Hudson's Bay Company chartered. **1682**—La Salle claims Mississippi valley for Louis XIV. **1764**—St. Louis founded. **1765**—Maj. Robert Rogers seeks George III's permission to explore a river "called by the Indians Ouragon." **1780**—Englishman Sam Harrison invents a steel pen. **1792**—Capt. Robert Gray aboard *Columbia* charts Oregon coast and enters Columbia River. Later, Lt. W. R. Broughton explores Columbia and claims region for England.

1803—Napoleon sells Louisiana—about 830,000 square miles —and President Jefferson sends Lewis and Clark to the Pacific. **1805**—John Edwards of England invents the life preserver. **1810**—Missionary groups in East organize to work among western Indians. **1811**—John Jacob Astor directs Wilson Price Hunt overland to mouth of Columbia to build a fur trading post. Astoria becomes first permanent settlement on Pacific coast. **1812**—Astorian Robert Stuart goes east via South Pass, the Sweetwater, Court House Rock, and the Platte to the Missouri—first on the route later used by emigrants to Oregon.

1818—Thomas Hart Benton of Missouri urges settlement of Oregon. **1821**—Dr. John Floyd's bill to organize Oregon is voted down: Congress insists on clear title. **1823**—The Supreme Court judges that although Indians are rightful occupants, U.S. has title to the land: that American "discovery gave exclusive right to extinguish the Indian title of occupancy either by purchase or by conquest." **1824**—Hudson's Bay Company builds Fort Vancouver on the Columbia. Jedediah Smith, James Clyman, and William Sublette use and help popularize Stuart's route through South Pass. **1825**—William Ashley and Tom Fitzpatrick pioneer the Platte route to Great Salt Lake. **1827**—Independence and Fort Leavenworth are founded. In England, John Walker invents the friction (lucifer) match.

1829—Hall Jackson Kelley of Boston boosts settlement of Oregon, ". . . the loveliest and most envied country on earth." **1830**—Smith, Jackson, and Sublette's fur caravan, with 10 wagons, reaches Rockies via Platte with "ease and safety." **1832** —Merchant Nathaniel Wyeth, with John Ball (later, first settler in Oregon), begins first trading trip to the Columbia. Capt. B. Bonneville takes wagons over Continental Divide. **1833**—Silk top hat in vogue, threatens beaver sales. Westport is founded. **1834** —Methodist Rev. Jason Lee builds mission in Willamette valley.

1835—Presbyterian missionaries Dr. Marcus Whitman and Rev. Samuel Parker are sent to the Flatheads and Nez Percés. **1836**—Whitman's mission is built near Fort Walla Walla. **1838**—Memorials are presented to Congress by Rev. Jason Lee on behalf of Oregon settlers seeking U.S. rule and protection. **1839**—The first overland group, the 18-man Peoria Party— "Oregon or the Grave"—heads west, led by Thomas J. Farnham. Charles Goodyear vulcanizes rubber.

1840—Rocky Mountain fur trade ends; trappers become guides for emigrants. U.S. population is 17,069,453; free Negroes 386,000; slaves 2,487,355; Oregon country 400. **1841**—

Bidwell-Bartleson party, with Fr. P.-J. DeSmet, the first emigrant train to California leaves Westport. Sen. Benton's "Log Cabin" bill passes: it says a settler on public lands with "extinguished" Indian titles can preempt a quarter section at $1.25 an acre. Groups called Oregon Societies spring up in New England; members collect information on trails, publish reports, enlist emigrants. **1842**—Dr. Elijah White, of the Willamette Mission, is promoter of emigration; over 100 enlist.

1843—About 1,000 emigrants embark for Oregon. The first large train, 455 people, is led by Dr. Marcus Whitman. St. Joseph is named. The Pioneer Lyceum and Literary Club, in "wolf (predator) meetings," seeks civil, military protection for the Oregon colony. On July 5 the "First Organic Law" for Oregon is adopted at Champoeg village to create a provisional government. An Oregon bill, by Missouri Sen. Lewis F. Linn, gives 640 acres to each settler head of family. John C. Frémont's report of his exploration (in 1842) to South Pass becomes chief guidebook for emigrants; father-in-law Sen. Benton distributes thousands of copies. *The National Intelligencer* reports "the Oregon fever has broke out, and is now raging. . . . "

1844—About 2,000 leave for Oregon. The Gilliam party enlists 1,400. In Independence (pop. 400), still a major jumping-off place, $50,000 is spent by emigrants. Food prices: sugar— 7¢ a pound; flour—$4 a barrel; bacon—$3 a hundred; coffee— 9¢ a pound. Dry goods: American calicoes—6¢ to 15¢ a yard; blankets—$4 a pair. Stock: a good horse—$20 to $50; a mule— $30 to $50; oxen—$20 to $25 a yoke. Adventist William Miller predicts October 22 for Christ's second coming; October 23 ends Millerite movement.

1845—About 3,000 emigrants leave for Oregon. An Oregon provisional government is confirmed. The "Oregon Waltz" is composed by W. B. Bradbury. Col. S. W. Kearny leads first military party up the Platte to Fort Laramie; recorder is Capt. Philip St.-G. Cooke. Hudson's Bay Company quits the Columbia region. Portland is founded—and named, on the "Maine" side of a coin toss.

1846—1,000 emigrants. Oregon has 7,000 settlers and, by U.S.-British treaty, a north boundary at 49°. Frémont proclaims California an independent republic. War with Mexico. Christy's Virginia Minstrels sing "Hand Me Down My Walkin' Cane," "Arkansas Traveler," "Frog Went a-Courting," "She'll Be Comin' Round the Mountain."

1847—Saints Pratt, Brown, and Snow leave Council Bluffs and find the Promised Land. Cayuse Indians kill Marcus and Narcissa Whitman. Emigrants—2,000.

1848—A rights movement begins, resolved "that woman is man's equal." President Polk signs an Act establishing a free territorial government for Oregon, from 42° to 49° N and from the Rockies to the Pacific. "Goald" found in California. Fort Kearny is built. **1849**—In a rush by leaps and bounds 20,000 leave the Missouri jumping-off places en route for California gold. Maj. Osborne Cross reports on the military expedition from Fort Leavenworth to Oregon City. Walter Hunt invents the safety pin.

1859—Oregon becomes the 33rd State in the Union.

Preface

HAVE SOUGHT with camera and original eyewitness accounts to present a cross-country view portraying the geographic and human spectacle along the entire Oregon Trail. The exclusive use of entries from emigrant diaries and journals provides a personal, untranslated contact with a famous yesterday. From this eyewitness record, organized chronologically and geographically, we learn the day-by-day experiences of the people who dared enter an unpeopled land.

I was astonished to see so much remaining of the land as it must have appeared to the emigrants in the middle 1800s. Along the mountain miles the snowy peaks reside in silent solemnity. Streams still flow. Prairie grasses bend to the winds. Sometimes the blowing sand nicked my eyes, and the grime of a day's journey reminded me of what emigrant John T. Kerns wrote: "Dirty faces are as numerous as the stars of every evening." In lonesome times, when the vastness of the land was all but overwhelming, I remembered the words of an old alert roamer, James Clyman. "It is remarkable . . . and strange," he wrote, "that so many of all kinds and classes of People should sell out comfortable homes in Missouri and Elsewhere pack up and start across such an emmence Barren waste to settle in some new Place of which they have at most so uncertain information but this is the character of my countrymen." The emigrants moved westward. I followed with camera wherever and whenever the traces appeared.

For my camera views I selected the places actually seen and recorded by emigrants. Many locations took considerable detective work in the field and in archives to avoid inaccuracy. The trail is visible here and there in Kansas, Nebraska, Idaho, and Oregon. In Wyoming, it is a priceless heritage, well preserved in most places by nature, which refuses to blow it away. On South Pass, wagon wheel ruts are deep and exciting to see. Rocky Ridge, in Idaho, was appropriately named for the emigrant road cut directly across slab rock laying at 45 degrees, and the deep ruts are polished smooth from traffic of the wheels. In Oregon, much of the trail has been lost, destroyed by the steps of man's economic pace or in the beauty of new forests. Some of the trail is used by hunters, fish and game wardens, and an occasional Sunday historian; parts are county roads.

Even so, the Oregon Trail remains as the greatest settlement road in our history and an event never equaled for courage, adventure, and accomplishment. At best the trail would pass arrow-straight across greening prairies or wind along ridges colorful in wildflowers, with plenty of game in the lowlands. On days less exhilarating, grass was scarce, the ground a hammer, the road filled with stifling dust, and the long day a deed of monotony. Summer heat was almost unbearable.

The daily journals and diaries kept by hundreds of the one-third million emigrants record all the emotions and tribulations of those who were determined, as Ernest S. Osgood has said, "to bring the distant near." They express, also, in some degree, a consciousness of each being involved in a truly historic episode. In their diaries they describe cooking with buffalo chips, the abandonment of personal property, perhaps the simple, hasty burial of a loved one. On the next page might be an entry of joy and comfort, telling that "things went better today, and we hope tomorrow we shall be another day closer to Oregon."

Every turn in the Oregon Trail, every bump, every inch of the way resounded to the noise of the wagons. In contrast with the Lewis and Clark trail, which was a silent journey through a newly purchased and unknown wilderness, the Oregon Trail was crowded by thousands of people with oxen striding west beside thousands of squealing wheels on a known road. This primitive road followed the path explored by men like Stuart, Ball, Fitzpatrick, Clyman, Bridger, who dealt in furs and survival; by missionaries like Whitman, DeSmet, White, Parker, who dealt in souls and whose urging words undammed a torrent westward if not upward; by colonizers like Bidwell, Applegate, Barlow, and Burnett, who dealt in fortitude and emigrants, those ordinary people who made this such an extraordinary event.

Although beset by personal problems and weariness, as well as conflict with weather, the emigrants were delighted with the novelty of the land. Almost everyone wrote about Chimney Rock and Scott's Bluff. The former was the most popular landmark. It was a "stack," a "funnel," a "tower." The first genuine obstacle, Ash Hollow, was "steep," "past perpendicular." Laurel Hill, the last one, took them down "like shot off a shovel." There were no humble or lowly landmarks — each was both guidepost and marker, showing a place one day closer to the "Land of Milk and Honey."

In this book I cannot show you views of emigrants slaving to cross a river, of faces burned by wind and sun, or of the desolation at being left behind by an impatient wagon train when the father dies from cholera. There are no scenes of emigrants dancing at night within the wagon ring or of horsemen searching gullies for strayed cattle. But you will see, as I saw, the places that gave pleasure, that brought comment, and the great and small oddities and marvels along the 2,000 miles from Independence to Oregon City. You will see rivers and mountains, grave markers and sunsets, forests and storms. The illustrations, hopefully, will bring you closer to these emigrants as you read their words. And if you "listen," as I did, you will forever hear the thankful, prideful, and cheering voices of all those who had "wheeled across the country."

— *Ingvard Henry Eide,*
Missoula, Montana

A facsimile reproduction
from Mitchell's *Universal Atlas*
1856

Interior of Emigrant Wagon

St. Louis

AMERICAN ENTERPRIZE

By information received from thefe gentlemen [Robert Stuart's party, eastbound from Astoria], it appears that a journey acrofs the continent of N. America, might be performed with a waggon, there being no obftruction in the whole route that any perfon would dare to call a mountain in addition to its being much the moft direct and short one to go from this place to the mouth of the Columbia river. Any future party who may undertake this journey, and are tolerably acquainted with the different places, where it would be neceffary to lay up a fmall ftock of provifions would not be impeded, as in all probability they would not meet with an indian to interrupt their progrefs; altho on the other route more north there are almost infurmountable barriers.

— St. Louis *Missouri Gazette, May 15, 1813*

I heard that . . . there was a time when there were no people in this country except Indians. After that the people began to hear of men that had white skins; they had been seen far to the east. Before I was born they came out to our country and visited us. The man who came was from the Government. He wanted to make a treaty with us, and to give us presents, blankets, and guns, and flint and steel and knives.

The Head Chief told him that we needed none of these things. He said, "We have our buffalo and our corn. These things the Ruler gave to us, and they are all that we need. See this robe. This keeps me warm in winter. I need no blanket."

The white men had with them some cattle, and the Pawnee Chief said, "Lead out a heifer here on the prairie!" They led her out and the Chief, stepping up to her, shot her through behind the shoulder with his arrow, and she fell down and died. Then the Chief said, "Will not my arrow kill? I do not need your guns." Then he took his stone knife and skinned the heifer, and cut off a piece of fat meat. When he had done this he said, "Why should I take your knives? The Ruler has given me something to cut with."

Then taking the fire sticks, he kindled a fire to roast the meat, and while it was cooking, he spoke again and said, "You see, my brother, that the Ruler has given us all that we need for killing meat, or for cultivating the ground. Now go back to the country from whence you came. We do not want your presents, and do not want you to come into our country."

— *Curly Chief, Pawnee [re: 1820]*

Jumping-off Places

St. Louis *Missouri Republican*, July 4, 1825:

Mr. Printer: I see by your last paper that something called "O'Regan" has given name to the river and the territory on the Pacific. I wish to know whether the Christian name of that family of the O'Regans is Teague; for if so be that name, at full length is "Teague O'Regan", why let us have it, and not be after robbing a whole country of the best parts of its name.

Yours to serve
Patrick

[General William Clark] . . . some of our chiefs make the claim that the land belongs to us. It is not what the Great Spirit told me. He told me that the lands belong to Him, that no people owns the land; that I was not to forget to tell this to the white people when I met them in council.

— *Kannekuk, Kickapoo, 1827*

Conestoga Wagon

St. Louis, October 29, 1830

Sir [John H. Eaton, Secretary of War]: The business commenced by General Ashley some years ago, of taking furs from the United States territory beyond the Rocky mountains, has since been continued by Jedediah S. Smith, David E. Jackson, and William L. Sublette, under the firm of Smith, Jackson, and Sublette. They commenced business in 1826, and have since continued it; and have made observations and gained information which they think it important to communicate to the Government. The number of men they have employed has usually been from eighty to one hundred and eighty; and with these, divided into parties, they have traversed every part of the country west of the Rocky mountains, from the peninsula of California to the mouth of the Columbia river. Pack-horses, or rather mules, were at first used; but in the beginning of the present year, it was determined to try wagons; and in the month of April last, on the 10th day of the month, a caravan of ten wagons, drawn by five mules each, and two dearborns, drawn by one mule each, set out from St. Louis. We have eighty one men in company, all mounted on mules; and these were exclusive of a party left in the mountains. Our route from St. Louis was nearly due west to the western limits of the State; and thence along the Santa Fe trail about forty miles [to Gardner, Kan.]; from which the course was some degrees north of west, across the waters of the Kanzas, and up the Great Platte river, to the Rocky mountains, and to the head of Wind river [Lander, Wyo.] where it issues from the mountains. This took us until the 16th of July, and was as far as we wished the wagons to go, as the furs to be brought in were to be collected at this place, which is, or was this year, the great rendezvous of the persons engaged in that business. Here the wagons could easily have crossed the Rocky mountains, it being what is called the Southern Pass, had it been desirable . . . . For our support, at leaving the Missouri settlements, until we should get into the buffalo country, we drove twelve head of cattle, besides a milk cow. Eight of these only being required for use before we got to the buffaloes, the others went on to head of Wind river. We began to fall in with the buffaloes on the Platte, about three hundred and fifty miles from the white settlements; and from that time lived on buffaloes, the quantity being infinitely beyond what we needed. On the fourth of August, the wagons being in the mean time loaded with the furs which had been previously taken, we set out on the return to St. Louis. All the high points of the mountains then in view were white with snow; but the passes and valleys, and all the level country, were green with grass. Our route back was over the same ground nearly as in going out, and we arrived at St. Louis on the 10th of October, bringing back the ten wagons, the dearborns being left behind; four of the oxen and the milk cow were also brought back to . . . Missouri, as we did not need them for provision . . . .

The usual weight in wagons was about one thousand eight hundred pounds. The usual progress of the wagons was from fifteen to twenty five miles per day. The country being almost all open, level, and prairie, the chief obstructions were ravines and creeks, the banks of which required cutting down, and for this purpose a few pioneers were generally kept ahead of the caravan. This is the first time the wagons ever went to the Rocky mountains; and the ease and safety with which it was done prove the facility of communicating over land with the Pacific Ocean. The route from the

Ox Yoke

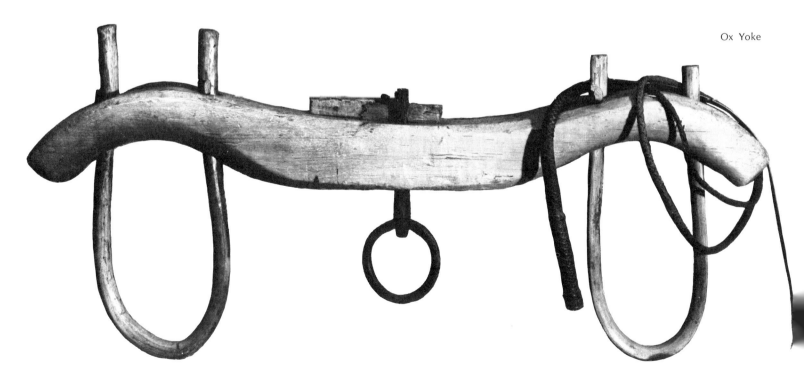

Southern Pass, where the wagons stopped, to the Great Falls of the Columbia, being easier and better than on this side of the mountains, with grass enough for horses and mules, but a scarcity of game for the support of men. One of the undersigned, to wit, Jedediah S. Smith, in his excursion west of the mountains, arrived at the post of the Hudson's Bay Company, called Fort Vancouver, near the mouth of the Multnomah river. He arrived there in August, 1828, and left the 12th of March, 1829, and made observations which he deems it material to communicate to the Government. Fort Vancouver is situated on the north side of the Columbia, five miles above the mouth of the Multnomah, in a handsome prairie, and on a second bank about three quarters of a mile from the river. This is the fort as it stood when he arrived there; but a large one, three hundred feet square, about three quarters of a mile lower down, and within two hundred yards of the river, was commenced the spring he came away. Twelve pounders were the heaviest cannon which we saw. The crop of 1828 was seven hundred bushels of wheat; the grain full and plump, and making good flour; fourteen acres of corn, the same number of acres of peas, eight acres of oats, four or five acres of barley, a fine garden, some small apple trees and grape vines. The ensuing spring eighty bushels of seed wheat were sown: about two hundred head of cattle, fifty horses and breeding mares, three hundred head of hogs, fourteen goats, the usual domestic fowls. They have mechanics of various kinds, to wit, blacksmiths, gunsmiths, carpenters, coopers, tinner and baker; a good saw mill on the bank of the river five miles above, a grist mill worked by hand, but intended to work by water. They had built two coasting vessels, one of which was then on a voyage to the Sandwich islands. No English or white woman was at the fort, but a great number of mixed blood Indian extraction, such as belong to the British fur trading establishments, who were treated as wives, and the families of children taken care of accordingly. So that every thing seemed to combine to prove that this fort was to be a permanent establishment. At Fort Vancouver the goods for the Indian trade are imported from London, and enter the territories of the United States, paying no duties; and from the same point the furs taken on the other side of the mountains are shipped. The annual quantity of these furs could not be exactly ascertained, but Mr. Smith was informed indirectly that they amounted to about thirty thousand beavers skins, besides otter skins and small furs. The beaver skins alone, at the New York prices, would be worth above two hundred and fifty thousand dollars. To obtain furs, both trapping and trading are resorted to. Various parties, provided with traps, spread over the country south of the Columbia to the neighborhood of the Mexican territory; and in 1824 and 5, they crossed the Rocky mountains, and trapped on the

waters of the Missouri river. They do not trap north of latitude 49 degrees, but confine that business to the territory of the United States. Thus this territory, being trapped by both parties, is nearly exhausted of beavers; and unless the British can be stopped, will soon be entirely exhausted, and no place left within the United States where beaver fur in any quantity can be obtained.

Detail from Double Ox Yoke, 1849

The inequality of the convention with Great Britain in 1818 is most glaring and apparent, its continuance is a great and manifest injury to the United States. The privileges granted by it have enabled the British to take possession of the Columbia river, and spread over the country south of it; while no Americans have ever gone, or can venture to go on the British side . . . .

In saying this, it is an act of justice to say, also, that the treatment received by Mr. Smith at Fort Vancouver was kind and hospitable; that, personally, he owes thanks to Governor Simpson and the gentlemen [including Dr. John McLoughlin, chief factor] of the Hudson's Bay Company, for the hospitable entertainment which he received from them, and for the efficient and successful aid which they gave him in recovering from the Umquah Indians a quantity of fur and many horses, of which these Indians had robbed him in 1828.

These facts being communicated to the Government, they consider that they have complied with their duty, and rendered an acceptable service to the administration; and respectfully request you, sir, to lay it before President Jackson.

We have the honor to be sir,
Yours, respectfully,
Jedediah S. Smith,
David E. Jackson,
W. L. Sublette. 1830

Hub Drill

1830 Frid., November 26

The Rocky Mountains. — The Cincinnati Commercial Advertiser, in copying the following article from the St. Louis Beacon, remarks: — it is but a few years since such a place as the Rocky Mountains was known to exist, except as a place inaccessible to man. They are already a source of great wealth to the enterprising citizens of the West; and where it was represented man could scarcely make his way, wagons go and come with perfect ease and facility—bringing loads of furs of immense value. In a few years, a trip to the Pacific, by way of the Rocky Mountains, will be no more of an undertaking than was a journey from the Atlantic cities to Missouri twenty years ago. Well and truly may it be said that "Westward the Star of Empire takes its way." We noticed, two weeks ago, the return of Messrs. Smith, Sublette, and Jackson, from the Rocky Mountains, and stated that they had taken two wagons out and back again. We now learn from them there was an error in the number two; the actual number was ten . . . .

Messrs. Smith, Sublette and Jackson are the first that ever took wagons to the Rocky Mountains. The ease with which they did it and could have gone on to the mouth of the Columbia, shows the folly and non-sense of those "scientific" characters who talk of the Rocky Mountains as the barrier which is to stop the westward march of the American people.

— Philadelphia *National Gazette, 1830*

[April] 4th . . . Eastern enterprise and influences are gaining ground since the town [of St. Louis] has been brought under the laws of the United States . . . Adventurers, of almost every description of character and nation, such as trappers, hunters, miners, and emigrants, collect here, as a starting point from whence to go into the still far west, many of whom seek a miserable fortune among the Rocky Mountains . . .

Dr. Marcus Whitman has already arrived here, who is appointed by the American Board of Commissioners for Foreign Missions to be my associate . . .

— *Rev. Samuel Parker, 1835*

THE OREGON SONG

To the far-far off Pacific sea,
Will you go - will you go - dear girl with me?
By a quiet brook, in a lovely spot
We'll jump from our wagon and build
our cot!

Then hip-hurrah for the prairie life!
Hip-hurrah for the mountain strife
And if rifles must crack, if we swords
must draw,
Our country forever, hurrah! hurrah!

— St. Louis *Missouri Republican, 1840*

Hub and Spokes

St. Louis, June 14, 1842

Lieutenant Fremont, of the corps of the topographical engineers, left . . . under orders from the war department, about ten days ago, with a party of twenty men on a tour to the Rocky Mountains. The object of the expedition is an examination of the country between the mouth of the Kanzas and the headwaters of the great River Platte, including the navigable parts of both these rivers, and what is called the Southern Pass in the Rocky Mountains, and intermediate country, frontiers of the Missouri to the mouth of the Columbia River. This expedition is connected with the proposition now before congress to occupy the territory about the Columbia River as proposed by Dr. [Lewis] Linn's bill.

The great River Platte is the most direct line of communication between this country and the mouth of the Columbia, and that route is known to be practicable and easy. It therefore becomes important to ascertain the general character of that river and the adjacent country, and the facilities it will be likely to afford in prosecuting contemplated settlements in Oregon. This Southern Pass, or depression in the Rocky Mountains, is near the source of the extreme branch of the River Platte, and affords an easy passage for wagons and other wheel carriages, which have frequently passed over the mountains on that route without difficulty or delay; and it is important that the latitude of this point should be ascertained, as it is thought that it will not vary much from the line established between the United States and Mexico by treaty with Spain, 1819. If this pass should fall south of that line (the forty-second degree of north latitude) it may become necessary to examine the country north of it, the line of the Yellowstone and south branch of the Columbia would, it is thought, afford our next best route . . . .

Since the attention of the country has been directed to the settlement of the Oregon Territory by our able senator (Doctor Linn), and by the reports of those who have visited that region in person, the importance of providing ample security for settlers there, and of opening a safe and easy communication from the western boundary of Missouri to the Columbia River has been universally admitted.

The day is not far distant when, if the general government shall do its duty in the matter, Oregon will be inhabited by a hardy, industrious, and intelligent population, and the enterprise of our citizens find a new channel of trade with the islands of the Pacific, the western coast of this whole continent, and perhaps with Eastern Asia. Notwithstanding the many obstacles at present in the way of the settlement of this territory, emigrants are rapidly pouring into it, and only demand . . . that protection which is due to all our citizens . . . .

We are pleased to learn that the proper authorities at Washington evince a disposition to do something toward encouraging the early occupation of Oregon by permanent American settlers. It is known that many of the islands of the Pacific have already been settled by Americans, and trading houses established, by which a large and profitable business is carried on with the Indian tribes on the northwestern coast of America, and with the East Indies and China. There is nothing to prevent trading establishments in Oregon from ultimately securing a large share of this trade, and adding much to the wealth and prosperity of the whole union . . . .

. . . . If Lieutenant Fremont shall be successful in his contemplated exploration of the route, and if the government shall furnish proper protection to those who shall seek a home in that distant region, the English may not only be completely dislodged from the foothold they have already acquired there, but prevented from making further inroads upon our western territory, and long monopolizing the greater part of the trade at present carried on with the Indian tribes at the Northwest and West.

— St. Louis *Missouri Reporter*, *1842*

Wagon Hub for 60-Inch Wheel

May 15. The middle district (of eastern Oregon) from the Cascade range to near the base of the Rocky Mountains, is the region called desert, and which, in the imaginations of many, has given character to the whole country. In some respects it is a desert — barren of wood — sprinkled with sandy plains — melancholy under the sombre aspect of the gloomy artemesia — and desolate from volcanic rocks, through the chasms of which plunge the headlong streams. But this desert has its redeeming points — much water-grass, many oases — the mountains capped with snow, to refresh the air, the land, and the eye-blooming valleys — a clear sky, pure air and a supreme salubrity.

— *Senator Thomas Hart Benton*, *1846*

Independence

The Town of Independence is laid out on high, handsome and rich land, surrounded by suitable stone and timber for building, contiguous to excellent never failing spring water; and is believed to be in the most healthy part of the state.

— Fayette *Missouri Intelligencer, 1827*

The Town of Independence . . . full of promise, like most of the innumerable towns springing up in the midst of the forest of the West, many of which though dignified by high-sounding epithets, consist of nothing but a ragged congeries of five or six rough log-huts, two or three clap-board houses, two or three so-called hotels, alias grogshops; a few stores . . . but nevertheless a thriving and aspiring place, in its way.

A little beyond this point [Independence], all carriage roads cease, and one deep black trail alone, which might be seen tending to the southwest, was that of the Santa Fe trappers and traders.

— *Charles Joseph Latrobe, 1833*

On the 21st of May, . . . the author and sixteen others arrived in the town of Independence, Missouri. Our destination was the Oregon Territory. Some of our number sought health in the wilderness — others sought the wilderness for its own sake — and others sought a residence among the ancient forests and lofty heights of the valley of the Columbia; and each actuated by his own peculiar reasons, or interest, began his preparations for leaving the frontier. Pack mules and horses and pack-saddles were purchased and prepared for service. Bacon and flour, salt and pepper, sufficient for four hundred miles, were secured in sacks; our powder-casks were wrapt in painted canvas, and large oil-cloths were purchased to protect these and our sacks of clothing from the rains; our arms were thoroughly repaired; bullets were moulded; powder-horns and cap-boxes filled; and all else done that was deemed needful, before we struck our tent for the Indian territory . . . .

— *Thomas J. Farnham, 1839*

We stopped at the best hotel in Independence. We were led to a poorly enclosed dormitory where eight large beds were strewn about so as to accommodate sixteen travelers.

— *Victor Tixier, 1840*

One of the preachers told me it was almost presumptious for so old a man as I to attempt such a hazardous journey . . . . Mr. Greene said there was a possibility of my returning, but not a probability.

— *Rev. Joseph Williams, 1841*

Sublette's Advice to Outfit and Regulations

That every male over 18 years of age should be provided with one mule or horse, or wagon conveyance; should have one gun, 3 pounds of powder, 12 pounds of lead, 1000 caps, or suitable flints, 50 pounds of flour or meal, 30 pounds of bacon, and a suitable proportion of provisions for women and children; that [Dr. Elijah] White should show his official appointment; that they elect a captain for one month; that there be elected a scientific corps, to consist of three persons, to keep a record of everything concerning the road and journey that might be useful to government or future emigrants.

This corp consisted of C. Lancaster, L. W. Hastings and A. L. Lovejoy. James Coats was elected pilot, and Nathaniel Crocker, secretary. It was ordered that H. Burns be appointed blacksmith, with power to choose two others, and also to call to his aid the force of the company; that John Hoffsletter be appointed Master wagonmaker, with like powers; that a code of laws be draughted, and submitted to the company, and that they be enforced by reprimand, fines, and final banishment; that there be no profane swearing, obscene conversation, or immoral conduct allowed in the Company, on pain of expulsion; that the names of every man, woman and child be registered by the secretary.

— *Elijah White, M.D., 1842*

As early as the year 1840, . . . I had heard of Oregon as a "Terra Incognita" somewhere upon the western slope of the continent, as a country to which the United States had some sort of claim, . . .

During the winter of 1841-2, being in Jefferson county, Iowa, I incidentally heard that a party contemplated leaving Independence in May or June, 1842, for Oregon, under the leadership of Dr. Elijah White, who had formerly been in Oregon connected with the Methodist missions, and who was then about returning to the Territory in the service of the U. S. Government as Sub-Indian agent. Thinking this a good opportunity to make the trip . . . I mounted my horse and rode across Western Iowa, then a wilderness, and arrived at Independence seventeen days after White and his party had left. I at first contemplated following them up alone, but learning that the murderous Pawnees were then hostile, I was advised not to attempt the dangerous experiment. I therefore abandoned the trip for the present, and spent most of the ensuing year in the employment of the government as a carpenter, in the construction of Fort Scott, in Kansas, about 100 miles south of Independence . . . .

Independence Courthouse, c. 1836

Without orders from any quarter, and without pre-concert, promptly as the grass began to start, the emigrants began to assemble near Independence, at a place called Fitzhugh's Mill. On the 17th day of May, 1843, notices were circulated through the different encampments that on the succeeding day, those contemplating emigration to Oregon, would meet at a designated point to organize.

Promptly at the appointed hour the motley groups assembled. It consisted of people from all the States and Territories, and nearly all nationalities. The most, however, from Arkansas, Illinois, Missouri and Iowa, and all strangers to one another, but impressed with some crude idea that there existed an imperative necessity for some kind of an organization for mutual protection against the hostile Indians inhabiting the great unknown wilderness stretching away to the shores of the Pacific, and which they were about to traverse with their wives and children, household goods and all their earthly possessions.

Many of the emigrants were from the western tier of counties of Missouri, known as the Platte Purchase, and among them was Peter H. Burnett, a former merchant, who had abandoned the yardstick and become a lawyer of some celebrity for his ability as a smooth-tongued advocate . . . . Mr. Burnett, or, as he was familiarly designated, "Pete," was called upon for a speech.

Mounting a log, the glib-tongued orator delivered a glowing, florid address. He commenced by showing his audience that the then western tier of States and Territories was overcrowded with a redundant population, who had not sufficient elbow room for the expansion of their enterprise and genius, and it was a duty they owed to themselves and posterity to strike out in search of a more expanded field and more genial climate, where the soil yielded the richest return for the slightest amount of cultivation, where the trees were loaded with perennial fruit and where a good substitute for bread, called La Camash, grew in the ground, salmon and other fish crowded the streams, and where the principal labor of the settler would be confined to keeping their gardens free from the inroads of buffalo, elk, deer and wild turkeys. He appealed to our patriotism by picturing forth the glorious empire we would establish upon the shores of the Pacific. How, with our trusty rifles, we would drive out the British usurpers who claimed the soil, and defend the country from the avarice and pretensions of the British lion, and how posterity would honor us for placing the fairest portion of our land under the dominion of the stars and stripes. He concluded with a slight allusion to the trials and hardships incident to the trip and dangers to be encountered from hostile Indians on the route, and those inhabiting the country whither we were bound. He furthermore

23

intimated a desire to look upon the tribe of noble "red men" that the valiant and well armed crowd around him could not vanquish in a single encounter.

Other speeches were made, full of glowing descriptions of the fair land of promise, the far away Oregon which no one in the assemblage had ever seen, and of which not more than half a dozen had ever read any account. After the election of Mr. Burnett, as captain, and other necessary officers, the meeting, as motley and primitive a one as ever assembled, adjourned, with "three cheers" for Capt. Burnett and Oregon.

On the 20th of May, 1843, after a pretty thorough military organization, we took up our line of march, with Capt. John Gantt, an old army officer, who combined the character of trapper and mountaineer, as our guide. Gantt had in his wanderings been as far as Green river and assured us of the practicability of a wagon road thus far. Green river, the extent of our guide's knowledge in that direction, was not halfway to the Willamette valley, the then only inhabited portion of Oregon. Beyond that we had not the slightest conjecture of the condition of the country. We went forth trusting to the future and would doubtless have encountered more difficulties than we experienced had not Dr. [Marcus] Whitman overtaken us before we reached the terminus of our guide's knowledge. He was familiar with the whole route and was confident that wagons could pass through the canyons and gorges of Snake river and over the Blue mountains, which the mountaineers in the vicinity of Fort Hall declared to be a physical impossibility.

— *James Willis Nesmith, 1843*

The best teams for this trip are ox teams. Let oxen be from three to five years old, well set, and compactly built, just such oxen as are best for use at home. They should not be too heavy, as their feet will not bear the trip too well; but oxen six, seven, and eight years old, some of them very large, stood the trip . . . very well, but not so well in general as the younger and lighter ones. Young cows make just as good a team as any. It is the travel and not the pulling that tires your team. If you have cows for a team, it requires more of them in bad roads, but they stand the trip equally well, if not better than oxen. We fully tested the ox and mule teams, and we found the ox teams greatly superior. One ox will pull as much as two mules, and in mud, as much as four. They are more easily managed, are not so subject to be lost or broken down on the way, cost less at the start, and are worth about four times as much here. The ox is a most noble animal, patient, thrifty, durable, gentle, not easily driven off and does not run off. Those who come to this country will be in love with their oxen . . . . The ox will plunge through mud, swim over streams, dive into thickets, climb mountains to get at grass, and he will eat almost anything.

— *Peter H. Burnett, 1843*

. . . Independence, a small town . . . situated six miles South of the Missouri River, and twelve miles from the Western line of the state, and now the principal starting point for all the companies engaged in the Western and New Mexican trade, and place of general rendezvous of persons from all parts of the United States . . . .

— *Overton Johnson and W. H. Winter, 1843*

For what do they brave the desert, the wilderness, the savage, the snowy precipices of the Rocky Mountains, the weary summer march, the storm-drenched bivouac and the gnawing of famine? — This migration of more than a thousand persons in one body to Oregon wears an aspect of insanity.

— *Horace Greeley, 1843*

1844 of May the 14th Left Independence & proceded on to Westport Roads extremely bad owing to the Leate greate rains

[May] 15. at Westport morning dull slight rains . . . . about 10 left West port continues to rain all day passed the head of Blue River came to camp at Elm Brook passed the methodist mission and several Shawnee Indian Formes in the course of the day made 18 miles.

[May] 16. It rained all night last night in one continued and rapid Shower This morning the whole prairie covered in water Shoe mouth deep no wood to be had except what we had hauled in waggons Started throug the rain about 8 miles over a roling prairie covered nearly knee deep in mud and water camped about ½ mile from timber packed some up to camp on our mules it continued to rain all night Slightly

— *James Clyman, 1844*

Drilling a Felloe

. . . we suppose that not less than two or three thousand people are congregating at this point.

— Independence *Western Expositor*, *May 3, 1845*

Having concluded from the best information I was able to obtain that the Oregon territory offers great inducements to emigrants, I determined to visit it with a view of satisfying myself in regard to it, and of ascertaining by personal observation whether its advantages were sufficient to warrant me in the effort to make it my future home . . . .

. . . a doubt arose in my mind whether the advantages which were expected to result from the trip, would be likely to compensate for the time and expense necessary to accomplish it, but I believe I was right, hoped for the best, and pressed onward.

— *Rev. Samuel Parker, 1845*

We rolled on without a hitch, crossed the Mississippi at Quincy, Illinois, and the Missouri river at Utica, Missouri. Went up on the south side all the way to Independence, where the grand start was to be made. There we lost one yoke of oxen, strayed or stolen, we never knew which, but they were the only animals we lost on the whole trip. Bought another yoke of oxen for twenty-two dollars and two or three cows for five dollars a head, to give milk on the road. We wanted father [Samuel K. Barlow] to buy one hundred cows . . . for five or six dollars apiece, and could get plenty of young men to drive them just for their board. Of course, we would have to furnish them each a horse or mule. Mules were better for the trip, but American mares were more profitable . . . .

. . . at Independence . . . again, five thousand strong or five thousand weak. At least two thirds of our company were women and children, and we had a thousand wagons at least.

The first thing to do was to organize. We called a representative meeting, elected a captain over all, and one little captain over every forty or fifty wagons, each company elected its own captain and he appointed his own lieutenants, etc. The guard was kept up for some time, and we stopped and started when the captain ordered. He always went on to look out a camping ground, taking into consideration wood, water and grass.

— *William Barlow, 1845*

There was so much fever and ague in Illinois, father decided to move [from Fulton County]. He had heard of Oregon. The thing that decided him to come to Oregon was he had heard there were plenty of fish here. Father was a great fisherman, and while he caught pike and red horse there, he wanted to move to a country where he could catch trout and salmon.

My father put in his spare time for some months making a strong sturdy wagon in which to cross the plains . . . . There were over 3000 people who started for Oregon in the spring of 1845.

Presley Welch was captain of one of the trains, Joel Palmer and Samuel K. Barlow being his lieutenants. Samuel Hancock was captain of another train. Both of these trains left from Independence, Mo. Another company with over 50 wagons left from St. Joe . . . .

. . . . I can well remember what a hullabaloo the neighbors set up when father said we were going to Oregon. They told him his family would all be killed by the Indians, or if we escaped the Indians we would either starve to death or drown or be lost in the desert, but father was not much of a hand to draw back after he had put his hand to the plow, so he went ahead and made ready for the trip. He built a large box in the home-made wagon and put in a lot of dried buffalo meat and pickled pork. He had made over a hundred pounds of maple sugar the preceding fall which we took along instead of loaf sugar. He also took along plenty of corn meal. At Independence, Mo., he laid in a big supply of buffalo meat and bought more coffee. He also laid in a plentiful supply of home twist tobacco. Father chewed it and mother smoked it . . . .

. . . Independence . . . was merely a trading post. . . . . There were several stores in Independence, a number of blacksmith shops and wagon shops as well as livery stables and hotels. At Independence, we joined the Barlow wagon train.

— *Benjamin Franklin Bonney, 1845*

[I] took my departure from Independence, Mo., in company with two hundred others, their wagons and the necessary teams, for the long, and . . . uncertain journey across the Plains. The destination of the party was Oregon . . . it was no trifling task to separate one's self from the old associations of early life and start upon such an enterprise, at such a time; for little was known of the route across from the Atlantic to the Pacific; it is true a small emigration crossed the year before, but little information was derived from these early pioneers other than that they reached Oregon after a long hazardous journey.

— *Samuel Hancock, 1845*

The landing at Independence — the store-houses — the Santa Fe waggons — the groups of peratical-looking Mexicans, employees of the Santa Fe Traders, with their broad, peaked hats — the men with their rifles seated on a log ready for Oregon . . . . The Baltimorians got shamefully drunk and one of them, an exquisite in full dress, tumbled into the water . . . .

Grease Bucket, c. 1840

. . . . The last arrival of emigrants came down the street with about twenty waggons . . . . What is remarkable, this body, as well as a very large portion of the emigrants were from the extreme western states [east of the Mississippi River] — N. England send but a small proportion, but they are better furnished than the rest . . . one remarkably pretty little girl was seated on horseback, holding a parasol over her head to keep off the rain . . . the men were hardy and good-looking . . . all looked well — but what a journey before them . . . as I passed their waggons I observed three old men, with their whips in their hands, discussing some point of theology — though this is hardly the disposition of the mess of the emigrants . . . . Woodworth parades a revolver in his belt, which he insists is necessary — and it may be a prudent precaution, for this place seems full of desperadoes, all arms are loaded . . . . Life is held in little esteem.

— *Francis Parkman, 1846*

[May 25.] The first five miles of the road leading from Independence to the Trace, we found in very bad condition for wagons. We have passed several emigrants and two large Santa Fe wagons badly stalled, notwithstanding the latter had six yokes of oxen each to draw them. This may prove another reason for Westport being made the point of rendezvous hereafter, unless the evil be remedied pretty soon.

— St. Louis *Reveille, 1846*

[March] . . . noise and confusion reigned supreme. Traders, trappers and emigrants filled the streets and stores. All were in a hurry, jostling one another, and impatient to get through with their business . . . . Mules and oxen strove for the right of way. 'Whoa' and 'haw' resounded on every side; while the loud cracking of ox goads, squeaking of wheels and rattling of chains, mingled with the oaths of teamsters, produced a din indescribable.

— *William G. Johnston, 1849*

At Independence the tents had hardly been set up and the women had just got about their cooking when we were visited by a dozen or more Kansas Indians, who were about as disreputable a looking lot as can be found in the country — dirty, ill-favored red men with ragged blankets cast about them, seeming more like beggars than anything else.

Any attempt to drive them away was useless, and it was in the highest degree necessary that sharp watch be kept else we would find much of our outfit missing after the visitors had taken their departure.

There were the wretched Kansans only half covered with their greasy, torn blankets; Shawnees, decked out in calicoes and fanciful stuff; Foxes with their shaved heads and painted faces; and here and there a Cheyenne sporting his war bonnet of feathers.

— *Jared Fox, 1852*

Wagon Jack

Westport

I went up the Missouri on the steamboat St. Peters to Choteau's Landing. Our trip lasted six days, because the water was at a very low stage; and offered nothing of special interest. The border village, West Port, is six miles distant from Choteau's Landing . . . . the village has perhaps thirty or forty houses, and is only a mile from the western border of the state of Missouri. It is the usual rendezvous for travelers to the Rocky Mountains, as is Independence, twelve miles distant, for those journeying to Santa Fe. I bought a horse and a mule, the former to ride, the latter for my baggage; and made other preparations necessary for my journey.

— *Frederick A. Wislizenus, M.D., 1839*

I was pleased with him [Kit Carson] and his manner of address . . . . He was a man of medium height, broad-shouldered and deep-chested, with a clear, steady blue eye and frank speech and address; quiet and unassuming.

— *Brevet-Capt. John C. Frémont, 1842*

Washington, March 1, 1843

Sir [Col. J. J. Albert, Chief, Corps of Topographical Engineers]: Agreeably to your orders to explore and report upon the country between the frontiers of Missouri and the South Pass in the Rocky Mountains, and on the line of the Kansas and Great Platte rivers, I set out from Washington City on the 2d day of May, 1842, and arrived at St. Louis, by way of New York, the 22d of May, where the necessary preparations were completed, and the expedition commenced.

I proceeded in a steamboat to Choteau's landing, about four hundred miles by water from St. Louis, and near the mouth of the Kansas river, whence we proceeded twelve miles to Mr. Cyrian [Cyprian] Chouteau's trading-post, where we completed our final arrangements for the expedition.

Gradually, however, everything — the material of the camp, men, horses, and even mules — settled into its place, and by the 10th we were ready to depart . . . I had collected in the neighborhood of St. Louis twenty-one men, principally Creole and Canadian voyageurs, who had become familiar with Prairie life in the service of the fur companies in the Indian country.

Mr. Charles Preuss, a native of Germany, was my assistant in the topographical part of the survey. L. Maxwell, of Kaskaskia, who had been engaged as a hunter and Christopher Carson (more familiarly known, for his exploits in the mountains, as Kit Carson) was our guide. (twenty-two persons were engaged in St.

Handloomed Coverlet, Jacquard Design, c. 1845

Louis) In addition to these, Henry Brant, son of J. B. Brant, of St. Louis, a young man of nineteen years of age, and Randolph, a lively boy of twelve, son of the Hon. Thomas H. Benton, accompanied me, for the development of mind and body which such an expedition would give.

— *Brevet-Capt. John C. Frémont, 1843*

The excitement in connection with the settlement of Oregon was stirring the hearts of the pioneers on the Mississippi frontier. My father heard about the Lynn bill [in the U.S. Senate] from the men at Fort Leavenworth. This bill . . . gave six hundred and forty acres of land to the head of every family that would settle in Oregon. Oregon became a sort of pioneer's paradise, and great were the stories told about it to induce emigrants to go. Mr. Peter H. Burnett was one of the wayside orators who sought to gather a company of men to go West across the plains to Oregon.

One Saturday morning father said that he was going into Platte City [near Weston in Missouri and Fort Leavenworth in Kansas] to hear Mr. Burnett talk about Oregon . . . . he told of the great crops of wheat which it was possible to raise in Oregon, and pictured in glowing terms the richness of the soil and the attraction of the climate, and then with a little twinkle of humor in his eye, he said, "and they do say, gentlemen, they do say, that out in Oregon the pigs are running about under the great acorn trees, round and fat, and already cooked, with knives and forks sticking in them so that you can cut off a slice whenever you are hungry." Of course at this everybody laughed . . . .

Father was so moved upon by what he had heard at Fort Leavenworth and what he heard from Mr. Burnett, that he decided to join the company that was going west to Oregon . . . .

We left our home near Platte City, on April 9, 1843, and drove to the Westport crossing of the Missouri River, where we camped three miles out. The grass not being strong enough for our teams to go on, we were compelled to make a considerable wait there. On the fifteenth of May Dr. Marcus Whitman came into our camp from Washington, D.C., saying that he was just from the Capital and that he had a promise from President Tyler that the President would do nothing contrary to the interests of Oregon settlers for one year. We had a pilot by the name of Captain Gant, whom we had hired for eight hundred dollars to pilot us [along the Independence Road] as far as Fort Hall, that being as far as he was acquainted with the country, so we engaged Dr. Whitman also to accompany us, father himself, paying eighty dollars to this end. There were one hundred and twenty-seven wagon in our company and something over four hundred and fifty-five souls.

— *Edward Henry Lenox, 1843*

The Liberty, Clay County Banner, says: We are informed that the expedition to Oregon, now rendezvoused at Westport, in Jackson County, will take up its line of march on the 20th of this month. The company consists of some four or five hundred emigrants — some with their families. They will have out one hundred and fifty wagons, drawn by oxen, together with horses for nearly every individual, and some milch cows, they will, we suppose, take as much provision with them as they can conveniently carry, together with a few of the necessary implements of husbandry. There are in the expedition a number of citizens of inestimable value to any community — men of fine intelligence and vigorous and intrepid character; admirably calculated to lay the firm foundations of a future empire.

— St. Louis *Daily Missouri Republican, May 27, 1843*

Sketch: A Shawnee Soiree (May 10, 1843)

About the middle of May, and while we were still laying encamped a mile or so outside the town of Westport, waiting for some necessary completions of our equipment that were still to be made, Old Parks — a sort of savage quadroon, being three parts white and one part Shawnee — told us of a great festival among the Indians about nine miles from where our tents were pitched. Parks assured us that the annual or rather semi-annual "Bread Dance" of the Shawnees was a very interesting and curious affair, at the same time favoring us with an invitation to be present, as "distinguished strangers," on the occasion. Of our whole camp, some six or seven only started off to this fashionable ball in Shawnee-town. We found the whole Shawnee Nation, or at least a very fair representation of it, assembled on the pleasure-ground, which we reached early in the evening. The monotonous tapping of a dull drum first smote upon our tympanums as we neared the scene, and then at once opened upon our vision as magnificent an exhibition of the wild and grotesque as we could have wished for. A few corn fields and clusters of log buildings were scattered about the vicinity, while the Indians were assembled in various thick groups upon a broad piece of level land in the center. We soon moved to where the revel seemed liveliest, and there a sort of ball-room was set apart, in which about two hundred dancers, men and women, were moving in sets and figures altogether new and curious to our observation. We thought of Fanny LaDeesse and were satisfied that with all her perfections of "the Academy," we saw here many refinements of the art of motion yet undreamed of by the Parisian muse. Fanny will smile and sweetly ejaculate, "C'est drole!" when she is told that the most distinguished perfection in dancing, among the ladies of Shawnee-land is to keep their ten toes all together, and never let them rise from the ground!

The dimensions of the ball-room were about one hundred and fifty feet by eighty; and a number of old barked logs, laid in this oblong manner, enclosed the now grassless spot used by the dancers. The logs were at once the limits of this open saloon, and convenient seats for the company within. The order of proceedings seemed to give the gentlemen precedence, who rose, one after another as a set commenced, and marched about, stamping in time with the before-mentioned drum, which was neither more nor less than a little empty powder or liquor keg, with a racoon skin stretched over it. This was beaten with a stick by a little, shrivelled, pock-marked, blear-eyed old man, who seemed to be a sort of blind Apollo among the revellers, and his dull-set instrument he accompanied with a sharp-set voice, in a low continuous sort of howl, that chimed with the song of the dancers in a way singularly wild. The large fires, lighting up the strange groups — the men going through contortions — the darkness outside the ball-room logs, while many a fire blazed in the woods around, where smaller groups were carousing — all this called still strange images to mind, and it seemed to be a dance of demons, while the voice of drummer Apollo came like a shrill yet hollow resonance from under ground, as of a captive enemy enchained.

— *Matthew C. Field*
New Orleans *Daily Picayune*
November 15, 1843

[Field was a member of Scottish sportsman Sir William Drummond Stewart's pleasure and hunting expedition to the Wind River Range. Among the "doctors, Lawyers, botonists, Bug Ketchers, Hunters," were William Sublette, Fr. Pierre-Jean DeSmet, and painter Alfred Jacob Miller.]

Sketch: Oregon Emigrants (May 21–June 1, 1843)

During our detention among the upper settlements, before starting out, a constant source of interest to us was the gathering of people bound to Oregon.

One Sunday morning, about the usual church hour in a larger place, five or six wagons passed through the town of Westport, and one old man, with silver hair, was with the party. Women and children were walking; fathers and brothers were driving loose cattle or managing the heavy teams; and keen-eyed youngsters, with their chins yet smooth, and rifles on their shoulders, kept in advance of the wagons, with long strides, looking as if they were already watching around the corners of the streets for game.

Many other bodies of these adventurous travellers crossed our notice at Independence, Westport, and at encampments made in the vicinity.

— *Matthew C. Field*
New Orleans *Daily Picayune*
November 21, 1843

[Westport] . . . full of Indians, whose little shaggy ponies were tied by dozens along the houses and fences. Sacs and Foxes, with shaved heads and painted faces, Shawanoes and Delawares, fluttering in calico frocks and turbans, Wyandots dressed like white men, and a few wretched Kanza wrapped in old blankets, were strolling about the streets, or lounging in and out of the shops and houses.

— *Francis Parkman, 1846*

Liberty

Monday, 20th . . . Our captain remarked at dinner today, that most of the accidents which happen to steam-boats take place on the Sabbath . . . we engaged a man to take us in a wagon to Liberty, Mo. [opposite Fort Leavenworth].

[21st] . . . we continued here about three weeks, waiting for caravans [going northward to Council Bluffs] . . . .

Liberty is a small village . . . . It has a Courthouse of brick — several stores, which do considerable business, a ropewalk, and a number of decent dwelling houses . . . . At this place it forms — men, horses and mules, and wagons, are collected and put in readiness; and from this place commences the long journey for the west . . .

It is amusing to observe the provincialism in this part of the country. If a person intends to commence a journey some time in the month, for instance, in May; he says, "I am going in all the month of May." For a large assembly of people they say, "a smart sprinkle of people." And the word "balance," comes into almost every transaction — "will you not have a *dessert* for the balance of your dinner?" — "to make out the *balance* of his night's rest, he slept until eight in the morning."

If your baggage is to be carried, it will be asked, "shall I *tote* your plunder?" This use of plunder is said to have originated in the early predatory habits of the borderers. They also speak of a "mighty pleasant day" — "a mighty beautiful flower" — "mighty weak." A

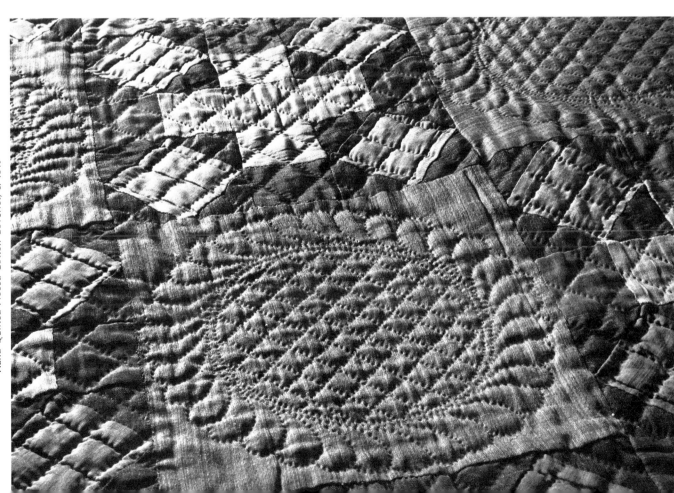

Hand-Quilted Pieced Cotton Coverlet, c. 1840

gentleman, with whom I formed some acquaintance, invited me, when I should make "an outing" for exercise, to call at his house; for his family would be "mighty glad" to see me.

— *Rev. Samuel Parker, 1835*

Sab 4 [June] Good Morn H & E [sister Harriet and brother Edward] I wrote last night till supper, after that it was so dark I could not see. I told you how many bipeds there was in our company last night now for the quadrupeds — 14 horses and six mules and fifteen head of cattle. We milk four cows we started with seventeen but we have killed one calf and the [American] Fur Company being out of provision have taken one of our cows for beaf it is usually pinching times with the company before they reach the buffalo, we have had a plenty because we made ample provision — at Liberty [Missouri] we purchased a barrell of flour and baked enough to last us with killing a calf or two untill we reach the buffalo. The fur Com is large this year, we are really a moving village, nearly four hundred animals with ours mostly mules, and seventy men the fur Com have seven wagons and one cart, drawn by six mules each, heavily loaded, the cart drawn by two mules carries a lame man one of the proprietors of the com. we have two waggons in our com. Mr and Mrs S [Henry Spalding] and Husband and myself ride on one Mr [William H.] Gray and the baggage in the other our Indian boys drive the cows and Dulin the horses. Young Miles [Goodyear] leads our forward horses four in each team. Now E if you wish to see the camp in motion look away ahead and see first the pilot and the Captain [Thomas "Broken Hand"] Fitzpatrick just before him — next the pack animals, all mules loaded with great packs soon after you will see the waggons and in the rear our company we all cover quite a space. The pack mules always string along one after the other just like Indians. There are several gentlemen in the Com who are going over the Mountains for pleasure, Capt [Sir William Drummond] Stewart — Mr. [Jason] Lee speaks of him in his journal He went over when he did and

returned he is an Englishman — Mr. Celan. We had a few of them to tea with us last Monday eve, Capts Fitzpatrick Stewart Maj [Moses "Black"] Harris and Celam. I wish I could discribe to you how we live so that you can realize it. Our manner of living is far prefferable to any in the States I never was so contented and happy before. Neither have I enjoyed such health for years. In the Morn as soon as the day breaks the first that we hear is the word — arise, arise, then the mules set up such noise as you never heard which puts the whole camp in motion. We encamp in a large ring, baggage and men tents and waggons on the outside and all the animals except the cows are fastened to pickets within the circle. This arrangement is to accommodate the guard who stand regularly every night and day also when we are not in motion, to protect our animals from the approach of Indians who would steal them. as I said the mules noise brings every man on his feet to loose them and turn them out to feed.

Now H & E you must think it very hard to have to get up so early after sleeping on the soft ground, when you find it hard work to open your eyes at seven o'clock just think of me every morn at the word arise we all spring. While the horses are feeding we get our breakfast in a hurry and eat it by this time the word catch up — catch up rings throu' the camp for moveing we are ready to start usually at six travel till eleven encamp rest and feed start again about two travel untill six or before if we come to a good tavern then encamp for the night.

Since we have been in the prairie we have done all our cooking when we left Liberty we expected to take bread to last us part of the way but could not get enough to carry us any distance we found it awkward work to bake at first out of doors but we have become so accustomed to now we do it very easy. Tell Mother I am a very good housekeeper in the prairie. I wish she could just take a peap at us while we are sitting at our meals, our table is the ground our table cloth is an Indian rubber cloth.

— *Narcissa Prentiss Whitman, 1836*

"Revere" Punched-Tin Candle Lantern, c. 1800

Miniature "Spark" Lantern, c. 1850

Hinged Tin Candle Lantern

St. Joseph, Missouri, 1854

St. Joseph

We rode on Monday, 18th, twelve miles to Blacksnake Hills. At this place [the future St. Joseph] Mr. Rubidoux [Robidoux] has a trading post, and an uncomonly fine farming establishment on the Missouri River . . . having a delightful prospect in front of more than a thousand acres of open bottom land . . . the hills on the north and east partially covered with woods . . . . Having obtained a supply of milk, I encamped out, preferring the field to the house.

Our mode of living from day to day, had . . . become uniform. Dry bread and bacon constituted our breakfast, dinner and supper. The bacon we cooked when we could obtain wood for fire; but when "out of sight of land", that is, when nothing but green grass could be seen, we ate our bacon without cooking. Some of the simplest articles of furniture were sufficient for our culinary purposes. The real wants of life are few; artificial ones are numerous.

— *Rev. Samuel Parker, 1835*

We stopped [in June] for two hours at the Blacksnake Hills. There I had a long talk with J. R. [Joseph Robidoux], who keeps a store and runs his father's fine farm . . . . This place is one of the finest on Missouri for the erection of a city.

— *Fr. Pierre-Jean DeSmet, S.J., 1838*

Mose Robidoux's warehouse [on May 20] . . . was a building of stockade fashion, split logs, set upright and roofed with clapboards . . . . His ample (old) log house for dwelling and trade . . . stood a short distance away on the gentle slope of a hill, with his little corn-cracking mill on a "branch" in the foreground. That very day the active, old gentlemen . . . was mounting his horse for a ride to the land office, to be opened next day at Plattsburg. He wanted to be on hand early to enter his quarter section, which it was said the people of Buchanan country intended to take from him for a county seat. They wanted to lay out a town and sell lots; but so did Mons. Robidoux . . . . With proper self-regard he named the town after himself, St. Joseph.

— *Richard S. Elliott, subagent, 1843*

Eastward and at the foot of these hills stands the town of St. Joseph . . . . In 1842 St. Joseph did not exist; . . . today there are 350 houses, two churches, a city hall, and a jail . . . . It's population is composed of Americans, French Creoles, Irish, and German.

— Fr. Pierre-Jean DeSmet, S.J., 1846

. . . knowledge of the [Indian] sign language was of the utmost importance to me, even in St. Joseph, for I came in contact there with Indians from so many different tribes that I was at first hopelessly confused by their various dialects.

One of my hobbies was to collect Indian weapons, decorations, and apparel. Before I had learned the sign for "swap" I rarely succeeded in making a purchase unless I had an interpreter. The reason was, as I found out, that, in my bungling manner, I had made the sign meaning "give." When a man presses the desired object to his breast and gives the Indian a questioning look he is requesting a gift; when he indicates or points out the article he wishes, then strikes his right forefinger twice across his left forefinger, he means barter or trade. I soon became better acquainted with the Indians, when I was able by means of signs to purchase moccasins, bows and arrows, tobacco pipes, embroidered purses, bracelets, and clothing. For a very slight compensation I was enabled thus to proceed with my studies. The Iowa I found especially friendly. The Fox Indians and the Potawatomi were far more reserved. The Iowa have been a well-disposed tribe from the first; there is no record of any hostile act on their part toward the white race. Both of the other two, on the contrary, have waged bloody wars for the retention of their lands, especially the Potawatomi. Whether, as some people assert, those two tribes are to be regarded for that reason as more warlike is a question. The Potawatomi, as a related tribe to the Chippewa, fought during the War of the Revolution with the English . . . .

Indians one meets here and in the surrounding country are, to be sure, no longer a true type of the savage. They have acquired much from living neighbors to the white man and, more's the pity, little that is good. How could it be otherwise? Do so-called Christians set them good examples? In the main, however, the Indian retains his traditional usages and customs . . . .

The manner of dress among Indians varies quite as much and sets them as distinctly apart from us as their copper-colored skin. As a rule, the men wear only breechcloths, moccasins, and woolen blankets; otherwise, they are nude. Sometimes they wear leggings, i.e., trousers of deerskin, that are cut differently according to the tribe to which the wearer belongs; that denotes tribal differences also in the way they are made and ornamented. The Indian women wear, nowadays, a short, bright-colored calico shirt . . . made with collar and with sleeves that are finished with cuff or wristband; they wear, besides, a sort of underskirt of red or blue woolen material that reaches to the calf of the leg and is held in place about the hips by a leather or woven girdle. Sometimes women use the same material for a kind of leggings that extend only to the knee and are fastened with knee bands, the straps and bands being often varicolored and richly ornamented with coral. On their arms they wear any number of bracelets, often as many as twenty, of brass wire that they themselves embellish in a really tasteful manner with files.

The fall of the Indian's blanket is similar to that of the Roman toga, but more graceful, because the drapery of a blanket is not so full — is less baggy in appearance. To put the blanket on, one takes hold of the longer upper edge with both hands, and bending forward, draws it up somewhat above the head, so that its weight is distributed equally on both sides, and therefore it does not drop when the belt (usually a strap of tanned buffalo hide) is worn to confine the folds about the hips. Though Indian women always belt their blankets, men never do except on their wanderings. In the under side of the belt or girdle at the back there is a slit through which a knife, in its sheath, is carried. Beneath the folds of the blanket, above the belt, women carry their children or other belongings. The blanket serves both as covering for the head and, in a way, as a veil. When the women are at work it is allowed to fall over the belt in order that they may move their arms freely . . . .

Often these braves carry a fan in the right hand as they strut about the village dressed in this way. That style is followed, however, only in warm weather. As these coverings are ornamented with one or more colored stripes along the border of their narrower sides that fall straight down in front, those stripes always attract one's attention. The buffalo robe is worn in the same way as the blanket, i.e., lengthwise around the body, the head end brought over from the right, the tail end carried forward from the left. But, as buffalo robes are much heavier than blankets, the women use little leather straps that are drawn through the robe and fastened, somewhat like the fastenings on a mantle, at the throat. This helps to place the weight of the robe on the shoulders. Blankets, as well as bison robes, are sometimes painted, but they are not as artistic, because the woolen surface does not admit of detailed drawing.

After a more extended acquaintance with the various tribes one becomes observant and notices definite marks of distinction. For instance, the Potawatomi skin is much darker than that of the other tribes in this region, their features less noble, their bearing not so stately. They wear their hair loose and unkempt. The men are fully clothed. They wear, usually, a coat and leggings of tanned deerskin, the leggings having a broad double projecting seam that distinguishes the wearer from members of any other tribe.

Frequently they wind around their heads and loins woolen scarfs or sashes that are embroidered with beads in a design of arrow heads in different colors (called, therefore, ceinture à fleche). The same design, both in drawing and in color, appears also in old Mexican paintings; the colors, in most instances, are white, black, and red.

The Iowa are a more cleanly people than the Potawatomi; they are also of a brighter color, handsomer, and more stately in bearing. The men stiffen their hair with grease or loam and wear it pulled back from the forehead in such a way that the brow, being entirely exposed, appears very high. They do not wear the shirt of deerskin nor do their leggings have the broad projecting seam, but the latter are often trimmed with beads . . . .

Even during the first month of my stay in St. Joseph I had chances every day to study Indians that came in bands from the different neighboring tribes. It was the time when the yearly payments were made for the land extorted from them. As soon as the father received the money for himself and members of his family (the Iowa received $8 a head from the United States Indian Agent) they came to St. Joseph to make their purchases, because they could supply their needs there at more reasonable rates than with the traders. Still many Indians were in debt to the latter and, in that case, the traders had the first claim for payment.

The Indians came in increasing numbers, pitched their tents of skins (or, as often happened, of white cotton cloth) in the depths of the forest on their side of the river and had themselves ferried across to St. Joseph . . . .

Forms more beautiful than those I found among the Iowa Indians I can not imagine, though I have been accustomed during my studies from life for many years to all that is finest in the human form. Another advantage was their habit of wandering about in a nude condition, which contributed much toward the proud, easy bearing, as well as to the natural, graceful movements that characterize the Indian. No individuals of the white race can compare with them in that regard. The Iowa arrange their hair in one or two braids on the crown of their head and fasten thereon some eagle feathers or other headgear. The women, on the contrary, part their hair above the brow, draw it backward and bind it at the neck; then they braid with that queue a cloth, either varicolored or else richly embroidered. The younger girls, the elite among them, at least, arrange their hair in two braids, one on each side of the head, that hang sometimes at the back, sometimes in front, and are also often adorned with bright-colored bands and beads.

Every Indian has straight black hair, dark brown eyes, copper-colored skin, more or less dark, rather prominent cheek bones, and small hands and feet. They rarely allow their beards to grow; in fact, they have hardly any hair at all on their bodies and the little that appears they very carefully pull out. When standing, an Indian's feet point directly in front of him; therefore, the footprints of an Indian can be easily distinguished from those of a white man. Any one who had to walk a great deal through tall grass or along narrow paths that animals use will understand at once the advantage of placing the feet that way . . . .

The Sauk and the Fox Indians shave the hair entirely from the crown of their heads and arrange what is left at the back in such a way that it looks like a tuft or brush. Some of them leave the long hair on their crowns for a support on which to fasten their head adornments. The braves have a proud warlike mien. They have this, at least, in common with the Potawatomi: they love the Americans just as little. They have no outlook for the future that inspires hope. Their thoughts dwell more on the past, when they were independent and free. Their daughters are not as beautiful as the maidens among the Iowa; consequently not so much exposed to the temptations of the white man . . . .

Saddle Bench

35

. . . . The Americans act as though they think the Indian domain is at their disposal for hunting and fishing as much as they like without being called to account; but if an Indian should be met hunting, on what is really his own ancient native ground that he has recently parted with, a bullet or a beating will certainly fall to his share.

Near the end of the year 1848 about 30 lodges of Iowa Indians camped in the forest across the river from St. Joseph . . . .

For three months I was a regular visitor at that camp and spent many a day and night in the variously constructed dwellings. The tents were, for the most part, conical in form and made of skins in the usual Indian fashion. There were among them, however, some lodges constructed of osier twigs or withes and covered with rush mats. There were others, besides, constructed with pieces of bark with a roof of the same material . . . .

In this Indian settlement I observed customs and modes of life. I sketched also as much as was possible during the cold winter season.

. . . in the United States, just now, a painter in the fine arts has no prospects whatsoever. He is looked upon as a "windbag," an intriguer, a "humbug." A house painter, on the contrary, makes a good income. In saying this, I bring no reproach against the Americans; they are republicans.

— *Rudolph Friederich Kurz, 1848*

My father had often heard Oregon spoken of and had taken considerable pains to get all the information possible of that country. Joel Palmer, who was a resident of the southern part of Indiana, had returned from Oregon in 1846, intending to return with a company in 1848. My father wrote to him for information as to the outfit needed for the trip, etc. He also obtained a book written or published by Lewis and Clark, giving their travels west of the Rockies. With this information, my father began to make preparations to emigrate to Oregon, by disposing of his lands, sawmills and other property. It was difficult to sell for money. He made a trade [in 1847] of his sawmill property to a man by the name of Swift, who owned a tannery in Fort Wayne [Indiana] and was interested in a mercantile establishment, for leather and different patterns of cloth and Kentucky jeans . . . .

We left Fort Wayne some time in April, by canal boat for Cincinnati, Ohio. We remained there a few days and left on the steamer *Phoenix* for Saint Louis.

We brought our wagons from Fort Wayne, consisting of one light two-horse for family use, two heavy ones for carrying loads, pulled by three or four yoke of cattle. We also bought a span of horses on our arrival at Saint Louis. Father concluded to let my brother Jefferson, L. D. Purdeau, Lawrence Burns and myself

take the span of horses and light wagon and go by land to Saint Joseph, our place of rendezvous. Before making our final start for Oregon, father and the rest of our company took passage on the steamer *Boreas, Number 3*, for Weston or Saint Joseph. I now have a receipt for money paid by my father to the steamer *Boreas, Number 3*, which gives the date of their arrival at Weston [April 29]: . . . Freight on two (2) wagons $22 . . . 3770 lbs. sundries @ 75c, $28.27 . . . 6½ passengers @ 03c, $16.50 . . . . Sister Annie was charged only half fare because she was under age . . . .

At Weston [opposite Fort Leavenworth] father bought our teams, oxen and some cows and one more wagon. In purchasing cattle, he bought one or two yoke from a man by the name of Staggs, who had been to Oregon in 1846. He had no good word for Oregon, and tried to discourage my father from going to that country. He said it was not fit to emigrate to . . . . After the purchase of our teams, we loaded our wagons and moved up to Saint Joseph, and in a few days, on May 4, crossed the Missouri River for our final start west. The ferryboat that brought our last wagon over took back . . . the noted mountaineer, Joseph L. Meek . . . .

We had our outfit, teams and necessary provisions for the trip, which consisted of 200 pounds of flour for each person (10 of us), 100 pounds of bacon for each person, a proportion of corn meal, dried apples and peaches, beans, salt, pepper, rice, tea, coffee, sugar and many smaller articles for such a trip; also a medicine chest, plenty of caps, powder and lead. Our company was made up of David O'Neill, one wagon, two boys; two Catholic priests and their servant; [and 16 adults and 11 children].

— *James D. Miller, 1848*

Independence is what is called in the west an old town. It is indebted to, and still depends entirely upon the Santa Fe trade for its prosperity and support . . . . St. Joseph is a new town, not yet six years old. Its situation is far superior to any town on the river . . . .

— *M. Thompson, 1849*

Imagine to yourself a biped five feet four inches high, with big whiskers, red mustachios, steeple-crowned hat, buckskin-coat, done up with hedge-hog quills, belt, pistol, hatchet, bullet pouch, bowie knife 20 inches long, red shirt . . . and five-inch spurs . . . it seems to me that the boys take pains to make themselves ridiculous.

— *Dr. Israel Lord, 1849*

The 7th [April], continued preparations [at St. Joseph]. While here Court was in session . . . . In July last, four men formed a plot to whip a man to death because he owed them a few dollars, which was ill-gotten gains, and which he refused to pay. For the accomplishment of their plot they secured handcuffs and went into the store and purchased cow hides, and then went to his own house in St. Joseph and compelled him to leave a sick bed and drove him by force out of town, handcuffed him and tied him to a bush, stripped him and commenced whipping him. While the whipping operation was going on they sent one of their number two or three times into town to buy liquor; thus they continued drinking and whipping him until he was dead, the operation lasting from four to six hours when death relieved the suffered from further bodily pain. Then they threw his clothes up in the bush over him to point out his remains.

— *Basil Nelson Longsworth, 1850*

[May 6] . . . . Just across the Missouri — almost within a stone's throw of us [in St. Joseph] — there is now in the midst of the wilderness the hum and bustle of a great city. Not less than 10,000 emigrants are encamped in the woods on the opposite bank. The poor Kickapoos and Pottawatomies . . . gaze upon the crowd and their doings with wonderment.

— *Ralph Ringwood, 1850*

To see [May 8] persons selling there outfits at auction daily since my stay here, it would seem that thousands were returning home . . . . Many have come here and gambled away their money . . . others have run short of funds to procure feed for their teams from the high rates they have been compelled to pay, and are forced to sell and return home. Others again, too impatient to wait for grass, set out on the plains and finding no grass after what little feed they had was fed out, fed their Bread and flour &c. . . .

St. Joseph is a beautiful scite for a town and at this time is doing a heavy business. It is only seven years since this place commenced and at this time I would suppose there was seventy five to a hundred houses of business including all kinds except dwellings.

— *Jefferson A. Drake, 1850*

The Missouri River has to be crossed to-day. There are several boats and among them one steamboat to ferry over the crowd that is waiting their regular turn; to wait until all who had secured regular tickets to cross over mean't the loss of two or three days, and as we were all ready . . . we cast about us to see if there was no other way to cross the big muddy.

As good luck would have it we discovered a small wood flat [boat] lying at the bottom of the river two feet beneath the surface of the water . . . . We soon had the boat in trim and commenced to load our animals.

Sad Iron, c. 1840

In this, however, our progress was very slow for as we got one mule on board and our attention directed to another the first one would jump overboard and swim ashore, to the great delight of the many who were looking on. After several turns of the kind, and finding that we gained but slowly in our endeavor to freight the boat by the single additions, we concluded to drive them all on together.

In this we succeeded admirably, for on they went and we put up the railing to keep them there. A shout of victory followed the putting up of the bars; a victory was gained over the frisky mule and the order given to "cast-off," but before the order could be obeyed the fiends in mule shape took it into their heads to look over the same side of the boat and all at the same time. Result, the dipping of the boat to the water's edge on one side, which frightened the little brutes themselves and they all, as with common consent, leaped overboard again. Three times, three cheers were given by the crowd on shore . . . . Of course there was no swearing done for nobody could be found that could do justice to the occasion. Finally the mules were got on board, securely tied, the lines cast off and the riffle made. This was our last trip. We had so much trouble with the mules that it was reasonable to expect a quiet time with our oxen; in this, however, we were mistaken for they seemed to have caught contrariness from the mules and were, if possible, more stubborn than the mules themselves . . . we got the horned brutes on board and landed them safely on the other shore. The balance of our property was soon crossed over and we camped for the day to "fix up" things. Here is a general camping ground, and as it is on the verge of civilization anything forgotten can be obtained by recrossing the river.

— *John Hawkins Clark, 1852*

April 5th. Arrived at St. Joseph today. Was quite disappointed at the appearance of this place. I had expected to find log houses and frame shanties, but instead I find brick houses, and plenty of whiskey. Every man I meet looks like an ale cask himself. To my opinion St. Joseph would rise a great deal faster if the people here did not take so much advantage of the emigrants.

Apr. 10. Elizabeth [Agnes's sister, Mrs. Fred Warner] and I took a walk today, and sitting on the ground I could see the Indians across the river. The vast territory lies stretched before me, and nothing but wide forests can be seen as far as the eye can reach, and yet it seems small compared to the great continent once all their own. But now the Government allows them [the Indians] part to themselves as a great favor and taken by them as such, but that does not make it right.

April 19. Done nothing today. Wish we were started.

May 3. We will leave this place today and glad to get away. I cannot like St. Joseph. There is beautiful scenery around here but I do not like it so well as my native hills [Alleganey City, Pennsylvania]. They were bare and shabby, but, oh dear, they were childhood's home. There first I learned to romp and play, and love others so well . . . .

The last load to cross the river in the evening which consisted of four men and one yoke of oxen met with trouble. The ferry ran onto a root of a tree in the water and upset. All the men were drowned, and the cattle, although yoked together, swam out and were recovered next morning. The men had been drinking too much and were reckless.

— *Agnes Stewart, 1853*

Weston/Ft. Leavenworth

Sunday morning. [May 6; Weston: "Little Switzerland."] Rainy, dismal cold chilly . . . . difficulties multiply as we proceed. A wagon with four yoke of oxen was stalled . . . a mile from town . . . a bad start . . . .

— *James F. Wilkins, 1849*

Before leaving Fort Leavenworth we were joined by a small party of emigrants for California, who desired to travel in our company for the sake of protection . . . . The cholera had for a considerable time been raging on the Missouri; and as we passed up, fearful rumors of its prevelance and fatality among the emigrants on the route, daily reached us from the plains . . . . One member of our little party was carried to the hospital in a state of collapse, where he died in twenty four hours.

My party consisted principally of experienced voyageurs, who had spent the best part of their lives among the wilds of the Rocky Mountains . . . . We followed the "emigration road" . . . . Over a rolling prairie, fringed on the south with trees . . . . Our first day's journey was only six miles, but we were now fairly embarked, and things gradually assumed the appearance of order and regularity.

— *Capt. Howard Stansbury, 1852*

"Fort Leavenworth," 1849, by James F. Wilkins

Weston, Missouri

Nebraska City

A small party of Otoe Indians camped on a small island in the Missouri about two miles above Nebraska City. It contained perhaps a hundred acres . . . . The men of the party had succeeded in Iowa in trading a pony for a five gallon keg of whiskey, which they brought to their village with the avowed intention of having a regular spree . . . .

In order that the liquors might be equally divided, no one to get more than another, they decided to make divisions by mouthfuls. They selected one of their number with an average sized mouth to make the divisions. This man served without pay. His method was to fill his mouth with the liquor and empty it in a cup held by one of the other men. This was kept up until the entire quantity had been served.

Unfortunately, the measuring mouth leaked and another had to be selected, the owner of the first one having become gloriously drunk. It must not be supposed that only one mouthful was given each man. The distribution was kept up until every one was drunk as a lord.

It is astonishing how quickly a corral can be broken and strung out on the road when teams are not broken and are not familiar with the routine. On unyoking, the yokes are stood up by the wagon to which the team belongs. As soon as the cattle are driven into the corral, the driver takes the yoke belonging to the cattle, walks to the off ox, yokes him, then calls his mate to come under. This order is obeyed promptly if the ox is near and this is nearly always the case with cattle that have been worked together long. This yoke is driven to its wagon and the others are treated in the same way, the second yoke fastened to the first by a log chain and so on until the wheelers are yoked. They are attached to their

Roads West

Independence Road

On the Trail

We found that William Sublette and his men were encamped near Independence, Missouri. He readily consented to our [Nathaniel J. Wyeth's expedition] joining his men; we must be under his full command and take our share in guarding camp and in defending in case of an attack by the Indians. Here we purchased more horses, having bought a few at Lexington to carry our baggage. Here a Mr. Campbell and his party also joined Mr. Sublette's party, making in all a party of eighty men and three hundred horses. Captain Wyeth's party consisted of twenty-five men. We took with us fifteen sheep and two yoke of oxen. Each man was to have charge of three horses, two packs and one to ride. We also took some extra horses in case some were stolen or worn out.

We were kept in strict military order, and marched double file. Those first ready took their places next to the commander. We always camped in the form of a hollow square, making a river or stream the fourth side. The horses were hobbled (fore feet tied) and turned out of camp to feed. When brought into camp at night they were left hobbled, and were tied to stakes driven close to the ground, giving each horse as much room as could be spared him within the square. The watch changed every four hours. If found asleep, the watch was obliged to walk the next day for punishment. Captain Sublette's camp calls were as follows: "Catch up; catch up," which was at sunset. Then each man brought his horses into camp. At dawn the call was "Turn out; turn out," and then horses were turned out of camp to feed, while we breakfasted. Then the horses were saddled and packed. At noon a stop was always made for half an hour. The horses were unpacked to rest them, each horse carried one hundred and eighty pounds. Not being able to trot with this load, they soon formed the habit of walking fast.

There was so little dew or rain that we did not need our tents, so we slept on the ground wrapped in our blankets, our saddles for pillows. I always wrapped myself first in my camlet cloak, pulling the cape over my head to shut off the wind or moon. This was our camp routine until we reached the Rocky Mountains.

May 12 — Left Independence, traveling west . . . .

— John Ball, 1832

Oregon Trail Ruts, East of Sapling Grove (Gardner, Kansas)

Here we left the last traces of civilization . . . . Not even a song of a bird broke upon the surrounding stillness; and, save the single track of the emigrants, winding over the hills, not a foot-print broke the rich unvaried verdure of the forest-begirt prairies; and in the little islet groves that dotted the plain — the wooded strips that wound along the course of the rivulet and the blue wall that surrounded, not a trunk was scarred nor a twig was broken.

It was a vast, beautiful and perfect picture, which nature herself had drawn, and the hand of man had never violated. No decoration of art mingled to confuse or mar the perfection. All was natural, beautiful, unbroken. The transition had been sudden, as the change was great. Everything was calculated to inspire the mind with feelings of no common kind . . . . Having pitched our tent and kindled a fire, supper was soon prepared, spread upon the ground, and we took our seats upon the grass around it . . . (then) we slept to dream of all that we loved and had left behind us, and awoke to know that they were far from us and that our home was the wild uncultivated field of nature.

— *Overton Johnson and W. H. Winter, 1843*

[To N. M. Ludlow, St. Louis:]

We have had some desperate rainy weather, and experienced the luxurious satisfaction of getting up in the middle of the night to creep out and dig a trench around our tent [at Camp William, Shawnee Land, Missouri Territory].

— *Matthew C. Field, 1843*

One afternoon, when the sun seemed to be about three hours high and we were traveling along at ox-team gait, over a level prairie, John East, a good, honest man, also from Missouri, who was walking and driving his team, was told that we were then crossing the Missouri line, whereupon he turned about facing the east, pulled of [off] his slouched hat, and waving it above his head said, "Farewell to America!"

— *Jesse Applegate, 1843*

It is four o'clock A. M.; the sentinels on duty have discharged their rifles — the signal that the hours of sleep are over — and every wagon and tent is pouring forth its night tenants, and slow-kindling smokes begin largely to rise and float away in the morning air. Sixty men start from the corral, spreading as they make through the vast herd of cattle and horses that make a semicircle around the encampment, the most distant perhaps two miles away.

The herders pass to the extreme verge and carefully examine for trails beyond, to see that none of the animals have strayed or been stolen during the night. This morning no trails led beyond the outside animals in sight, and by 5 o'clock the herders begin to contract the great, moving circle, and the well-trained animals move slowly towards camp, clipping here and there a thistle or a tempting bunch of grass on the way. In about an hour five thousand animals are close up to the encampment, and the teamsters are busy selecting their teams and driving them inside the corral to be yoked.

The corral is a circle one hundred yards deep, formed with wagons connected strongly with each other; the wagon in the rear being connected with the wagon in front by its tongue and ox chains. It is a strong barrier that the most vicious ox cannot break, and in case of an attack of the Sioux would be no contemptible intrenchment.

From 6 to 7 o'clock is a busy time; breakfast is to be eaten, the tents struck, the wagons loaded and the teams yoked and brought up in readiness to be attached to their respective wagons. All know when, at 7 o'clock, the signal to march sounds, that those not ready to take their proper places in the line of march must fall into the dusty rear for the day.

There are sixty wagons. They have been divided into fifteen divisions or platoons of four wagons each, and each platoon is entitled to lead in its turn. The leading platoon today will be the rear one tomorrow, and will bring up the rear unless some teamster, through indolence or negligence, has lost his place in the line, and is condemned to that uncomfortable post. It is within ten minutes of seven; the corral . . . barricade is everywhere broken, the teams being attached to the wagons. The women and children have taken their places in them. The pilot (a borderer who has passed his life on the verge of civilization and has been chosen to the post of leader from his knowledge of the savage and his experience in travel through roadless wastes), stands ready, in the midst of his pioneers and aides, to mount and lead the way. Ten or fifteen young men, not today on duty, form another cluster. They are ready to start on a buffalo hunt . . . .

It is on the stroke of seven; the rush to and fro, the cracking of whips, the loud command to oxen, and what seemed to be the inextricable confusion of the last ten minutes has ceased. Fortunately every one has been found and every teamster is at his post. The clear notes of a trumpet sound in the front; the pilot and his guards mount their horses; the leading divisions of the wagons move out of the encampment, and take up the line of march; the rest fall into their places with the precision of clock work, until the spot so lately full of life sinks back into that solitude that seems to reign over the broad plain and rushing river as the caravan draws its lazy length towards the distant El Dorado . . . .

It is not yet 8 o'clock when the first watch is to be set; the evening meal is just over, and the corral now

"Fording," 1849, by James F. Wilkins

free from the intrusion of cattle or horses, groups of children are scattered over it. The larger are taking a game of romps; "the wee toddling things" are being taught that great achievement that distinguishes man from the lower animals. Before a tent near the river a violin makes lively music, and some youths and maidens have improvised a dance upon the green; in another quarter a flute gives its mellow and melancholy notes to the still night air, which, as they float away over the quiet river, seem a lament for the past rather than a hope for the future. It has been a prosperous day; more than twenty miles have been accomplished of the great journey. The encampment is a good one; one of the causes that threatened much future delay (a childbirth case) has just been removed by the skill and energy of that "good angel" of the emigrants, Doctor [Marcus] Whitman, and it has lifted a load from the hearts . . . .

But time passes; the watch is set for the night; the council of old men has been broken up, and each has returned to his own quarter; the flute has whispered its last lament to the deepening night; the violin is silent, and the dancers have dispersed; enamoured youth have whispered a tender "good night" in the ear of blushing maidens, or stolen a kiss from the lips of some future bride — for Cupid here, as elsewhere, has been busy bringing together congenial hearts, and among these simple people he alone is consulted in forming the marriage tie. Even the Doctor and the pilot have finished their confidential interview and have separated for the night. All is hushed and repose from the fatigues of the day, save the vigilant guard and the wakeful leader, who still has cares upon his mind that forbid sleep. He hears the 10 o'clock relief taking post and the "all Well" report of the returned guard; the night deepens, yet he seeks not the needed repose . . . the last care of the day being removed, and the last duty performed, he too seeks the rest that will enable him to go through the same routine tomorrow.

— *Jesse Applegate, 1843*

From one of the wagons, they drew forth a large jug of whiskey, and before bed-time all the men were completely intoxicated. In the crowd was a mountaineer who gave us a few lessons in the first chapter of a life among the mountains. At midnight, when all were quiet, I wrapped myself in my blanket, laid down under an oak tree, and began to realize that I was on my journey to Oregon.

— *Joel Palmer, 1845*

Sapling Grove

May 5, 1834. Today we left the settlements. After a twenty mile horse-walk we have reached and made our camp in Sapling Grove. We are a mighty band to meet and contend with a whole village of red-skins. We count thirty-seven, in all, with ninety-five horses and mules. I presume I am not [now] out of the United States, and in the territory of our good Uncle Sam. But does his law, or power, still protect me? Shall I say to the red-man, "take care what you do! If you strike me, I will sue you for assault and battery; if you steal my horse, I will send you to the penitentiary."

May 6, 1834 . . . . This evening, one Monsieur Wolf and I gave each other a mutual scare. He, however, tucked his tail between his legs, and put off at a great rate of speed. Had I been able, I have no doubt I should have done the same thing, tail and all.

— *William Marshall Anderson, 1834*

On May 4th the different parties who were to join the expedition met for their first night camp at Sapling Grove, about eight miles from West Port. [In the caravan were Asahel Munger, his wife, and newly married Rev. and Mrs. J. S. Griffin going to work among the Oregon Indians.]

My first day's journey began under evil auspices, for I had not yet learned to pack my mule . . . . My baggage weighed 150 to 200 pounds, a quite ordinary load for a mule; but I had not divided the burden properly, so that I had to repack repeatedly . . . .

Our caravan was small. It consisted of only twenty-seven persons. Nine of them were in the service of the Fur Company of St. Louis [Choteau, Pratte & Co.], and were to bring merchandise to the yearly randezvous on the Green River. Their leader was Mr. Harris, a Mountaineer without special education, but with fine sound senses, that he well knew how to use.

The first day we marched over the broad Santa Fe road, beaten out by the caravans. Then leaving it to our left we took a narrow wagon road, established by

"Coyote or Prairie Wolf," 1843, by John W. Audubon

former journeys to the Rocky Mountains, but often so indistinctly traced, that our leaders at times lost it, and simply followed the general direction [northwestward].

Our way led through prairie with many undulating hills of good soil . . . watered with a few brooks and rivalets. On the prairie itself there is no wood. Several times we had to content ourselves with muddy standing water; but usually we found pleasant, even romantic camping places on clear brooks . . . .

All the rest joined the expedition as individuals . . . some others spoke of a permanent settlement on the Columbia; again, others intended to go to california. Almost all, however, were activated by some commercial motive. The majority of the party were Americans; the rest consisted of French Canadians, a few Germans, and a Dane.

The Fur Company transported its goods on two wheeled carts, of which there were four, each drawn by two mules, and loaded with 800 to 900 pounds. The rest put their packs on mules or horses, of which there were fifty to sixty in the caravan.

Our first camp, Sapling Grove, was in a little hickory wood, with fresh spring water . . . .

At dawn, the leader rouses the camp with an inharmonious: "Get up! Get up! Get up!" Every one rises. The first care is for the animals. They are loosed from their pickets and allowed an hour for grazing. Meanwhile we prepare our breakfast, strike our tents, and prepare for the start . . . in the early days of the journey we are apt to lead the pack animals by rope; later on, we leave them free, and drive them before us.

At first packing causes novices much trouble on the way. Here the towering pack leans to one side; there it topples under the animal's belly. At one time the beast stands stock still with its swaying load; at another it rushes madly off, kicking out till it is free of its burden. But pauseless, like an army over its fallen, the train moves on. With bottled-up wrath the older men, with raging and swearing the younger ones, gather up their belongings, load the beasts afresh, and trot after the column. Toward noon a rest of an hour or two is made, if a suitable camp can be found, the chief requisites being fresh water, good grass, and sufficient wood.

We unload the beasts to let them graze, and prepare a mid-day meal. Then we start off again, and march on toward sunset. We set up the tents, prepare our meal, lie around the fire, and then, wrapped in our woolen blankets commit ourselves to our fate till the next morning. In this way twenty to twenty-five miles are covered daily. The only food the animals get is grass. For ourselves, we take with us for the first week some provisions, such as ham, ship-biscuits, tea and coffee. Afterwards, we depend on hunting.

Such are the daily doings of the caravan.

— *Frederick A. Wislizenus, M.D., 1839*

May 7. After traveling about fifteen miles we halted and procured an extra set of horseshoes and a few additional wagon bows. The main body of emigrants is twenty-five miles in advance of us; we have now passed the Missouri, and are traveling in an Indian country — most of which is rolling prairie.

May 8. We started at seven o'clock A.M. and traveled about twenty miles, Towards evening we overtook an emigrating company, consisting of thirty-eight wagons, with about one thousand head of loose cattle . . . we passed this company, expecting to overtake a company of about one hundred wagons, which were but a few miles before us. The night, however, became so dark that we were compelled to encamp upon the prairie. Soon after we had staked our horses, a herd of wild Indian horses came galloping furiously by us, which so alarmed our horses and mules, that they broke loose and ran away after them. Dodson and myself pursued, but were distanced, and after running two or three miles, abandoned the chase as hopeless, and attempted to return to camp.

May 9 — At daylight, Dodson and I resumed the search for our lost stock. After a fatiguing tramp of several hours, I came upon one of the mules, which being hobbled, had been unable to keep with the herd. Dodson was unsuccessful, and returned to camp before me; during our absence, however, the herd had strolled near the camp, and Buckley had succeeded in taking our two horses. Having taken some refreshments, we started again in search of the lost animals. As I was returning to camp, hopeless, weary and hungry, I saw at a distance Dodson and Buckley mounted upon our two horses, and giving chase to the herd of Indian horses, among which were our two mules. The scene was wild, romantic and exciting. The race was untrammeled by any of those arbitrary and ruthless rules with which the "Knights of the turf" encumber their races, and was pursued on both sides, for a nobler purpose; it was to decide between the rights of property on the one side, and the rights of liberty on the other.

The contest was for a long time doubtful, but the herd finally succeeded in winning the race, and poor Buckley and Dodson were compelled to yield; the former having lost his reputation as a sportsman, and the latter — what grieved him more = his team and both had ruined the character of their coursers in suffering them to be beaten.

Sad and dispirited, they returned to camp, where, after a short consultation, it was unanimously resolved, — inasmuch as there was no other alternative, — to suffer the mules freely and forever to enjoy the enlarged liberty which they had so nobly won.

— *Joel Palmer, 1845*

47

Trail Junction

May 12 — Left Independence, traveling west on the Santa Fe road. The fifteenth we [Nathaniel Wyeth's expedition] left Santa Fe trail.

— John Ball, 1832

During our journey, it was the customary practice to encamp an hour or two before sunset, when the carts were disposed so as to form a sort of barricade around a circle some eight yard in diameter. The tents were pitched, and the horses hobbled and turned loose to graze, before the cooks of the messes, of which there were four, were busily engaged in preparing the evening meal.

At night fall the horses, mules, and oxen were driven in, and picketed — that is, secured by a halter, of which one end was tied to a small steel shod picket, and driven into the ground, the halter being twenty or thirty feet long, which enabled them to obtain a little food during the night.

— Brevet-Capt. John C. Frémont, 1842

[May] 16 . . . about non to day left the Sant a fee trace these are two of the longest roads that are perhaps in the world the one to Sant Afee and the other to oregon doubled teams nearly all the way Both teams Swamped down and had to unload our team breakeing an axeltree

[May] 20 . . . the women & children are coming out again haveing been confined to the waggons for 2 days past went to a camp of 4 waggons in the fore noon . . . . 2 fine looking yong Ladies in camp

[May] 23. We have been passing through lands sofar belonging to the Shawnee nation or Tribe of Indians nearly all of which Tribe have Quit hunting and gone into a half civilized manner of living cultivating small Lots of ground in corn Beans Potatoes and grains and vegetables their country is almost intierly striped of all kinds of game but is fine and Productive in grains and Stock both horses and cattle Timber is scarce but finely watered in part the trail passes through

[May] 24. It rained all night by day our teams ware moving to the river which we had been expecting [to] fall but which began to rise again . . . . me[n] women and children dripping in mud and water over Shoe mouth deep and I Thought I never saw more determined resolution even amongst men than most of the female part of our company exhibited The leaving of home of near andear friend the war whoop and Scalpin Knif The long dreary Journey the privations of a life in a Tent with all the horrors of flood and field and even the element seemed to combine to make us uncomfortable But still there was a determined resolution sufficient to overcome all obsicles with the utmost exertion we crssed over 20 waggons by about 10 o'clock when the waters became too deep to cross and in about an hour it rose so as to swim a horse.

they [women] seem to have been ignored; yet they performed their toils with as much fidelity as the men, and have been as useful in their way.

— James Clyman, 1844

May 26 . . . . The road on our side of the river for miles ahead are lined with teams and from our camp to the missouri behind is one continuous line of wagons.

— Samuel Clark McKeeby, 1850

To the Kansas River

The fifteenth [of May] we left Santa Fe trail, going northwest to the Kansas River to a government agency there. The country was mostly hilly, the hills being of shell-filled sandstone and boulders of quartz and granite. The last white man we saw was a blacksmith for the Indians, who had his smithy on the Kansas.

— John Ball, 1832

As we advanced the prairie became more gently undulating. The heaving ridges which had made our trail thus far appear to pass over an immense sea, the billows of which had been changed to waving meadows the instant they had escaped from the embraces of the tempest, gave place to wide and gentle swells, scarcely perceptible over the increased expanse in sight. Ten miles on the day's march; the animals were tugging lustily through the mud, when the advance guard shouted "Elk! Elk!" and "steaks broiled," and "ribs boiled," and "marrow bones," and "no more hunger!" "Oregon for ever, starve or live," as an appointed number of my companions filed off to the chase.

— Thomas J. Farnham, 1839

On the fifth day after our start we reached the Kanzas, or, as it is commonly called, Ka [or Kaw] River, not deep, but rather broad and swift. Its course is from west to east . . . . Some miles from us, on the same side of the river, was a village of the Kas, or Kanzas Indians; across the river, somewhat farther off, were two villages of the same tribe. Near the first village there is a trading house, a smith, and a Methodist mission. The Kas formerly lived forty miles to the west; but in 1826 in pursuance of treaties, the United States Government assigned them the district which they now inhabit; and has set apart for them for twenty years the annual sum of $3,500 . . . which is given them principally in kind.

. . . The whole tribe is said to number 1,500 souls. The attempt to civilize the Kas and lead them to agriculture as yet has had little success. The government has sent them some mechanics, has established a sort

We had a rainy march on the 12th (June) . . . we encamped in a remarkably beautiful situation on the Kansas bluffs, which commanded a fine view of the river valley.

— *Brevet-Capt. John C. Frémont, 1842*

June 12, Sunday . . . . Eternal prairie and grass, with occasional groups of trees. Frémont prefers it to every other landscape. To me it is as if someone would prefer a book with blank pages to a good story. The ocean, has, after all, its storms and icebergs, the beautiful sunrise and sunset. But the prairie? To deuce with such a life; I wish I were in Washington with my old girl.

June 13 (Monday) . . . . Slept badly on the saddle cover. Just above me two owls with their disgusting hooting. Chased them away three times, but after a minute they were there again. Finally, I let them howl.

— *Charles Preuss, 1842*

The Doctor [Marcus Whitman] spent much time in hunting out the best route for the wagons, and would plunge into streams in search of practicable fords, regardless of the depth or temperature of water; and sometimes, after the fatigue of a hard day's march, would spend much of the night in going from one party to another to minister to the sick.

— *James Willis Nesmith, 1843*

His [Whitman's] constant advice, which we knew was based upon a knowledge of the road before us, was, "Travel, *travel*, TRAVEL; nothing else will take you to the end of your journey; nothing is wise that does not help you along; nothing is good for you that causes a moment's delay."

— *Jesse Applegate, 1843*

. . . and here [past the Wakarusa River, 60 miles out] let me say there was one young Lady which showed herself worthy of the bravest undaunted poieneer of [the] west for after having kneaded her dough she watched and nursed the fire and held an umblella over the fire and her skillit with the greatest composure for near 2 hours and baked bread enough to give us a verry plentifull supper.

— *James Clyman, 1844*

of model farm, and furnishes them yearly a number of cattle and swine. But they usually burn the fencing of the farm in winter and slaughter the animals. In other respects, they live, like the rest of the Indians, from hunting; and as their country, though containing some deer, and elk, has no buffalo, they go twice a year some hundreds of miles away on a buffalo hunt, and bring the dried meat back with them. A tendency toward civilization, on the other hand, is indicated by their permanent residence in villages . . . .

— *Frederick A. Wislizenus, M.D., 1839*

I can hardly describe my feelings as I was traveling up the Caw (or Kanzas) River . . . . I could scarcely follow the wagon tracks, the ground was so hard in the prairie. I had almost concluded at last to turn back, and got down on my knees, and asked the Lord whether I should do so or not . . . . about an hour before sunset, I got down off my horse, and prayed again. and instead of sleeping in the prairie, I got to an encampment where there was fire, and plenty of wood, and good water. I roasted my meat, sweetened some water, and with my biscuits, made a hearty supper.

— *Rev. Joseph Williams, 1841*

Kansas (Kaw) Crossing

. . . up to this point, the road we had traveled was a remarkably fine one, well beaten, and level — the usual road of a prairie country . . . the boat [ferry] was twenty feet long and five broad, and on it were placed the body and wheels of a cart, with the load belonging to it, and three men with paddles . . . but as night was drawing near, and, in our anxiety to have all over before the darkness closed in, I put upon the boat the remaining two carts with their accompanying load. The man at the helm was timid on water, and, in his alarm, capsized the boat. Carts, barrels, boxes, and bales were in a moment floating down the current, but all the men who were on the shore jumped into the water, without stopping to think if they could swim, and almost everything — even heavy articles, such as guns and lead were recovered . . . all the sugar belonging to one of the messes wasted its sweets on the muddy waters; but our heaviest loss was a bag of coffee, which contained nearly all our provision . . . . It was a loss which none but a traveler in a strange and inhospitable country can appreciate.

— *Brevet-Capt. John C. Frémont, 1842*

June 14 (Tuesday) . . . . And they actually came at eleven o'clock. They had lost the road and had had to find their way across the creeks themselves. Fremont had sense enough to order a halt immediately. A strong coffee was brewed and enjoyed by all. The beef was just to my taste, especially since I had been obliged to skip two meals.

At two o'clock we reached the Kansas, and while I am writing this our baggage is being ferried across in the rubber boat. This boat, which is inflated and used for the first time, performs quite well. Horses and men swam across quickly, but the oxen struggled hard. So far only one has consented to go across. The river is between three and four hundred feet wide, but only at a distance of forty to fifty feet is it deep enough to swim. Just now I hear shouting from the opposite shore . . . .

A sack with 150 pounds of coffee has not been recovered; otherwise nothing is missing, but much sugar and bread is spoiled. Today we have a day of rest. Many Indians visit us. We are having salad, butter, onions, and milk for lunch. Who would have expected that! Two oxen were traded for a cow with calf; now we can drink our tea with milk. The remainder of the coffee will not last very long. Today I washed a shirt again. Turned out a little better than the first time.

— *Charles Preuss, 1842*

In their largest force we saw them [the "adventurous travellers" bound for Oregon] just after crossing the Kansas River, about the 1st of June. The Oregonians were assembled here to the number of six or eight hundred, and when we passed their encampment they were engaged in the business of electing officers to regulate and conduct their proceedings. It was a curious and unaccountable spectacle to us, as we approached. We saw a large body of men wheeling and marching about the prairie, describing evolutions neither recognizable as savage or civic, or military. We soon knew they were not Indians and were not long setting them down for the emigrants, but what, in the name of mystery, they were about, our best guessing could not reduce to anything in the shape of a mathematical probability.

— *Matthew C. Field, 1843*

We came up on the south side of the Caw [Kansas] River and camped below and near an Indian town of the Caw tribe. There were huts and cabins ranging along the river on either side of a street. It was said those Indians grew corn, beans, and pumpkins. I admired several of the Indian men I saw there. They were more than six feet tall, straight, and moved with a proud step; wore blankets drawn around their shoulders, and leggins. Their hair was shorn to the scalp, except something like a rooster's comb on top of the head, colored red. I remember standing and gazing up into the face of one of those tall Indians, probably to see if he were a good or bad Indian. I was not afraid of them. I had lived near the Osage River and I saw that the Caw River looked to be hardly half as wide. The current was slow and the water I thought was very deep. The men in some way made the wagon boxes water tight and used them as boats. In crossing the river the Indians assisted our people in swimming our cattle and horses. I noticed that the Indians did not swim like white men, but with an overhanded stroke, "dog-fashion," they said. These Indians were friendly and accommodating. They told us we would soon reach the country of the Cheyennes and Pawnees, and that they were bad Indians.

— *Jesse Applegate, 1843*

[The Kansas River] was considerably swollen on acount of recent rains. There were no boats and of course, no bridges then, but a Frenchman in the neighborhood had three dugouts made of logs. These my father secured the next morning and with them made a platform, fastening the dugouts about four feet apart, and on this very primitive raft, the wagons were one by one ferried across. The better part of two days was spent in crossing the river . . . .

William Vaughn . . . was swimming the river, leading some stock when he was suddenly seized with cramps, in the middle of the stream, and with a quick cry for help, went down . . . . J.W. [Nesmith] brought him up, but Vaughn after the manner of drowning men, clutched his rescuer so that Nesmith himself was in danger of being strangled. To this day, I can seem to hear Nesmith cry, "Let me go and I will save you!" But Nesmith was compelled to release himself by diving again. This time with the help of Stewart, he brought the now unconscious Vaughn to the shore. Nesmith called to me for a keg. I remembered that there was one in father's tent, and brought it as quickly as a boy's legs could carry me. Vaughn was laid over the keg and the water rolled out of him, while Stewart and I were kept busy pumping his arms. Even with these vigorous measures, Nesmith was on the point of giving up, for the man seemed to be utterly dead, but some almost imperceptible, convulsive motions gave him courage, and at length consciousness was restored to Vaughn.

— *Edward Henry Lenox, 1843*

[May 26] Ladies passing from Tent to Tent Early our ferrying continues to progress Slowly Some young men got a hymn Book and sung a few familiar reformation camp meeting songs last night which had a peculiar Symphonic and feeling Effect in connection with the time and place. a call was made this morning for a regular organization . . . . about 2 oclock we got all our Teams waggons and Baggage over & assertained that there ware 92 men present made some regulations to prepare for keeping of a night and day guard as we are now not more [than] 2 days easy travel from the

Crossing, on the Kansas River (Belvue, Kansas)

Kaw Indian villagis the first of the wild roveing tribes that we meet with on our way this evening two waggons that ware in the rear came up opposite side & we ware told that 12 or 15 Teams are yet comeing on it has been fine and clear & the evening pleasant the Ladies gave us a few hymns in the afternoon which had a pleasant meloncholly affect

[May] 28. after a verry tidious & toilsome d[a]ys drive I arived at my mess wet as water could make me and found them all sheltering themselves the best way they could about the waggons they ware fortunate enough however to have furnished themselves with a fair supply of wood & now commenced the tug of war for the rain again renued its strength & fell in perfect sluces as though the windows of heaven had again been broken up and a second deluge had commenced intermingled with vived flashes of Lightning and deep growling thunder which continued until about dark when it slaked up for the night . . . .

[June] 3. this is [the] third season that a considerabbl emegration has pased right through the Kaw village and crossed the Kanzas at this place

. . . . Last year I understand that the Emigrant lost that never ware returned 3 or 4 horses & 20 or thirty head of neat cattle and a considerabl amount of other property and we have Lost 200 Dollars worth or horses mules and other property which might be mostly recovered if time would permit and we had an intirperter that would look to our intrest but as it is we must submit without recourse the Kaws are now starting on their summer hunt and our Stolen horses cannot be obtained untill they return which will not be untill some time about the first of august or latear

— *James Clyman, 1844*

By means of a rope, one end of which was coiled around a tree, the wagons were let down the steep banks of the river [Kansas], and placed in the boat. Two wagons and 12 mules were taken over at a time, the boat being propelled by poles. A Frenchman [Charles Beaubien or Lewis Ogee] and his two sons, half-breed Kaws, own and work the ferry. Their charge is $4. for each wagon, 25¢ for a mule, and 10¢ each man. Double teams are required to haul the wagons up the northern bank, and through the deep sands extending ¼ mile back from the river.

Fist fight came off this evening between two members of Captain Kirkuff's mess. [He who] provoked the quarrel . . . was rewarded with rings around his eyes bearing a strong resemblance to ebony goggles.

— *William G. Johnston, 1849*

"Papin's Ferry," c. 1854, by Samuel Reader

52

To the Blue River

Friday, June 17 . . . . A party of emigrants to the Columbia river, under the charge of Dr. [Elijah] White, an agent of the government in Oregon Territory, were about three weeks in advance of us . . . . There were sixty-four men, and sixteen or seventeen families . . . a considerable number of cattle, and were transporting their household furniture in large heavy wagons . . . there had been much sickness among them, and . . . they had lost several children.

— Brevet-Capt. John C. Frémont, 1842

And what a day that first day was, west of the Caw [Kansas River]. Rain, rain, rain, and mud up to the hubs of the wagons, stalled teams, and maddened, worn out drivers. My own oxen, which were far better fed than most of the oxen in the company, were hardly able to make any progress at all with our heavily loaded wagon. Our family generally rode in a lighter wagon. My wagon carried eleven hundred pounds of flour, three hundred pounds of bacon, one hundred pounds of sugar, one hundred pounds of dried apples, fifty pounds of coffee, fifty pounds of salt, a keg of syrup, a keg of tar, and innumerable other articles in smaller quantities. At the end of that weary day, I asked the pilot how far we had come, and he answered, to my dismay, "About two and a half miles." It seemed to me, that at that rate it would take us all eternity to reach the Pacific Coast. But we made a little better progress the next day . . . . It was on the evening of this dreary day of such slow progress that my father asked J. W. Nesmith to take a little book which he handed him, and go through the camp and make a careful list of every man and boy over fourteen years of age, for guard duty . . . .

The large bands of cattle owned by Jesse and Lindsay Applegate, and Daniel Waldo could hardly be rounded up in the morning before ten o'clock, and so delayed us in our morning start, that after a few days it was amicably agreed to divide the company. Father took our two teams and thirty-one other teams, whose occupants chose to accompany us, we went ahead. Those who were left behind, chose Jesse Applegate as Captain [of the "Cow Column"] . . . .

On that first Sunday morning father was resting in his tent, and mother and the four girls were taking it easy after an arduous week, when several from the families around us broke in impatiently upon us and wanted to know at what hour we were going to get off. "How is this, Captain Lenox," said one of them, "that you are not up and off this fine morning?" "We are not going to travel to-day," replied my father. "This is the Lord's day. The cattle need rest, and we need rest, and your families need rest." "Oh, you can't cram that down our throats," was the vigorous and irreverent reply;

"We are going on." "Well," said Captain Lenox, "I have no authority to stop you, but you will find it to your interest to travel with a well guarded company, rather than to go it alone." Dr. [Marcus] Whitman was standing near, and broke in with the advice, "Gentlemen, you will do well to pay attention to your captain, and take his word. Otherwise, you may lose your scalps, and those of your families." This settled the matter and ever afterwards we had our Sunday rest.

— Edward Henry Lenox, 1843

I think it was the second day after we had crossed the Caw we met a war party of Caws, marching afoot, about a hundred of them painted and feathered and armed with bows, spears, war-clubs, tomahawks, and knives. Some were wounded and limping. Some with blood on faces, arms in slings, and bandages around their heads . . . seemed to be tired and in a hurry. They told us they had been out on a buffalo hunt and had been attacked by a war party of the Pawnees and had a fight with them . . . there was a Mexican in the train who cut off an Indian's hand at the wrist and hung it on a stake about three feet high in the encampment. I saw it there myself, an was afraid of it, for I saw it was a man's hand. An indignation meeting was the result of this ghastly exhibition . . . the Mexican was compelled to leave the company.

— Jesse Applegate, 1843

June] 7. Judge of my feeling a rapid hail Storm out side a hog wallow within all in unison the Thunder Lightning & hail the schreems an yells within and my object to recover stolen property being instantly known all eyes ware directed on me a loud angry Quarrel commenced between my Friends and enemies and my situation was far from being envious for Knives ware soon drawn and one Flurrished over my head the indian that held it was soon grappled & a half dozen ware as soon wallowing in the mud on the ground floor of the Lodge.

— James Clyman, 1844

Red Vermillion

June 18 (Saturday). Continued up the Kansas. Met a few Delaware Indians in their tent. They were engaged in drying their game on a fire to make it ready for transportation.

Stopped at [Red (Little)] Vermillion Creek. Since the calf was only getting thinner by constant walking, it was slaughtered, and, just as with oxen, a portion was prepared right away for the evening meal. I stuck to the beef.

— Charles Preuss, 1842

Vieux's Ford

June 18th. I rode for some miles to the left, attracted by the appearance of a cluster of huts near the mouth of the Vermillion. It was a large but deserted Kansas village, scattered in an open wood along the margin of the stream on a spot chosen with the customary Indian fondness for beauty of scenery. The Pawnees had attacked it in the early spring. Some of the houses were burned and others blackened with smoke; the weeds were already getting possession of the cleared places. Riding up the Vermillion river I reached the ford [Louis Vieux's ford] in time to meet the carts, and crossing, encamped on the western side.

We breakfasted the next morning at half past five, and left our encampment early. Quitting the river bottom I rode along the uplands over the rolling country, generally in view of the Kansas, from eight to twelve miles distant. Many large boulders of a very compact sandstone, of various shades of red, some of them four or five tons in weight, were scattered along the hills. We traveled nineteen miles and pitched our tents . . . . We crossed at 10 a. m. [June 20th] the Big Vermillion. Making our usual halt at noon, after a half day's march of twenty-four miles we reached the Big Blue.

— *Brevet-Capt. John C. Frémont, 1842*

. . . emigrants forded the Red Vermillion river at this point [Vieux's ford] for many years. After Mr. Vieux had constructed his log cabin, near this ford, he built a toll bridge. . . . Louis Vieux sometimes made as much as $300 a day revenue from the toll bridge . . . charged only $1 for each outfit that crossed.

He furnished hay and grain to travelers . . . He was of French descent, a big man among the Pottawatomie Indians — business agent for the tribe, interpreter and named a chief . . . .

Here some fifty pioneers succumbed to the cholera. They were all buried on the east bank of the Red Vermillion in the shadow of the hill a short distance to the east. It was where Louis Vieux . . . now lies buried . . . . From the hillside in the immediate vicinity large slabs of . . . lime rock were carried by the survivors, a stone was erected at the head of each grave, and the name and date of burial carved on each stone . . . .

(Only three remain of those created, one carving is distinguishable: T. S. Prather, May 27, 1849. He died of cholera.)

— *William E. Smith, 1850*

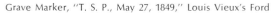

Grave Marker, "T. S. P., May 27, 1849," Louis Vieux's Ford

Near the Blue

June 20 (Monday) .... After a ride of twenty-four miles we now pitch our tent at Blue River. A prairie chicken was shot. If the cook cannot prepare it any better than the turtle, let him gulp it down himself.

— *Charles Preuss, 1842*

This is the middle ground between the Kanzas and Pawnee Indians. The day before we crossed the Big Blue River, we met a war party of Kaus (Kanzas), returning from the Pawnee country. They told us they had seen the Pawnees, and had beaten them in battle; but we learned afterwards, from a more creditable source that it was exactly the other way. They had one or two fresh scalps and as many wounded men, and

Alcove Springs

Rock Inscription, "J. F. Reed—26 May 1846," Alcove Springs

Alcove Springs, Near the Big Blue River (Marysville, Kansas)

56

were leaving the world behind them as fast as possible. We saw their battleground afterwards, and found on it two or three dead bodies. Here the Emigrants, finding that it was inconvenient and retarding to their progress, to travel in so large a body, dissolved their first organization and formed themselves into smaller companies.

— *Overton Johnson and W. H. Winter, 1843*

The Prairie, June 6, 1843

Dear Friends:

We have just touched a good wooding and watering place known as Rocky Creek, about two hundred miles from the Missouri line. I have persuaded some trading people from the mountains who are passing us to wait and carry on a line for me. We are all very well and growing fat; not on buffalo however, for the lords of the Prairie are yet far in advance of us, but exercise and fasting have infinitely more to do with our improvement. Antelopes are running around the green, but they seem to shun any more acquaintance with us pertinaciously. We had turtle soup however last night for supper and that ain't bad, even when eaten out of tin plates and "squatting" tailor fashion on the grass. We shall reach the "Big Blue" tomorrow and hope to find buffalo the next day. At present we are disappointed at not having reached them, and our supplies, laid in under other expectations, are now fast running out, which fact may possibly remove any danger of the gout or an alderman's death from among us for a long time. We are in full situation to travel fast but have so many difficult crossing-places, rafts have to be constructed, and the animals made to swim the river loose, that our progress is rather vexatiously retarded. Still, however, we continue in the best of spirits and full of excitement and interest in the adventure. Now and then some greenhorn of an attendant takes a grumbling fit, but gets so quizzed and befooled for his foolishness that he soon picks up sense enough to be silent if not satisfied.

— *Matthew C. Field*
New Orleans *Daily Picayune, July 30, 1843*

. . . today struck our old trail made on our [William Sublette and Mose Harris] return from the mountains in 1827 . . . .

— *James Clyman, 1844*

Cholera, taken in the premonitory stage, is a mild and manageable disease; but requires vigilance and prudence to prevent it from running into confirmed cholera. These symptoms are a mild looseness, with indigestion, and attended with little or no pain; of longer or shorter duration. — Commonly preceding an attack from one to three or four days. In this mild form, or stage of the disease, the patient should take from fifteen to twenty drops of laudanum [opium], four or five times a day, to check, and to hold in check, this looseness of the bowels; they should, at the same time, be attentive to diet and to exercise, avoiding all imprudences and excesses.

But sometimes the attacks come on more violently, without giving any previous notice; so that, in an hour or two, the patient is completely prostrated, and the disease assumes all its characteristic features — such as the rice-water, and the milk-and-water-like discharges, either from stomach and bowels, or both, accompanied with partial or general spasm. In all such cases, I gave from sixty to eighty drops of laudanum, with fifteen or twenty drops of essence of pepper-mint, in a good portion of strong toddy; or, if the pepper-mint was not at hand, in its place I used a tea-spoonful of the tincture of camphor, or two or three table-spoonfuls of strong, red-pepper tea; sometimes, also, a tea-spoonful of the tincture of kino [an astringent, to arrest hemorrhage].

It should be always borne in mind, that if the dose of medicine is cast up by puking, it should be repeated so soon as the stomach becomes a little settled.

— *Ferdinando Stith, M.D., 1844*

June 22nd . . . . We were congratulating ourselves on being done with cholera but here was the prospect of losing two or more of our esteemed members . . . and of another long delay. Owing to this disease we were already forty or fifty days behind, and, as the game had been driven from the road by earlier hunters, our supplies were being rapidly consumed, and we were liable to be caught in the early snows on the mountains, making the outlook very discouraging.

Five of our comrades had previously become the prey of this dread disease, and yet, like a sleuth-hound, it was still pursuing us . . . . Medical treatment, sympathy and brotherly care proved of no avail. Both patients passed into a state of collapse before midnight and died early next morning.

Their bodies were laid out in clean clothes, after which they were sewed up in their blankets and at twelve buried in one grave . . . . We erected a neat and substantial cairn . . . . burning all the clothing in which they had died . . . . that both [men] should be stricken with cholera at the same time within a few minutes of each other was beyond our comprehension.

— *Reuben Cole Shaw, 1849*

I passed through a camp where people were dying and rottening, alive, unhurt and untouched, I slept among the dying and dead for over a month, handling and attending on cholera patients, and returned safe and sound.

— *Fr. Pierre-Jean DeSmet, S.J., 1851*

Independence Crossing

...we encamped on the Little Blue, where we established for the time being a sort of fury converting our wagon beds into boats for transportation, having before started proved ourselves with those which would answer the double purpose of both land and water craft... there were more wolves than I ever saw, or might say ever heard of before, for they made the night hideous with their yelling, and to a person unaccustomed to such sounds, and in a strange country it is anything but musical; at least it seemed to me as if all the wolves for a thousand miles around had congregated at this particular place, for our special benefit. In the morning they could be seen dispersing in droves (packs), and were by no means loath to part with these "traveling musicians".

...after a long day's drive encamped for the night on what is called the Big Blue; here we saw indications of the encampment of the little party called "The first immagration;" who preceded us in the year 1843, from these indications we supposed they must have had rather an unpleasant time just here; in fact, I have since learned that they were obliged in consequence of high waters to remain here for three weeks or more, the whole country contiguous to the River being completely inundated. Our party here being more fortunate than our predecessors, had no difficulty in crossing.

— Samuel Hancock, 1845

Independence Crossing, Big Blue River (Marysville, Kansas)

St. Joe Road

Across the Missouri

When a new outfit is to be got ready, wagons are purchased, all alike if possible, and shipped to the starting point on the Missouri river . . . . Oxen are purchased in Missouri and Iowa and driven to the point fixed upon. Drivers are hired and sent to the camp nearby.

The wagons are provided with double canvas sheets [usually Osnaburg] to protect the goods from rain while in camp. The oxen are yoked up and driven about as a sort of drill since many are very far from being broken, in order to make them biddable. Usually six yokes of oxen are intended for each wagon. One yoke is placed astride the tongue of the wagon, the other five chained to the end of the tongue by which the load is pulled. The front yoke or leaders as they are called must be well broken, biddable oxen, subject to and obedient to the command of the driver without bit or rein. When the leaders and wheelers are biddable, the four yokes between the two are controlled although they may be very raw oxen. They soon become sober oxen after pulling heavy loads a few days.

When the goods arrive by steamer, the wagons are driven to the landing, the goods loaded and the wagons sent back to camp. When all the wagons are ready, the start is made. Such is the newness of everything that a very short drive is made for a day or two, then the drives are lengthened until from 16 to 20 miles can be made during the day. It is the practice of some wagon masters to make this drive each day and to eat only two meals.

As soon as it is light enough to see to yoke the cattle, a drive of five or six miles is made, then there is a stop for breakfast. The oxen are unyoked, put to graze and watered while the men are eating and greasing the wagons. This greasing is done every two or three days. It is called "greasing" but should be called "tarring" as tar is used mostly. The oxen are again yoked and a drive of about the same distance is made, though if convenient this should be the longest drive. The oxen are again unyoked, watered and put to graze. Now the men prepare their meal at leisure, eat, clear up everything and are ready for the third drive.

Starting about sun down, they drive until the driver of the first or leading team sees the wagon master sitting by the side of the road, when he turns his team, follows the direction of the wagon master and stops. The next team is driven by the side of the first, quite close, the third one stops his wagon with the off front wheel almost touching the near hind wheel of the first. The fourth team is stopped so that the near fore wheel is stopped near the off hind wheel of the second wagon, and by

alternating the other teams as they are driven up, a corral is formed. When completed a fair circle is made. As soon as a team is at its place, the oxen are unyoked and the night herder takes them in charge when all are freed from their yokes. The wagon master selects a place for grazing. No more is seen of the oxen or herder until daylight the next morning when the routine of the preceding day is re-enacted.

As soon as the corral is made the men are ready for slumber; some in the wagons when the goods are not piled to the bows; some under the wagons; others wherever most convenient.

There are many unexpected hindrances in travel. All is smooth sailing until we reach a spongy crossing at a point which was once a creek. It may be two wagons are driven across safely but when the third one is driven in or on, down it goes to its hubs. You either double the team or unload and haul the empty wagon out. Now it will not do to try another wagon, so every one takes his butcher knife and a blanket, cuts as much grass as he can carry in the blanket, piles it on the marshy draw and tramples it down. Then a wagon is driven on and nearly always over. Sometimes before all the train is over the grass has to be replenished.

Sometimes we come to a stretch of sandy road two or three miles long when time is saved by doubling teams to pull half the wagons over and returning for the other half.

Sometimes an unaccountable nervousness comes over the cattle of a train which makes them very difficult to handle and frequently very dangerous. They will stampede and run with the loaded wagon, leaving the road and overturning it . . . .

It is well established that cattle are very much afraid of snakes. I once had a confirmation of this fact in a very simple and scarcely to be believed story.

As a driver was using his whip, it became detached from the handle and fell across the road over which the oxen had to pass. Our ox, seeing the whip which resembled a snake, jumped all four feet off the ground, gave an unusual bawl, and the whole train in a twinkling was on the run. Fortunately, we were on a level road, yet it required great effort to quiet the cattle. Very little damage was done, two or three spokes were broken out of the wheels by one wheel running against another.

— Lewis Bissell Dougherty, 1848

When we left St. Joseph a number of reflections crossed my mind. St. Joseph is a hard place. Mechanics charge extravagantly high for their work. It contains 4,000 people and is a stirring place. A few days before we were there four negroes were sold at public sale, an old man, woman and two children.

[Later] . . . . This morning we started and traveled over a very muddy road and about 2:00 or 3:00 in the evening we came to a large prairie which was eight miles across. We drove pretty fast and reached a lodging on the west side. There were no buildings, but prairie hens, cranes, ravens and turkeys. This prairie is one of the beauties of nature. It is rolling or hilly country and would certainly be rich and very productive if cultivated.

This night we pitched our tents and for the first time found ourselves enjoying the realities of a trip to Oregon. The wind blew a gale, and a threatening storm hurried us on our preparations. We kindled a fire, made our coffee and fried meat and spread a quilt in our tent, placed our supper on it, seated ourselves on the ground and commenced helping ourselves.

— Basil Nelson Longsworth, 1850

When farely over the [Missouri] river we began to fix things up; put the wagons together, mate the oxen, mules and horses; stow away provisions, appoint each man to do a certain duty, for a period of time. The man who cooked for two weeks, was to drive oxen for the next two weeks, and the man who had been driving oxen was to take his place. Teamsters, guards, and all concerned, were to change places every two weeks....

There are many musicians belonging to the different encampments surrounding us, and after supper all commenced to practise the sweet tunes that were to enliven us while sitting around the camp fire on the far plains. Never shall I forget the hoarse bellow of the portly frog or the sharp twang of the wee ones, mingled as they were with soft strains of instrumental music.... This concert lasted until near midnight, when all was hushed except the crackling of the log fires as they were every now and then replaced by the watchful sentinel as he kept watch and ward over the sleeping multitude....

May 7. — .... We are twenty persons in number, mostly young men, and all from Cinncinnati except two Canadians who joined the company while coming up the river.

May 8. — Bright was the morning and light our hearts as we rolled out of camp on this, our first day's journey of 2,000 miles....

— John Hawkins Clark, 1852

After a particular route has been selected to make the journey across the plains, and the requisite number have arrived ... their first business should be to organize themselves into a company and elect a commander. The company should be of sufficient magnitude to herd and guard animals, and for protection against Indians .... In the selection of a captain, good judgement, integrity of purpose and practical experience are the essential requisites .... His duty should be to direct the order of the march, the time of starting and halting, to select the camps, detail and give orders to guards, and,

indeed, to control and superintend all the movements of the company. An obligation should be drawn up and signed by all the members of the association, wherein each one should bind himself to abide in all cases by the orders and decisions of the captain and to aid him by every means in his power ... and they should also obligate themselves to aid each other, so as to make the individual interest of each member the common concern of the whole company.

— Randolph B. Marcy, 1857

Missouri River Crossing from St. Joseph

Rolling Hills West of the Missouri River (near Elwood, Kansas)

Wolf Creek

In crossing rivers where the water is so high as to come into the wagon beds, but is not above a fording stage, the contents of the wagons may be kept dry by raising the beds between the uprights, and retaining them in that position with blocks of wood placed at each corner, between the rockers and the bottom of the wagon-beds. The blocks must be squared at each end, and their length, of course, should vary with the depth of the water, which can be determined before cutting them.

When rivers are wide, with a swift current, they should always, if possible, be forded obliquely down stream, as the action of the water against the wagons, assists very materially in carrying them across . . . .

When it becomes necessary, with loaded wagons, to cross a stream of this character against the current, I would recommend that teams be doubled, the leading animals led, a horseman placed on each side with whips to assist the driver, and that, before the first wagon enters the water, a man should be sent in advance to ascertain the best ford.

— *Randolph B. Marcy, 1857*

Wolf Creek in 1859 (Doniphan County, Kansas)

Wolf Creek

Presbyterian Mission

On May 20, 1853, our train of fourteen wagons, bound for Oregon, crossed the Missouri river in the *Highland Mary*, at a few scattering houses called St. Mary, I believe. Our first camp outside of organized territory was made in the high grass on the bank of the Missouri river, a short distance below the Omaha Indian Mission [Presbyterian] which was the last house we saw until we reached Fort Dalles, about the middle of October.

Our train effected no organization, other than a common understanding that each would do his part. We had no captain to hold responsible for the petty annoyances of the road. There was no pompous strut of brief authority, or irritating insubordination. As free men the journey was commenced, and as such prosecuted. The cares and duties of home, farm and citizenship were transferred to camp and road; the duties were changed but responsibility remained. The family was the unit; its integrity was unaffected. Each yoked its teams in early morning, plodded on until nightfall, and unyoked.

— George B. Currey, 1853

To the Big Blue

Within a few hours time [the morning of May 6] we began to sight vast heards of buffalo on their way to and from the plains to the river where they made regular excursions to get water . . . . The order was given to stop, then veer to the left, as these animals were in a wild race commonly called a stampede, and had never been known to stop for anything that proves an obstruction to their progress. We were barely able to give them right of way ere the great moving mass of apparently crazed beasts came alongside our teams . . . . For more than two hours our progress was stayed and the time seemed to pass quickly too, for we were so spellbound in our wonder at the vastness of the herd . . . .

My mother drove "Blackey" and "Sorrel" hitched to the Virginia carriage which father bought for the especial trip. At first we were ruled out of the train on account of the horse team but we found that horses were much better fitted for such a journey than oxen . . . .

All along this part of the road there was great scarcity of wood and many times we were compelled to cook our food with buffalo chips. This caused many ladies to act very cross and many were the rude phrases uttered, far more humiliating to refined ears than any mention of the material used for fuel could have been, but fane of surroundings was a great level, and, ere long, each member of the various households was busily employed in the search for fuel. The fires burned clear and with great heat, so that by good management with our old fashioned "Dutch ovens" and closed kettles, a clean and wholesome meal could be quickly prepared over a fire of buffalo chips. Almost every family was provided with one or more good milch cows, and after a night's rest and graze the fresh morning milk, good warm bread, meats and sauce, for there was an abundance of dried fruits in each provision wagon.

Right here I wish to state that many of those emigrants were well equipped for setting up a new home in a far off land. Whole bolts of sheeting, linsey wool, jean for men's clothing, carpets, homeknit hoisery and mittens of colors, both grave and gay, were stored away by careful hands to circumvent the day of need. Books also were not entirely forgotten. My husband and I brought our Bible, dictionary, arithmetic, grammar, charts and maps, also our diplomas of graduation.

— Sarah Cummins, 1845

October 3 . . . . The country between the frontiers of the Missouri and the Big Blue for about 200 miles, presents a remarkable uniformity in all its leading features. Clay soil, rolling prairies and the shores of the rivers well wooded. You meet forests of oak and nut trees of all varieties, with maple and cottonwood and a variety of trees found in the east.

The hillsides in several places abound in fine springs of water surrounded by beautiful groves, arranged with as much order and tact as if planted by the hand of man.

— Fr. Pierre-Jean DeSmet, S.J., 1851

May 17 . . . . It is very warm today, but a nice breeze flying makes it pleasant. It is nice when all is well and happy. Passing a muddy little run. I don't know its name. Take in wood and water and go on again. How beautiful everything looks. As far as I can see it is beautiful green hills and I can see many trees in the distance, and I can see a thunder cloud in the distance, too, — black, black it rises, then it rolls, and all is so grand. The sun beaming through in one place makes the clouds blacker. In appearance the forked lightning flashes and seems to drop to the ground. I must get in the wagon and not get wet if I can help it. It makes one so uncomfortable. Oh, such a windy day. We could not have a fire to cook breakfast. We had to travel five miles to a hollow place. 'Tis dreadful cold. Oh, the wind goes to a person's heart. I will shiver to death. I feel for the men gathering the cattle and yoking them up. It was so cold for them, and no warm breakfast. Camping under the heavens as usual.

May 19. We present a sight watching the cattle with a whip while the men are yoking them up, some packing up the wagons. Little Janet Warner . . . passing around with a coverless umbrella . . . . Cattle lying on the ground. What awkward attempts some of the men making at yoking the cattle. Some of them scarcely ever saw cattle before they started on this journey. Some of them

Oregon Trail (near Beattie, Kansas)

swearing. I think they might do without that, sinning their souls away for nothing. How plain we are told, "Thou shalt not take the name of the Lord, thy God, in vain" . . . .

It is a beautiful day. The sun is shining bright and warm, and a cool breeze blowing makes it very nice indeed, and it seems very much like home. If I had a horse — but, no, I would not like that either. Oh, they are just starting, so I must stop for today. Oh, I feel so lonesome today. Sometimes I can govern myself, but not always, but I hold in pretty well considering all things. Trying to write walking but it won't do. We stopped for the night in a pretty place.

— *Agnes Stewart, 1853*

Big Blue Crossing

May 15. — Started early to make the Big Blue river, but rain commenced falling and retarded our progress so that we lay up short of the mark. Camped before sundown one mile from wood and water; good grass, however, which reconciled us to the many other inconveniences which we experienced. No hot coffee nor warm bread; a cold snack and well-filled pipes our only comfort.

May 16. — The wind commenced blowing and the rain to fall just before daylight. It was a tedious journey of six miles from camp to the Big Blue river; the wind and rain from the northwest, as we were going in that direction had to "face the music" of the elements in all their disagreeableness. Six miles in six hours and we are on the banks of the Big Blue. Here we set fire to a pile of driftwood, cooked our dinner and smoked our pipes. On the east bank of this river is located a private post-office, a dramshop, hotel and a ferry, the business all under one roof. If we mail a letter we pay $1; if we take a dram of whiskey, seventy-five cents; a square meal, [?] $1.50; if it is a wagon we want carried over the river, $4, and no grumbling. The proprietor is doing a rushing business. During our stay of two and a half hours he crossed forty wagons, his clerks were busy handing out whiskey and the cooks getting out the bacon, biscuits and coffee. How many letters he received for transportation during the same time I am unable to say, but our company handed in fifteen or twenty. The boss has a good thing just now; how long he will be able to keep it depends on the overland immigration.

Rather than to pay $4 per wagon for being ferried we concluded to ford the river, which we did without much trouble or danger. Took in wood and water and pushed on onto the open prairie.

— *John Hawkins Clark, 1852*

64

Ft. Leavenworth Road

Toward the Ridge

Friday, June 1 .... In the course of the afternoon we passed the travelling train of Mr. Allen, consisting of about twenty-five ox-teams .... They had been on the spot several days, detained by sickness. One of the party had died but the day before of cholera, and two more were then down with the same disease. In the morning early, we had met four men from the same camp, returning on foot, with their effects on their backs, frightened at the danger, and disgusted already with the trip.

It was here that we first saw a train "corralled".

Monday, June 4 .... We are now fairly on the broad open prairie; the air fresh, cool, and delightful; the view on all sides very extensive.

In the afternoon we were met by a small band of Sauk Indians, who presented a paper, written by some philanthropic emigrant, representing that, as we were now passing through their country consuming their grass, water, and wood .... they wished to receive something by way of remuneration, whether money, biscuits, (of which they are very fond,) or tobacco. They were rather a fine looking body of men, and seemed quite peacably disposed.

— *Capt. Howard Stansbury, 1852*

Big Vermillion Crossing

June 7 — The road lies through a rolling prairie, and a ridge dividing the waters of the Missouri from those of the Big Blue river, a tributary of the Kansas.

Met a Mr. Brulet, a French trader, from Fort Laramie, with a large train of wagons, laden with packs of buffalo robes, bound for St. Louis. He had been forty days on the road, and had met not less than four thousand wagons, averaging four persons to a wagon. This number of emigrants appeared to him to be getting along rather badly, from their want of experience ....

A small party, with a single wagon drove into camp just as we were leaving the ground. They had formed part of a company from St. Louis, had proceeded within sixty miles of Fort Kearney, but had quarrelled, and became disgusted with the trip and with each other, and had separated. These persons were on their return to St. Louis. They gave discouraging accounts of matters ahead. Wagons, they said, could be bought upon the route of emigration, for from ten to fifteen dollars apiece, and provisions for almost nothing at all.

— *Capt. Howard Stansbury, 1852*

June 9 — We crossed the Big Vermillion — the stream is seventy yards wide, flowing with a back current. We found the trees and stumps on its banks carved all over

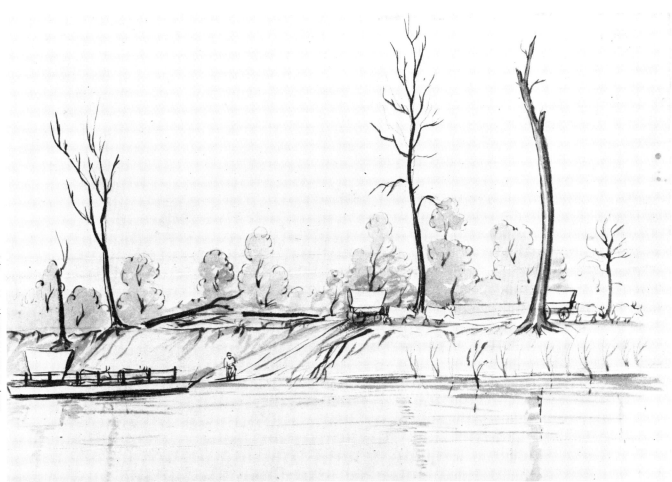

"Ferry of the Nodaway," 1849, by James F. Wilkins

with the names of hundreds of emigrants who had preceded us, the dates of their passage, the state of their health and spirits, together with an occasional message for their friends who were expected to follow . . . . Just above us was a wagon with a small party of emigrants. They had lost most of their cattle on the journey; and the father of three of them having died on the road, they, in conformity with his dying wishes, were now on their return to the settlements . . . .

. . . encamped on the right bank [east] of the Big Blue, near a spring of fine water [Alcove Springs] on the margin of a level prairie, bordered with huge trees, under the welcome shade of which we pitched our tents, after a fatiguing march of twenty-six miles.

. . . . Since crossing the Vermilion, the character of the country has changed from that of a high and rolling prairie to a comparatively flat and elevated plateau.

— Capt. Howard Stansbury, 1852

Trail Junction

Sunday, June 10 — The camp rested, it having been determined . . . wise to keep the Sabbath . . . .

. . . . Several large catfish and some soft-shelled turtles were caught in the stream by the men. The rich bottom in the rear of the camp produces strawberries of fine quality in utmost profusion; the men gathered them by hatfuls. Two large terrapins were also found here on the prairie.

In the afternoon, the advance of a train from St. Joseph, belonging to Messrs. Bissonet and Badeau, bound on a trading expedition among the Sioux, passed the camp and halted on the bluff beyond. Mr. Bissonet, who is an old trapper . . . informed me that the stream called by our guides the Legerette is in fact the Nemaha; and that the streams called the Fremont, Great and Little Nemahas, are the waters of Turkey Creek, and flow into the Blue to the north of the road.

— Capt. Howard Stansbury, 1852

Monday, June 11. At half-past five o'clock, a most violent storm of wind and rain set in, and raged with great fury for three hours . . . . Several large trees were blown down and one fell across an emigrant wagon close by us. The owners, who had sought refuge in it from the tempest, narrowly escaped with their lives . . . .

Eight miles from the Blue, we struck the emigration road from Independence. Here we found a company of seventy or eighty persons with some twenty wagons on their way to California, among whom I recognised several former campagnos de voyage on the Missouri . . . .

Passed six graves today.

— Capt. Howard Stansbury, 1852

Council Bluffs Road

ɯ

Along the North Side

. . . [the 25th] we went forward and arrived at Elkhorn, a very considerable river . . . we constructed a boat of a wagon body, so covered with undressed skins as to make it nearly water tight. The method was very good . . . but night came on before we finished . . . .

On the 27th . . . *met Messrs. Campbell and Sublette with a small caravan, returning from the Black Hills [Laramie Range, Wyo.].* When mountain traders meet under such circumstances there must be mutual exchanges of friendship, more ceremonious and complicated than can be gone through with in the passing "how do you do." The two caravans encamped.

Wednesday July 1st. I rested the last night as quietly as I should have done upon a bed, in a civilized country. . . . My bed is made by first spreading down a buffalo skin, upon this a bear skin, then two or three mackinaw blankets, and my portmanteau constitutes my pillow.

We proceeded a few miles up the Loups Fork . . . found a good fording place, where we crossed . . . . We halted for the night. The manner of encamping is to form a large hollow square, encompassing an area of about an acre, having the river on one side; three wagons forming a part of another side, coming down the river and three more in the same manner on the opposite side; and the packages so arranged in parcels, about three rods apart, as to fill up the rear, and the sides not occupied by the wagons.

The horses and mules, near the middle of the day, are turned out under guard, to feed for two hours, and the same again toward night, until after sunset, when they are taken up and brought into the hollow square, and fastened with ropes twelve feet long, to pickets driven firmly into the ground.

The men are divided into small companies, stationed at the several parcels of goods and wagons, where they wrap themselves in their blankets and rest for the night.

— Rev. Samuel Parker, 1835

Monday, May 24th. We camped on the banks of the River Platte. Beautiful place for camping, but the Pawnee Indians are plenty and the Italian Gypsy cannot beat them in begging. We are expecting a scrap with this tribe within the next few days. They tell us we cannot pass through their country without giving them one steer out of every team, and this is impossible. Therefore, guess we will have to fight. We have joined with twelve other teams, making in all twenty-four teams, and we number sixty-five fighting men, if none runs. Hope for the best. Tonight we are again encamped in the midst of a large city, dwelling in tents. Music, singing and merrymaking can be heard in all directions. At one camp they are dancing after the inspiring strains of the violin. At the adjoining camp they are holding a religious meeting and still at another many families are seated around a large campfire, prepared by the young men of that train, for a special evening chat. Everybody seemingly happy. No fear of being attacked by Indians in such a crowd as this.

— *Enoch W. Conyers, 1852*

Of the fortitude of the women one cannot say too much. Embarrassed at the start by the follies of fashion, they soon rose to the occasion and cast false modesty aside. Long dresses were quickly discarded and the bloomer donned. Could we but have had the camera trained on one of those typical camps, what a picture there would be. Elderly matrons dressed almost like little girls of today. The younger women were rather shy in accepting the inevitable but finally fell into the procession, and we soon had a community of women wearing bloomers. Some of them went barefoot, partly from choice and in some cases from necessity.

The same could be said of the men, as shoe leather began to grind out from the sand and dry heat. Of all the fantastic costumes, it is safe to say the like was never seen before. The scene beggars description. Patches became visible upon the clothing of preachers as well as laymen; the situation brooked no respect of persons. The grandmother's cap was soon displaced by a handkerchief or perhaps a bit of cloth. Grandfather's high crowned hat disappeared as if by magic. Hatless and bootless men became a common sight. Bonnetless women were to be seen on all sides. They wore what they had left or could get, without question as to the fitness of things. Rich dresses were worn by some ladies because they had no others; the gentlemen drew upon their wardrobes until scarcely a fine unsoiled suit was left.

— *Ezra Meeker, 1852*

Loup River (Sarpy County, Nebraska)

Across the Great Plains

After we came to the Platte [opposite Fort Kearny], we pursued our way up the river . . . the country begins to diminish in its fertility . . . the men of the caravan complain of delay, and had reason to do so, having nothing to eat but boiled corn, and no way to obtain any more before finding buffalo . . . the intellectual powers of these Indians [Pawnees] are very good, but need cultivation. They are fond of ornaments, and not having the same means of gratifying their vanity as civilized people have, they resort to almost anything to decorate their persons; such as porcupine quills, beads, wreaths of grass and flowers, brass rings upon their wrists, birds feathers, and claws of wild beasts. The claws of a grizzly bear are an ornament of the first order, and the tails of white wolves are in high estimation. But their favorite and almost universal ornament is painting their faces with vermillion . . . .

I had heard of the prairie horse-fly, but was not aware that it would be so very annoying and even tormenting to our horses. Its bite is like the thrust of the point of a lancet, and when the fly is surfeited, or brushed off, the blood immediately gushes out . . . but when a horse is separated from the company, he is severely bitten by them. On one occasion, when I rode forward to find a crossing place over a deep muddy stream of water, they came around my horse in such swarms that he became frantic, and I was obliged to return in full speed. I have no doubt that a horse left alone in the season of these flies would be killed by them.

— *Rev. Samuel Parker, 1835*

The Linn Ct. [County] Co. camped close by. They gave us a splendid serenade . . . . After the singing the men felt like walking twenty miles and concluded to have a French Four with Cotillion, formed a ring and chose their partners . . . the way the prairie grass suffered was a sight.

— *Bryan Dennis, 1850*

. . . scarcely out of sight of grave diggers [for cholera].

— *Abraham Sortore, 1850*

The dead [from cholera] lay sometimes in rows of fifties or more . . . people were continually hurrying past us in their desperate haste to escape the dreadful epidemic.

The dust was intolerable. In calm weather it would rise so thick at times that the lead team of oxen could not be seen from the wagon. Like a London fog, it seemed thick enough to cut.

— *Ezra Meeker, 1852*

Plain—Approaching the Platte River

Native Grasses at the Platte

May 17 we have a dreadful storm of rain and hail last night and very sharp lightning. It killed two oxen . . . . We had just encamped in a large flat prairie [opposite Fort Kearny], when the storm commenced in all its fury and in two minutes after the cattle were taken from the wagons every brute was gone out of sight . . . all gone before the storm like so many wild beasts . . . . The wind was so high I thought it would tear the wagons to pieces. Nothing but the stoutest covers could stand it. The rain beat into the wagons so that everything was wet, in less than 2 hours the water was a foot deep all over our camp grounds. As we could have no tents pitched, all had to crowd into the wagons and sleep in wet beds, with their wet clothes on, without supper.

— *Amelia S. Knight, 1853*

June 20th. Traveling on the fresh traces of the Oregon emigrants, relieves a little of the loneliness of the day . . . .

Our midday halt was Wyeth's Creek . . . . Here a pack of cards, lying loose on the grass, marked an encampment of our Oregon emigrants.

June 24 (Friday). Broke camp at six and continued along Little Blue River. I now have to do my surveying at the rear of the caravan because they maintain it is too dangerous to ride ahead alone. I don't like this . . . . I was lucky to engage one of the men to do my laundry . . . . If I only had a bottle of wine . . . oh, those good times, where are they now!

June 25 (Saturday). . . . that silly brant (Brant) came galloping up and claimed he had seen Indians on the other side of the river. We halted, and our two sharpshooters set out to reconnoiter while the others made ready their rifles and pistols for an emergency. After half an hour it became clear that Mr. Brant had seen elk instead of Indians. After we laughed at him, we moved on quietly in the roasting heat of the sun. (94° Fahrenheit)

— *Charles Preuss, 1842*

When about twenty days out, and no sign of buffalo or even antelope . . . an uneasy sensation began to pervade the camp quite generally. Some had let their good spirits forsake them a week after leaving Westport, some kept up brave faces for a fortnight longer, but about this time nearly everybody looked serious. On the morning of the 12th of June the last slice of bacon in the possession of "Our Mess" went into the frying pan for breakfast, and we rode along the [Little] Blue, after finishing our scanty meal, in very dull spirits indeed.

This Blue is a beautiful stream within the range of the Pawnee Indians. It cuts deep through an elevated region of prairie, and when high, as it was at this time [June], a varying width of from a hundred to a hundred and thirty feet is displayed by its surface. Crossing the uplands from the Blue to the Platte the traveller finds himself upon a most wild and desolate district; and, after leaving the tops of the timber in the Valley of the Blue behind him, nothing is seen around but grass and sky — excepting only the flowers, the beautiful prairie flowers, that spring up everywhere, like sweet emotions that come sometimes to the most desolate heart. It was in this vicinity that we first found the splendid gaura coccinea expanding its delicate blossoms, with its rosy shade in the morning, its heightened scarlet in the noontide, and its pale hue of the moon as evening comes on, when it emits its most delicious fragrance. The sida coccinea displayed itself, also, upon the banks of the Blue . . . .

It is proper to mention that the traveller to the mountains by this route crosses two streams with cerulean cognomenation, the distinction between them being that one is little and the other large, whereby one is known as the "Big Blue", and the other contents itself to murmur through the wilderness under the appellation of the "Little".

— *Matthew C. Field*
New Orleans Daily Picayune
December 31, 1843

It continued to rain, at intervals, of several days, and the road . . . became quite muddy and bad. After leaving Big Blue River . . . the proportion of timber was less, until we came to the Little Blue River — a distance of 70 miles; and here, the hills bordering on the stream, are a little sandy.

— *Overton Johnson and W. H. Winter, 1843*

. . . we came in sight of quite a large Indian village (Sioux) . . . the Indians soon visited, and seemed disposed to cultivate a friendly inter-course which we gave them to understand we appreciated. Seeing we were in need of food, they brought . . . dead prairie dogs, and some screech owls; doubtless these are considered delicacies among them, but fortunately we had plenty of food more familiar and palatable to us, and we declined partaking of these rare dishes . . . . They brought deer skins, buffalo robes, and many other things which they were desirous of trading and some of which we purchased. . . . . These Indians are considered pretty numerous and are rather good looking, both male and female; in their rude and uncultivated way they seemed to have some regard to their appearance and deportment, at least during our sojourn amongst them . . . the children who were too small to use bow and arrow are permitted to run at large, in a state of nudity, this exposure in all probability prepares them for subsequent hardships they have to endure.

— *Samuel Hancock, 1845*

Such sharp and incessant flashes of lightning, such stunning and continuous thunder, I had never known before. The woods were completely obscured by the diagonal sheets of rain that fell with a heavy roar, and rose in spray from the ground; and the streams rose so rapidly that we could hardly ford them.

Toward sunset, however, the storm ceased as suddenly as it began . . . . The thunder here is not like the tame thunder of the Atlantic coast. Bursting with a terrific crash directly above our heads, it roared over the boundless waste of the prairie, seeming to roll around the whole circle of the firmament with a peculiar and awful reverberation. The lightning flashed all night.

— *Francis Parkman, 1846*

[Found here near the Little Blue] a company that got into a fight among themselves ... burnt fragments of wagons, stoves, axes, etc., with a great quantity of harness cut to pieces; and with a quantity of torn shirts, coats, hats ... all besmeared by blood.

— *James W. Evans, 1850*

Sunday — intended to lay by, but grass of no account so go 18 miles.

— *Walter G. Pigman, 1850*

Wednesday, June 12. — In the bottom of the creek a species of larkspur and wild onion abound; our men used the latter freely, and we found them quite palatable in flavoring our bean-soup .... Indeed, the appearance of a tree, in all these regions of naked prairie, is to the traveller a certain indication of the presence of water; numerous tracks are to be seen, leading off from the main road to some sheltered and sequestered grove, affording the welcome indulgence of shade, wood, water, and grass to the weary imigrant and his still more wearied beasts.

Elsewhere, during the long fatiguing day, shade there is none; unless it is beneath his [the emigrant's] wagon, which to him is literally his home. In it he carries his all, and it serves him as tent, kitchen, parlor, and bedroom, and not unfrequently as a boat, to ferry his load over an otherwise impassable stream.

An immense number of black beetles and other insects swarmed around the camp [on Walnut Creek] .... Attracted by the light, they annoyed us beyond measure, and would be heard all night, pattering against the tents like large drops of rain in a heavy shower.

... [Sunday] was devoted to rest. Most of the people availed themselves of the opportunity to take a hunt, as we had killed no game up to this time. In fact, we had had no opportunity, the game having been driven from the vicinity of the travelled route [Oregon Trail] by emigration which had already passed over the road.

The results of their efforts was accordingly not very magnificent, the whole party bringing in only a duck, a musk-rat, a large snapping turtle, and one miserably poor antelope.

The constant use of salt meat, without vegetables, had affected us all with a cutaneous irritation, to be allayed

The Narrows (near Hastings, Nebraska)

only by the use of fresh meat; and hence the arrival of this antelope was hailed by our voyageurs with lively satisfaction. The little carcass was cut up and divided among the several messes, a portion being sent to our travelling companions [emigrants]; and it was amusing to see how soon every one was seduously engaged in preparing this most welcomed addition to our homely fare.

... June 18. We have been traveling for the last three days up the valley of the Little Blue .... In the morning we passed a government ox-train laden with provisions for the new post about to be established in the neighborhood of Fort Hall. It consisted of thirty-one oxen, and about forty men.

The valley of the Little Blue has not presented any great novelty in the way of flowers. The only new plants met with have been a lupine, the flower of which, of a bright purple, rises directly from the root, the plant is totally leafless — a splendid variety of the mallow, of a bright carmine color, its trailing stems sending up flowers in little patches of a few yards square, presented a rich and beautiful appearance, enhancing the monotony of the prairie by its brilliant hues. The aloe occurred in some places in abundance, and there were a few cacti and a species of a leguminous plant, having a flower of pale purple color, resembling a vetch; also a species of pale blue digitalis.

— Capt. Howard Stansbury, 1852

Oak Roots, The Narrows

The Little Blue ran hard by, about fifty feet wide by three or four deep, fringed with emerald green oak groves, cottonwood, and long-leaved willows; its waters supply catfish, suckers, and a soft-shelled turtle, but the fish are full of bones, and taste, as might be imagined, much like mud.

— Richard Burton, 1860

The Coast of Nebraska

Crossing on the way several Pawnee roads to the Arkansas, we reached, in about twenty-one miles from our halt on the Blue, what is called the coast of the Nebraska, or Platte river. This had seemed in the distance a range of high and broken hills; but on a nearer approach were found to be elevations of forty to sixty feet, into which the wind had worked the sand. They were covered with the usual fine grasses of the country, and bordered the eastern side of the ridge on a breadth of about two miles.

— Brevet-Capt. John C. Frémont, 1842

June 26 (Sunday) .... We crossed over from Little Blue to the Platte. We marched twenty-five miles without water, made no stop, and are now very tired. Tomorrow we shall move up this river almost to the culminating point of our journey. Low, wet prairie. Legions of mosquitoes.

— Charles Preuss, 1842

June 28 .... We had a specimen of the false alarms to which all parties in these wild regions are subject .... A man who was a short distance in the rear, came spurring up in great haste, shouting Indians! Indians! I immediately halted, arms were examined and put in order; and Kit Carson, springing upon one of the hunting horses, crossed the river, and galloped off ....

Mounted on a fine horse, without saddle, and scouring bareheaded over the prairies, Kit was one of the finest pictures of a horseman I have ever seen. A short time enabled him to discover that the Indian war party of twenty-seven consisted of six elk, who had been gazing curiously at our caravan as it passed by, and were now scampering off at full speed ... and its excitement broke agreeably on the monotony of the day.

— Brevet-Capt. John C. Frémont, 1842

June 28 (Tuesday). Just as we had made a halt and had sat down for our lunch, the cry "Indians, Indians" was heard. Everybody jumped up and at the horizon there were actually a dozen figures to be seen. Some ran to collect the horses which grazed outside camp; the others

Coast of Nebraska (near Grand Island, Nebraska)

prepared their rifles and pistols. Our young commander makes it a point to treat every such trivium with great importance. Our two hunters rode toward the figures and returned soon with the intelligence that they were whites on their return trip to Missouri. Soon they arrived, twelve or thirteen, all on foot and rather ragged. Our party treated them, gave them tobacco, and after about an hour we marched on toward the west and they toward the east.

— *Charles Preuss, 1842*

After striking this stream [Little Blue] we continued to travel up it 10 miles; then leaving it, turned across in a north westerly direction, for the main Platte River. On the Little Blue River we found a few Antelopes, which were the first wild animals of any size, which we had seen since we left the States; and after leaving the waters of the Kanzas we found no bees, and this, from all that we could learn, is the farthest point West which they have yet reached: Nor did we find any of the wild fowls, or smaller animals, common in the Western States, until we passed the Mountains. We reached the Platte River in the evening; the distance across being about 25 miles, which is the greatest, on the whole route, without water.

— *Overton Johnson and W. H. Winter, 1843*

[June] 9. Several Teams remained at last encampment to await the appearance of a young emigrant who came on & overtook us at 5 oclock P. M. in riding this forenoon a Short distance south of the trail we fell in a deep vally amid the bare clay Bluffs which realized allmost all the fabled scent of the much Fabled Spice groves of arabia or India for more than 2 miles the odours of the wild rose & many other oderiferous herbs scented the whole atmosphere But the groves ware wanting nothing but gnarled cotton woods ware seen

[June] 10. roled out across the devide between the head of Kanzas & the great Platt and from the eye I should Judge that the main platte is as high or higher than the Kanzas near our last nights encampment a narrow row of low sand hills running paralel with and not more than 6 or 8 miles from the platte being the only deviding ridge.

[June] 11th. no wood but a few dry willows and Quite small no timber except a few cotton wood Trees & them all confined to the Islands in the river which are numerous but generally small the Prairie ponds are well stored with wild ducks [these] with a few antelope constuite all the game yet seen & but feew of them

— *James Clyman, 1844*

On June 25th, we had a succession of rolling prairies and deep, miry streams, one of which was quite difficult to cross. Two of our wild pack mules mired, stuck fast, and gave up to die; but, with a rope about the neck, they were pulled out more dead than alive, and the ordeal seemed to have changed their dispositions, as after their mud bath they became very tame and gentle . . . .

[Later] . . . posted on a large tree was found the following: NOTICE — We camped here on the 10th day of May. Jim Lider went up the creek to hunt deer and never came back. We found his dead body two miles up the creek after two days hunt, his scalp, clothes and gun all gone. The Pawnees did it. Look out for the red devils. — John Slade, Captain, Otter Creek Co.

June 26th . . . . After thirty miles travel the Platte was sighted.

— *Reuben Cole Shaw, 1849*

We crossed the ridge dividing its water from those of the Platte River . . . . On arriving at the western edge of the plateau, the country became more elevated . . . . A range of small hills of a sandy, reddish clay, with a sharp outline toward the river forming the "Coast of Nebraska", and also constituting the bluff bounding the river valley on the south . . . beyond this verdant carpet of two miles in breadth, flows the river of which we had heard so much.

— *Capt. Howard Stansbury, 1852*

May 30. Helen [a sister] found a pocket book. Some one will wish they had not lost it. It contained some friendship lines, some lines of poetry, a lock of hair, but lost to him now. Camping on the vast prairie and in sight of the Platte River.

— *Agnes Stewart, 1853*

. . . wife's old love affair with . . . the tailor seems to have started all over again.

— *Hans P. E. Hoth, 1854*

Platte River Road

Grand Island

The Grand Ile [Grand Island] terminated two miles back, so according to our ideas it is 72 miles long and if we may calculate its width in the same ratio, it will be (about) 24 broad) — It has throughout pofsefsed great bodies of Timber affording shelter and subsistence to a good many Deer, some Elk and a few Beaver — Ever since we lost sight of the Buffaloe their dung and other sign of last winter, and also Indian encampments of same time have been seen every where, from which we are confident a number of the Panee nation must have wintered on the Platte, and from the snow being yet visible on the last Hills we saw on the north, that season must have been (very) severe, else the Buffaloe would not have come so low . . . .

Every appearance of Savage and Buffaloe is at an end all the freshest roads seemed to crofs the Big Island which we suppose the route to their present Towns on the Loup Fork.

— *Robert Stuart, 1813*

May 21 — We encamped on a branch of the Kansas called the Big Blue, which we crossed the next day and passed Captain [Benjamin] Bonneville's party on a trading excursion by wagon. We stopped a few moments to salute and passed on . . . . We kept up the waters of the Blue to its source, and thence reached the Platte in one day's march of twenty-five miles over barren, dry prairie.

We found no timber of any amount after leaving the waters of the Blue. We could not carry our percussion caps on our guns for fear of discharging them, the air was so very dry. We reached the Platte opposite a big island, probably Grand Island, on May 28 . . . .

The Platte is a broad, turbulent stream and warm. Its bed is a mile or two wide . . . .

There was a great deal of grumbling among Captain Wyeth's men. Some deserted and turned back. We all felt gnawings of hunger and were very thirsty. The warm water of the Platte was not refreshing. June 3 we saw a frightful drove of buffalo appearing as far as the eye could reach, as if the ground was a sea of them. Such armies of them see and fear nothing . . . .

The warm water of the Platte caused diarrhoea. Dr. Jacob Wyeth, the captain's brother, was quite ill. But for the guidance of Captain Sublette we must have perished for the want of subsistence in this desert of the Missouri.

— *John Ball, 1832*

May 17, 1834. We breakfasted on the prairie.... We did not arrive at the Platte at the appointed time, in consequence of an offset, made to mislead a small party of reds, who dropped down upon us, out of the clouds. Like ghosts from the grave, they came unheard, uninvited and undesired.... 3 O'clock, P. M. this day, I saw one of the greatest lies in the world, if a lie can be seen, the Platte. The name is not a lie, for the outward seeming is always in French, Indian, or English, platte, Nebraska, flat, but there it ends. In appearance, is like the Mississippi, broad, boisterous and deep; in appearance, capable of bearing the navies of the world, and yet the infernal liar is hardly able to float a canoe. This fussy, foaming, seething thing is like some big bragging men I have seen, all blubber and belly.... opposite Grand Island, and the question arises, whether, in the sense of magnitude, there is a grander fresh water island in the world....

May 18, 1834.... I picked up today a human skull, and carried it for many miles.... I built it up as a living being, as a companion, invested with flesh, vivified with spirit. It told me, that, impelled by the love of adventure, he had, years gone by, bade adieu to his kin and country, and sought to behold the wonders of these unknown wilds; that he once rejoiced in the beauties of nature; that, like me, he had seen, with admiration, the glorious up-rising and down-going of the sun in the ocean of verdant prairie, and whilst beholding with satisfaction these plains.... he had fallen the victim of an unseen foe.

May 20, 1834. We are now one month out from St. Louis. Found another skull on the plain today, but did not enter into conversation, in fool-sympathy, with the rest smiled at the jest and ribaldry of some reckless packer, and passed on to finish another day — tramp in the march of time.

— *William Marshall Anderson, 1834*

The Platte has its source on the eastern slopes of the Rocky Mountains, and has two Main branches [North and South], which, on their union, flow in an easterly direction toward the Missouri. A short distance below the meeting point the river divides afresh, and forms a great long island.

At this island we reached the Platte. The river, of which we saw but a small part, is not broad at this point, with sparse borders of cottonwood. The river is a mile or two broad on either side, and bounded by small hills or bluffs. The river is shallow, but ... one may sink in the quicksands. The very valley is covered with pure river sand.

— *Frederick A. Wislizenus, M.D., 1839*

Platte River (near Grand Island, Nebraska)

Coast of Nebraska (West of Kearny, Nebraska)

From the sandhills, it [the Platte] had the appearance of a great inland sea. It looked wider than the Mississippi and showed to much better advantage, there being no timber on the banks to check the scope of the human eye. Grand Island which lays just opposite in the middle of the river is one hundred miles long, and has some cottonwood trees upon it. There is no tree timber here growing upon the margin of the river, not even a willow switch. There are, however, some timber and brush growing upon the various small islands in the river which can be obtained by wading rapid sloughs two or three hundred yards across. My first impression on beholding Platte River was, that as it looked so wide and so muddy, and rolled along within three feet of the top of the bank with such majesty that it was unusually swollen and perfectly impassable. Judge my surprise when I learned that it was only three or four feet deep .... The water is exceedingly muddy, or should I say sandy; and what adds greatly to the singular appearance of this river, the water is so completely filled with glittering particles of micah or isingglass that its shining waves look to be rich with floating gold ... the plains are so low and level that if Platte River could rise five feet it would cover a country at least ten miles wide!

— *James W. Evans, 1850*

Fort Kearny

June 6. We advanced twenty miles today. We find a good road [near Fort Kearny] but an utter absence of ordinary fuel. We are compelled to substitute for it buffalo dung which burns freely . . . .

June 7 . . . . the grass is very poor in the Platte bottoms, having been devoured by the buffalo herds. These bottoms are from two to four miles in width, and are intersected, at every variety of interval, by paths made by the buffaloes, from the bluffs to the river. These paths are remarkable in their appearance, being fifteen inches wide, and four inches deep, and worn into the soil smoothly as they could be cut with a spade.

We formed our encampment on the bank of the river, with three emigrating companies within as many miles of us; two above and one below; one of fifty-two wagons, one of thirteen, and one of forty-three — ours having thirty-seven. We find our cattle growing lame, and most of the company are occupied in attempting to remedy the lameness. The prairie having been burnt, dry, sharp stubs of clotted grass remain, which are very hard, and wear and irritate the feet of the cattle. The foot becomes dry and feverish, and cracks in the opening of the hoof. In this opening the rough blades of grass and dirt collect, and the foot generally festers, and swells much. Our

80

mode of treating it was, to wash the foot with strong soap suds, scrape or cut away all the diseased flesh, and then pour boiling pitch or tar upon the sore. If applied early this remedy will cure. Should the heel become worn out, apply tar or pitch, and singe with a hot iron.

— *Joel Palmer, 1845*

At the fort [Kearny], as it is misnamed (for there is neither wall nor picket, nor fortification of any kind) they get very good water only three feet below the surface. The grass is all fed very short, and but for having some blacksmithing done, we should have left early . . . . The place is built of turf with two or three exceptions. It was commenced last fall, and the buildings look well considering the material. Some of them are shaved down so true and smooth as to look really well. The largest are perhaps 25 or 30 feet wide, and 70 or 80 long — and there may be 20 in all. One frame building is now nearly completed, and a great number more will be erected this season. They have a steam saw mill in operation, and are making large quantities of brick. The soldiers have extra wages, if they choose to work, which most do. There are a great many tents pitched about . . . . They have a store filled with goods, and they were just receiving a large supply by land from the Missouri.

Vegetation is backward. The gardens have been planted three or four times, and the seed has mostly rotted. Potatoes were two inches high, and peas in full bloom, five inches. Rope sells for 4s. a pound, salt 10 cents, 4 quart pans 50 cts., cheapest suspenders 4 to 6 shillings, etc. The weather has been so cold till the last three days as to require overcoats in the middle of the day.

— *Dr. Israel Lord, 1849*

Every year the Pawnee Indians would pass the Fort [Kearny] on their way to buffaloes for their summer hunt. There were so many that a whole day would pass and still they would be tramping to camp . . . . They had many contrivances to move their belongings. Travi [travois] was most generally used.

— *Lewis Bissell Dougherty, 1849*

May 31. Passing Fort Kearney. There has passed here 13,000 people, 3,000 wagons, and about 90,000 head of stock. It is a little village 310 miles from St. Joseph west. Time seems to roll. Camped near Ft. Kearney. Wednesday three Indians passed us strangely dressed. Bought one yoke of oxen. Gave $80.00 for them. We are near the Platte River which they say is four miles wide . . . . The next day Thursday. Saw three men chasing two wolves from a grave.

"Hunting Buffalo," 1844, by Felix Darley

[June 2] Friday . . . . Mother fell in the creek today while crossing [Plum Creek] and got all wet. Mother still keeps better. Tonight for the first time we cooked supper on a fire made of buffalo chips. I do not like such a use of them. I would rather have wood, but cannot get it and use water from a puddle hole . . . .

June 6 . . . . Saw some rare specimens of wild flowers, some more beautiful than . . . seen cultivated in gardens. We passed one wagon while they were at dinner, that has six pups under it. Rather a large family for the plains . . . . Where we stopped at noon there was a grave dug up by the wolves, and we saw a rib in the place, so Lizzie and I carried stones and filled the hole again. Some person had done the same before, not liking to see the lifeless clay thrown about.

— *Agnes Stewart, 1853*

West to the Forks

I was often struck with admiration at sights of the picturesque scenes which we enjoyed all the way up the Platte. Think of the big ponds that you have seen in the parks of European noblemen, dotted with little wooded islands, the Platte offers these by thousands.

— *Fr. Pierre-Jean DeSmet, S.J., 1840*

After leaving the waters of the Kanzas, the character of the country changes rapidly. The hills, on either side of the narrow valley of the Platte, which is from five to ten miles wide, are little else than huge piles of sand. The valley itself, is quite sandy; but it nevertheless produces a rich grass, which our animals were very fond of. It is also covered, in many places, with the Prickly Pear, the thorns of which frequently get into the feet of the loose cattle and produce lameness. The River is from one to three miles in width, and the bed of the channel is entirely of quicksand. When we came to it, it was quite full, and the water was every where running level with its banks, but seldom overflowing them, and was running with a strong, even current. There is, in many places along the Platte, a kind of salt, with which the ground, in spots, is covered; and the water in the River is slightly impregnated. In some of the sloughs and pools, back from the River, the water is very strong. We found but little wood here, and none except immediately on the River. We were frequently unable to procure it, and were compelled, sometimes, to make a strange substitute in the excrement of the Buffalo, in order to do our cooking. The varieties of timber are few; the principal kind being what is commonly called Cotton Wood. We saw great numbers of Antelopes, as we passed up the River; but they were so wild, and the valley was so level, that it was difficult to approach them. We also saw a singular little animal, which has been called the Prairie Dog. Its size, shape and color, are very much the same as the large wharf rat, and its barking resembles that of the common Gray Squirrel. They burrow in the ground, and live in villages, frequently of several hundreds. There is a small Owl, that sometimes lives in the same hole with the dog.

— *Overton Johnson and W. H. Winter, 1843*

We traveled up the south bank of the Platte . . . though not so remarkable as the famed and mysterious Nile . . . the Platte is still a remarkable river. Like the Nile it runs hundreds of miles through a desert without receiving any tributaries. Its general course is almost . . . a direct line . . . .

In making our monotonous journey up the smooth valley of the Platte, through the warm, genial sunshine of summer, the feeling of drowsiness was so great that it was extremely difficult to keep awake during the day . . . drivers went to sleep on the road, sitting in the front of their wagons; and the oxen, being about as sleepy, would stop until the drivers were aroused from their slumbers. My wagon was used only for the family to ride in; and Mrs. Burnett and myself drove and slept alternately during the day.

— *Peter H. Burnett, 1843*

[A] severe thunder storm . . . took place in the middle of the night. The thunder seemed almost incessant, and the lightning was so brilliant you could read by its flashes. The men chained the oxen so they would not stampede, though they were very restive. Our tents were blown down as were the covers off our prairie schooners and in less than five minutes we were wet as drowned rats . . . . You have no idea of the confusion resulting . . . with the oxen bellowing, the children crying and the men shouting, the thunder rolling like a constant salvo of artillery; with everything as light as day from the lightning flashes and the next second as black as the depth of the pit.

— *Benjamin Franklin Bonney, 1845*

We were now fairly in the Platte River Country and the rain for the past twenty-four hours pouring down in torrents . . . . Smoke could be seen at some distance and fearing interruption from the Indians our guard was instantly placed on duty . . . when informed that morning discovered several of our horses missing . . . myself with nine others of the party armed and mounted on fine horses started in pursuit . . . . We had at times some difficulty in keeping on their track, for the Indians displayed considerable ingenuity, traveling in the creeks for the purpose of avoiding detection.

We traveled that day perhaps fifty miles, and at

"Nooning on the Platte," by Albert Bierstadt, c. 1858

last . . . we espied our horses standing in close proximity to some Indians who were apparently engaged in preparing food for themselves. We commenced a charge . . . but they did not discover us until we were within two hundred yards, when they sprang for the horses; but . . . we commenced a tremendous yelling, and urging our horses forward, succeeded in preventing the Indians reaching them. In this charge we not only recovered our own horses but captured seven additional ones from the retreating Indians, who, to the number of about thirty, took refuge in a thicket.

— *Samuel Hancock, 1845*

June 1. The emigrants were encamped a mile ahead of us. Started early and passed them. Weather clear, but astonishingly cold and bitter. Road through the flat bottom of the Platte, with the low line of sand buttes just visible on right and left . . . at nooning, weather changed — the sky was filled with dark windy clouds, and sharp, cold gusts of rain kept coming on . . . . traveling always in the face of an infernal bitter driving mixture of icy wind and sleet. Once it came so furiously, driving in horizontal lines, that all the animals turned tail to it and could not be moved — cart, waggon and turned about . . . . There are plenty of emigrants ahead. Among the different bands that we have passed there is considerable hostility and jealousy, on account of camping places, etc.

— *Francis Parkman, 1846*

The 2d of September, 1851, we found ourselves on the Great Route to Oregon, over which, like successive ocean surges, the caravans, composed of thousands of emigrants from every country and clime, have passed during these latter years to reach the rich gold mines of California, or to take possession of the new lands in the fertile plains and valleys of Utah and Oregon. These intrepid pioneers of civilization have formed the broadest, longest and most beautiful road in the whole world — from the United States to the Pacific ocean . . . .

Our Indian companions, who had never seen but the narrow hunting paths by which they transport themselves and their lodges, were filled with admiration on seeing this noble highway, which is as smooth as a barn floor swept by the winds, and not a blade of grass can shoot on it on account of the continual passing . . . . They styled the route the Great Medicine Road of the Whites . . . . How wonderful will be the accounts given of the Great Medicine Road by our unsophisticated Indians when they go back to their villages, and sit in the midst of an admiring circle of relatives!

— *Fr. Pierre-Jean DeSmet, S.J., 1851*

I am very surprised to find such a well-beaten road . . . . as broad as 8 or 10 common roads in the States, and with a very little work could be made one of the most beautiful roads in the world . . . .

Where the prairie is rolling the pitches are very steep in some places, and often there are mud holes at the bottom. Over the level prairie the road is not as smooth. The water does not run off so soon after rain, and it is very much cut up by cattle going over it.

— *Rebecca Ketcham, 1853*

Buffalo Country

May 21, 1834. The numbers of buffalo, or bison, properly speaking, have multiplied by thousands and tens of thousands . . . where is the limit of their feeding range? My friend, Mr. Sublette, assures me he has seen such bands on the waters of the Arkansa . . . . The Platte is still the Platte, from two to three miles wide and fully knee deep.

— *William Marshall Anderson, 1834*

I relish it well, and it agrees with me. My health is excellent. So long as I have buffalo meat, I do not wish anything else.

— *Narcissa Prentiss Whitman, 1836*

Where a buffalo herd has grazed for some time the ground is absolutely bare; for what they do not eat is trampled with their ungainly feet. Their bellowing can often be heard for miles. It is deeper and more muffled than that of our cattle, and at a distance not unlike the grunting of a great herd of swine. To their watering places they form narrow paths, over which they leisurely move on, one behind the other. A buffalo region is crossed by such paths in every direction . . . . Should it, however, ever come to the extermination of these animals, then the whole of this country must necessarily assume some other shape; for to the inhabitant here the buffalo is more important than is his camel to the Arab. It supplies his prime necessities: food, dwelling and clothing.

The hunt for buffalo is one of the grandest and most interesting of which I know. The hunting is done either a-foot by stalking, or on horseback by running. In both cases one must seek to be on the windward, to get as near as possible. For stalking, a hilly country is most favorable . . . .

A good buffalo hunter prefers to ride without a saddle. He sticks one pistol in his belt, holds the other in his right hand, and starts off at top speed. He rushes into the midst of the fleeing herd, and for some minutes buffaloes and rider disappear in a thick cloud of dust. But suddenly he reappears at one side close behind a buffalo which he has picked for his prey and separated from the herd. The hunted animal exerts all its strength to escape its pursuer; but the emulous horse races with him, following all his turnings, almost without guidance by the bridle. Now he has overtaken him; he is racing close to his left side; but the buffalo turns sharply and the horse shoots past him. The race begins afresh. Again, the horse overtakes the buffalo; again they are running parallel, and the rider discharges his pistol point-blank in the buffalo's flank. He now gallops slowly after the exhausted animal, and if necessary, gives him a second shot.

— *Frederick A. Wislizenus, M.D., 1839*

The meat of the buffalo cow is the most wholesome and the most common in the west. It may be called the daily bread of the traveler, for he never loses his relish for it. Though some prefer the tongue, others the hump, or some other favorite pieces, all parts are excellent food. To preserve the meat it is cut into slices, thin enough to be dried in the sun; sometimes a kind of hash is made of it, and this is mixed with the marrow taken from the largest bones. This kind of mixture is called bull or cheese, and is generally served up and eaten raw, but when boiled or baked it is of more easy digestion, and has a more savory taste to a civilized palate.

— *Fr. Pierre-Jean DeSmet, S.J., 1841*

These immense plains are generally clad with a short, curly [buffalo] grass, very fine and nutritious, and well adapted to the sustenance of the countless herds of buffalo and other wild animals that feed upon it. Their soil is generally of a thin vegetable mound, upon a substratum of indurated sand and gravel.

In many places it is quite sterile, producing little other than sand-burrs and a specimen of thin, coarse grass, that sadly fail to conceal its forbidding surface; in others, it is but little better than a desert waste of sand-hills, or white sunbaked clay, so hard and impervious that neither herb nor grass can take root to grow upon it; and in others, it presents a light superfice, both rich and productive, beclad with all that can beautify and adorn a wilderness of verdure.

— *Rufus B. Sage, 1841*

The air was keen the next morning at sunrise, the thermometer standing at 44°, and it was sufficiently cold to make overcoats very comfortable. A few miles brought us into the midst of the buffalo, swarming in immense numbers over the plains, where they had left scarcely a blade of grass standing. Mr. Preuss, who was sketching at a little distance in the rear, had at first noted them as large groves of timber. In the sight of such a mass of life, the traveller feels a strange emotion of grandeur. We had heard from a distance a dull and confused murmuring, and, when we came in view of their dark masses, there was not one among us who did not feel his heart beat quicker. It was the early part of the day, when the herds are feeding; and everywhere they were in motion. Here and there a huge old bull was rolling in the grass, and clouds of dust rose in the air from various parts of the bands, each the scene of some obstinate fight. Indians and buffalo make the poetry and life of the prairie, and our camp was full of their exhilaration. In place of the quiet monotony of the march, relieved only by the cracking of the whip, and an "avance donc! enfant de garce!" shouts and songs resounded from every part of the line, and our evening camp was always the commencement of a feast, which terminated only with our departure on the following morning. At any time of the night might be seen pieces of the most delicate and choicest meat, roasting en appolas, on sticks around the fire, and the guard were never without company.

— *Brevet-Capt. John C. Frémont, 1842*

Perhaps the flesh of no animal is more delicious than that of a young buffalo cow, in good order. You may eat as much as you please, and it will not oppress you.

— *Peter H. Burnett, 1843*

[July] 11. This river Platt has a channel not much less than three miles wide and the intervale from Bluff to Bluff as much as 12 miles wide the bank from 2 to 4 feet high above the water whare it is 4 feet high it is remarkable dry and hard formed of a fine pale tenacious clay and fine dead sand remarkabel hard and smoothe

[July] 16. Throughout the night all the companis of Oregon Emigrants mountaineers & californians &c &c ahead of us had had buffaloe for several days & being anxious my self to get amess I laid my couse S.W. over the cut Bluffs nearly perpendicular and passed main range the country became more regual and level found the Buffalo in great Quantities Killed one verry fine one loaded my mule and started for camp had hard riding to pass the cut Bluffs & obtain the open plain through which the river passes before sundown But here commenced our Toils the camp having made 18 miles at 12 of which we had to ride after night the moketoes with uncommon Blood thirsty appetite commenced & ware Litterly so thick that with all our exertions we could hardly breath

— *James Clyman, 1844*

"Bison," by Albert Bierstadt, c. 1858

I am sure we could see five thousand head [of buffalo] at once in lots of places, and wolves were very nearly as thick. Some of the boys made a terrible slaughter both among the buffalo and wolves. They just shot them down to see them fall, did not even skin them and the hides were worth from four to eight dollars each. Father called a meeting of his company, and admonished the boys in the kindest kind of words, not to kill any more than just enough for meat. For, he said, it was robbing the Indians of their natural food and might arouse the wrath of the great Sioux nation, whose country we were now crossing. He said, as long as we went straight through and did not kill too many of their buffalo, they would not molest us. Up to this time, we had not had a mishap. No sickness, but peace and kindness reigned supreme. Stock had actually improved all the time, but just now . . . we had quite a mishap. Somebody's untrained, worthless dog . . . had gone over the bank of the Big Platte River to cool off. He stayed there until all the teams had passed. The loose stock was just coming up some distance behind, when the big dog made a bound from the water to the top of the bank and gave himself a big shake to throw the water out of his hair. Away went the cows, horses, bulls and all, with such a rattle and jam that it would almost raise the hair on a dead man's head. When the stampede started, the animals were half a mile behind the wagons, which was the distance they were allowed to keep. But on they came with renewed fury at every bound. The old Captain, who happened to be back with his company, took in the situation at a glance, clapped spurs to his

noble mare and bounded along the line with a trumpet voice to those in the wagons to halt and drop their wagon tongues. But it was too late for all to accomplish. Some of the hind teams were all ready on hearing the order. Our four family wagons and Gaines' two were ahead that day. James Barlow's big team was in the lead, but failed to stop when he said "whoa." So he dropped his lead ox in his tracks with the butt of his whip stock. J. M. Bacon's team was next. In this wagon, Mother Barlow rode, and it had to stop as it was jammed up against James' wagon. That gave mother time to jump out and run to the bank of the river about twenty yards off and jump down the bank, only a few feet high. I had been quick enough to get my team loose from the wagon, but J. L. Barlow and Gaines' two teams got under considerable headway, but fortunately one of Gaines' oxen fell down, and that was more than the balance of the team could pull. This gave my sister, Mrs. Gaines, good time to get out with the baby, about a year old, and get down the bank of the river. She always said that that ox-broken neck saved her life, as she was just fixing to jump, and it might have been her neck instead of the ox's. It was her natural disposition to make the best of everything.

The cleanup of this stampede were a few broken wagon tongues, a few smashed-up wagon wheels, one ox with a broken neck, another with a broken leg and two days' layover for repairs. Fortunately, no human being was even crippled. Some were slightly bruised.

— *William Barlow, 1845*

"Caravan on the Prairies," by William T. Ranney, c. 1850

June 15. An unoccupied spectator, who could have beheld our camp today, would think it a singular spectacle. The hunters returning with the spoil; some erecting scaffolds, and others drying the meat. Of the women, some were washing, some ironing, some baking. At two of the tents, the fiddle was employed in uttering its unaccustomed voice among the solitudes of the Platte. At one tent I heard singing; at others the occupants were engaged in reading, some the Bible; others poring over novels. While all this was going on, that nothing might be wanting to complete the harmony of the scene, a Campbellite preacher named Foster, was reading a hymn, preparatory to religious worship. The fiddles were silenced, and those who had been occupied with that amusement, betook themselves to cards. Such is but a minature of the great world we had left behind us, when we crossed the line that separates civilized man from the wilderness.

— *Joel Palmer, 1845*

. . . after a long day's drive, reached a place where we could obtain plenty of grass and water; up to this point in our journey, we were able to have in camp an old fasioned wood fire, but here there was no wood obtainable, and we were obliged to take blankets and sally forth to procure "buffalo chips", this the young men disliked very much, being the first time they were ever engaged in such business; particularly as there were some ladies in our company . . . but there being no alternative the ladies were obliged to divest themselves of all fastidiousness and make use of this fuel for all cooking purposes, which after the first shock proved an excellent substitute for fire wood. Holes were dug in the ground and filled with these chips, at which the ladies soon cooked us excellent suppers. "Buffalo Chips" was the absorbing subject of conversation . . . .

— *Samuel Hancock, 1845*

I am reminded of the many ways travelers can put the buffalo hide to useful purposes. Sometimes a spoke is broken out of a wheel which may let the wheel down. We find and fit a piece of timber next to the broken spoke and wrap it with fresh hide, the hairs in, and take a hot iron and dry the hide around the stick. When perfectly dry the hide holds tight and is nearly as strong as hoop iron.

We treat a broken tongue, sometimes replace a broken link of chain with hide. Horses become sorefooted until blood appears. We shoe them with buffalo hide. We . . . put the horse's foot in the hide, draw up the outer edge around the hoof with the lace which holds, as the hoof is smaller at top than bottom.

This sort of horse shoe will last four or five days depending on the gravel on the road and the amount of travel.

Oxen shod with dry hide cut to fit the claw and put on with tacks. This has to be done often as most oxen have a twist to their hoofs in walking and the hide wears rapidly.

— *Lewis Bissell Dougherty, 1848*

June 28th . . . . I will briefly explain . . . using buffalo chips as fuel along the Platte.

Selecting a spot a short distance from the steep river bank, a hole about six inches in diameter and eight to twelve inches deep was excavated. An air tunnel was then formed by forcing a ramrod horizontally from the river bank to the bottom of the cavity, giving the oven the required draught. In making a fire . . . a wisp of dry grass was lighted and placed at the bottom of the oven, opposite the air tunnel, feeding the flame with finely pulverized dry chips, which readily ignited . . . after filling the fireplace with broken chips and placing around the oven two or three small rocks on which to rest the cooking utensils, we had a combination which at first gave us a grand surprise, as but a little smoke and only slight odor emitted from the fire, and we found, . . .after having eaten our first meal cooked in this manner, that the prejudice previously entertained against buffalo chips as a fuel had vanished into thin air.

— *Reuben Cole Shaw, 1849*

The roads that are made by these animals [buffalo] so much resemble the tracks left by a large wagon-train, that the inexperienced traveller may occasionally imagine himself following the course of an ordinary wagon road. These tracks run for hundred of miles across the prairies and all usually found to lead to some salt-spring, or some river or creek where the animals can allay their thirst.

— *J. J. Audubon and J. Bachman, 1849*

Early in the morning a large herd of buffalo were seen quietly feeding on the side of a high hill, about a mile to the southward . . . . Keeping himself concealed behind a large rock, the hunter very leisurly shot down four of these monsters . . . .

The skinning process commences by making an incision along the top of the back bone, and separating the hide downward so as to get the more quickly . . . the choice parts of the animal.

These are the "bass," a hump projecting from the back of the neck just before the shoulders, and which is generally removed with the skin attached. It is about the size of a man's head, and, when boiled, resembles marrow, being exceedingly tender, rich, and nutritious.

Next comes the "hump" and the "hump ribs," projections of the vertebrae just behind the shoulders, some of which are a foot in length. They are generally broken off by a mallet made of the lower joint of one of the fore legs, cut off for the purpose. After that comes the "fleece," the portion of the flesh covering the ribs; the "depuis," a broad, fat part extending from the shoulders to the tail; the "belly fleece," some of the ribs, called "side-ribs," to distinguish them from the hump-ribs; the thigh or marrow-bones, and the tongue.

Generally, the animal is opened and the tenderloin and tallow secured. All the rest, including the hams and shoulders — indeed, by far the greater portion of the animal — is left on the ground. When buffalo are plenty, the hump, bass, and tongue — very frequently only the latter — are taken, and occasionally a marrow-bone for a tid-bit.

This is called butchering "mountain fashion," and a most barbarious fashion it is.

— *Capt. Howard Stansbury, 1852*

Crossing South Platte

After we had ridden perhaps ten miles, we were lucky enough to kill three head [of buffalo]. The last one was a cow. For a while she looked on as we flayed a bull, but forfeited her life by her curiosity. She had a calf with her that took to flight. The cow's udder was full of milk. We sucked out the milk and found it refreshing and palatable. Laden with the hides, we returned at evening to the camp, where in our absence the Indians had also arrived. Many squaws paid us their respects today . . . .

They were continuously about us in our tents; all objects that were new to them they stared at and handled, not failing to appropriate some when unobserved. The two wives of the Missionaries [Congregationalists Asahel Munger and J. S. Griffin] were special objects of their curiosity . . . .

— *Frederick A. Wislizenus, M.D., 1839*

we reached the junction of the north and south arms of the Platte. The bluffs, like the wings of a stage, on either side, had now become more interesting. I climbed one of the highest points to enjoy the view . . . .

Arriving at the top I found considerable strong "Medicine." Thirty buffalo skulls, adorned with all kinds of gewgaws, lay before me in a magic circle . . . .

On the third day [June 6] we left the river, going across a plateau in a northwesterly direction toward the North Fork. On this plateau we saw for the first time wild horses. They were very skittish. Their sense of smell is said to be very keen . . . . camped near Ash Creek.

— *Frederick A. Wislizenus, M.D., 1839*

[May 28th] . . . . All this region, clear up to the Great Mountains, is a veritable barren, rocky and sandy, covered with scaria and other volcanic substances, with no fertile spots save on the rivers and creeks.

— *Fr. Pierre-Jean DeSmet, S.J., 1840*

July 2. The morning was cool and smoky [at junction of North and South Plattes] . . . . We passed near an encampment of the Oregon emigrants . . . . A variety of household articles were scattered about.

— *Brevet-Capt. John C. Frémont, 1842*

July 2 (Saturday) — continued to move along the Platte . . . . It was so shallow that we did not need the boat. Camped among millions of mosquitoes.

— *Charles Preuss, 1842*

July 4th . . . . I had halted earlier than usual . . . and all hands were soon busily engaged in preparing a feast . . . the kindness of our friends at St. Louis had provided us with a large supply of excellent preserves and rich fruit cake; and when these were added to macaroni soup, and variously prepared dishes of the choicest buffalo meat, crowned with a cup of coffee, and enjoyed with prairie appetite, we felt, as we sat in barbaric luxury around our smoking supper on the grass, a greater sensation of enjoyment than the Roman epicure at his perfumed feast.

— *Brevet-Capt. John C. Frémont, 1842*

July 4 (Monday). Today is the day we have talked about for a long time. Like everybody else in the United States, we were supposed to celebrate it, at least by a day of rest. But that stubborn Fremont started off as usual after he had treated us at breakfast with some of his miserable red wine . . . .

However, we stopped earlier than usual, and for supper the brandy keg was opened. We did our share, to a very modest extent, to be sure.

— *Charles Preuss, 1842*

Graves abound in these regions, and the mortal remains of a vast number of emigrants repose there. With these emigrants have also sunk beneath the valley of the Platte that ardent thirst for gold, those desires and ambitions, projects for wealth, greatness and pleasure . . . . they are buried in these desert strands.

— *Fr. Pierre-Jean DeSmet, S.J., 1842*

We made several attempts to cross the [Platte] South Branch, but always found the water too deep, and continued to travel up the South side . . . eighty five miles above the Forks, having determined to construct boats. For this purpose we procured in the first place, a sufficient number of green Buffalo hides, and having sewed two of them together for each boat, we stretched them over the wagon beds as tight as we could, with the flesh side out, and then turned them up in the sun to dry . . . .

. . . . The crossing was effected in six days, and without any serious accident. We passed here the fourth day of July.

— *Overton Johnson and W. H. Winter, 1843*

It is the second of July, and we begin now to ferry our effects over the big South Platte River. We work hard at this until the night of the 4th, when our company including cattle and mules have all crossed . . . .

. . . . Mataney was about six and a half feet tall, and when he was on his donkey, his feet nearly touched the ground. To him the boys would say, "Get off that rabbit and carry him!" Presently, J. W. [James Willis] Nesmith bought the jack for five hundred dollars, mounted him, and rode off without paying for him, so Mataney sued Nesmith. The company appointed [Peter H.] Burnett as Judge. A trial was held at night. Nesmith pleaded non-jurisdiction, and won the case. The next day Nesmith rode the jack, and Mataney walked and knew not what to do, but along toward night, Nesmith having had his fill of the fun, got off, saying, "Here Mataney take this rabbit, I wouldn't have such a thing." Mataney mounted the little creature, and was happy once more.

— *Edward Henry Lenox, 1843*

Tuesday, July 4 — The glorious Fourth has once more rolled around. Myself, with most of our company, celebrated it by swimming and fording the South Fork of the Big Platte, with cattle, wagons, baggage . . . . However, there seems to be some of our company reminating upon the luxuries destroyed in different parts of the great Republic on this day. Occasionally you hear something said about mint julips, soda, ice cream, cognac, porter, ale and sherry wine, but the Oregon emigrant must forget these luxuries.

— *James Willis Nesmith, 1843*

Tuesday, July 3. To-day we crossed the ridge between the North and South Forks of the Platte, a distance of eighteen and a half miles . . . . The road struck directly up the bluff, rising rapidly at first, then very gradually for twelve miles.

— *Capt. Howard Stansbury, 1846*

"Ford on the Platte," 1866, by Frank Buchser

Today passed over from south to north branch of the Platte. It is the roughest country here that the mind can conceive of. Indicative of volcanic action. I think of the shape of the earth — no level land — all ridges, mounds and deep hollows, without any herbage whatever.

— Elizabeth Geer, 1847

Our teams . . . were well-seasoned, good travelers. We made good time as far as the crossing of the South Fork of Platte river, almost due south of Ash Hollow on the North Fork, about 15 miles distant.

— Lewis Bissell Dougherty, 1848

Young shot Scott dead. The company had a trial and found him guilty. They gave him a choice to be hung or shot. He preferred being shot, and was forthwith.

— Charles Gould, 1849

We crossed the south fork of the Platte by fording. The treacherous quicksand kept the mules in constant motion.

— Reuben Cole Shaw, 1849

The Banks of the South Platte seemed to be lined with large trains . . . . they could be seen as far as the eye extended . . . . I had a good opportunity of ascertaining the number of persons with each wagon and it was a small average to estimate four to each one; which make nearly 20,000 persons ahead of us. The number of oxen were very seldom less than ten to each wagon.

— Maj. Osborne Cross, 1849

I have never known why this early trail led up the South Platte instead of crossing the main stream at the junction and moving directly up the North Platte, as was done by all the emigrant trains.

— J. W. Gibson, 1850

California Hill

Dry Stream Bed, Approaching Ash Hollow (near Lewellen, Nebraska)

Tuesday, June 7. What a beautiful morning. The sun shines bright, but not too hot. The birds sing and the flowers bloom just the way they did at home. The horses are lost and I do not know what we will do. — The horses are found again. Today I am 21 years of age . . . . No one congratulates me or anything, and I am glad of it. It is evening, and no one knows how strange one feels out here on a birthday . . . .

I am seated on a hill above the camp and the South Fork of the Platte River runs before me. It is a muddy stream . . . . The hills and valley are covered with flowers, blue, yellow and white and lilac. Everything looks beautiful . . . .

Friday, June 10. We will cross the south fork today in about an hour from now.

Saturday, 11. Three of our wagons crossed the river [upper ford] yesterday, and six to cross today. Helen, Mary, father and I came over on the first wagon on the tenth. I was very much afraid but we got over all safe enough. David Love's wagon went into a hole where the wagon oxen, and men, were all swimming. James . . . and Charles were carried under the oxen but came up on the other side. Dave lost his cap, Charles his hat, and John lost his whip. It was frightful. Our wagon took a circle and came out another way. They are preparing to bring mother's wagon over. — All the wagons are over, and all are safe.

— *Agnes Stewart, 1853*

Ash Hollow

March 26, 1813. [Ash Hollow camp, eastbound to St. Louis.] 3 miles lower, another Branch joined the main stream from the south, it is thickly wooded a short distance from its mouth, but with what kinds we could not well distinguish — for a considerable way above but more particularly below its junction the River Bluffs are very near and sometimes constitute its banks — they are composed principally of [a blue lime] stone and possess many cedars on which account we call the last mentioned Branch, Cedar Creek.

— *Robert Stuart, 1813*

Ash Hollow, which appeared to be only a depression in the unusually level plain, where were scattered ash timber trees.

— *Jesse Applegate, 1843*

We reach the brink of a hill near one-third of a mile high which we have to descend to reach the level of the hollow. We detach all the oxen from the wagon except the wheel yoke, lock the two hind wheels with the lock chain attached to the body of the wagon and wrap a log chain around the tire so it will cut into the ground when the wagon is in motion. Frequently the other five yokes of oxen are hitched with their heads to the wagon

Approach to Ash Hollow

behind. They being unaccustomed to this treatment, pull back and help to slow down the wagon.

Everything in the front of the wagons must be tied securely, as out comes the goods when the descent is begun. I cannot say at what angle we descend but it is so great that some go as far as to say "the road hangs a little past the perpendicular!"

— *Lewis Bissell Dougherty, 1848*

June 15 . . . we were compelled to let the wagons down into it [ravine] by ropes.

— *Maj. Osborne Cross, 1849*

June 18, Reached what is generally known as Ash Hollow, so called by its containing a quantity of ash timber. We stopped here early in the afternoon to do some repairing. June 19. Rachel [age 18] taken sick in the morning, died that night.

— *Nathan Pattison, 1849*

Tuesday, July 3 . . . . Before and below us was the North Fork of the Nebraska [Platte] winding its way through broken hills and green meadows; behind us the undulating prairie rising gently from the South Fork, over which we had just passed; on our right, the gradual convergence of the two valleys was distinctly perceptible; while immediately at our feet were the heads of Ash Creek, which fell off suddenly into deep precipitous chasms on either side, leaving only a high narrow ridge, or backbone, which gradually descended, until, toward its western termination, it fell off precipitately into the bottom of the creek. Here we were obliged, from the steepness of the road, to let the wagons down by ropes .... The bottom of Ash Creek is tolerably well wooded, principally with ash and some dwarf cedars. The bed of the stream was entirely dry, but toward the mouth several springs of delightfully cold and refreshing water were found, altogether the best that has been met with since leaving Missouri. We encamped at the mouth of the valley, here called Ash Hollow. The traces of the great tide of emigration that had preceded us were plainly visible in remains of camp-fires, in blazed trees covered with innumerable names carved and written on them.

Wednesday, July 4. This being a national festival, I determined to spend the day here and celebrate it as well as our limited means would permit. A salute was fired morning and evening, and a moderate allowance of grog served out to the men, which, with a whole day's rest and plenty of buffalo-meat, rendered them quite happy.

[Later, same day.] We had observed yesterday, on the opposite side of the river, a number of Indian lodges, pitched on the bank; but the total absence of any living or moving thing about them induced us from curiosity to pay them a visit.

We proceeded to the lodges which had attracted our curiosity. There were five of them, pitched upon the open prairie, and in them we found the bodies of nine Sioux, laid out upon the ground, wrapped in their robes of buffalo-skin, with their saddles, spears, camp-kettles, and all their accoutrements, piled up around them. Some lodges contained three, others only one body, all of them which were more or less in a state of decomposition. A short distance apart from these was one lodge .... It contained the body of a young Indian girl of sixteen or eighteen years, with a countenance presenting quite an agreeable expression: She was richly dressed in leggins of fine scarlet cloth, elaborately ornamented; a new pair of moccasins, beautifully embroidered with porcupine quills, was on her feet, and her body was wrapped in two superb buffalo-robes, worked in like manner. She had evidently been dead but a day or two; and to our surprise a portion of the upper part of her person was bare, exposing the face and a part of the breast, as if the robes in which she was wrapped had by some means been disarranged, whereas all the other bodies were closely covered up. It was, at the time, the opinion of our mountaineers that these Indians must have fallen in an encounter with a party of Crows; but I subsequently learned that they had all died of the cholera, and that

this young girl, being considered past recovery, had been arrayed by her friends in the habiliments of the dead, enclosed in the lodge alive, and abandoned to her fate — so fearfully alarmed were the Indians by this, to them, novel and terrible disease. But the melancholy tale of this poor forsaken girl does not end here. Her abandonment by her people, though with inevitable death before her eyes, may perhaps be excused from the extremity of their terror; but what will be thought of the conduct of men enlightened by Christianity, and under no such excess of fear, who, by their own confession, approached and looked into this lodge while the forsaken being was yet alive, and able partially to raise herself up and look at them, but who, with a heartlessness that disgraces human nature, turned away, and, without an effort for her relief, left her alone to die!

We recrossed the river and returned to our encampment, where preparations had been made for a Fourth of July dinner. Although deprived of the vegetable luxuries upon which our Eastern friends were doubtless feasting, still our bill of fare would not have been unacceptable even to an epicure. Buffalo-soup, buffalo-ribs, tender-loin, and marrow-bones roasted, boiled ham, stewed peaches, and broiled curlew, relished with a couple of bottles of cool claret, (which had been carefully preserved for the occasion,) and crowned by a cup of coffee and a segar, made a meal which, notwithstanding the cup was of tin and our table the greensward, we thought not entirely unworthy of the day. In the evening two men came into camp and requested our hospitality: they had been emigrants, but were on their return to the 'States disgusted, having fallen out with their company by the way.

— *Capt. Howard Stansbury, 1849*

About four miles from camp we reached the commencement of the approach to Ash Hollow. A large winding passage, through the hills, which are here cut in every direction by rains, ends in a precipitous descent of considerable difficulty .... Gravel trails have been opened down this place and ox-teams pass without much risk, but mule-teams require to be eased down with a rope. The command [of Col. W. W. Loring and Maj. Osborne Cross] descended without accident.

... scenery of Ash Hollow was a delightful change from the general monotony of the valley.

— *George Gibbs, 1849*

When we were on Ash Hollow Hill, a wagon wheel went over a boy's head; and he came very near losing his life. The Elders administered to him and he got better. His name was Jonathan Prothers. We had to lock both wheels to go down this hill . . . . Next morning we were off again, and after I got out a ways from this place, the wagon wheel went over my foot. I took some oil and anointed my foot, and in a short time it was all right.

— John Johnson Davies, 1850

. . . arrived on the Platte, at . . . Ash Hollow [on the way east to St. Louis], we turned our steps toward the South Fork, fifteen miles away, over a beautiful rolling country of great elevation. Here we met Prince P., accompanied only by a Prussian officer, on their way to enjoy a hunt in the Wind River Mountains. We exchanged our little news . . . . His excellency must be indeed courageous, to undertake at his age so long a journey in such a wilderness, with but one man as suite, and in a wretched little open wagon, which carried the prince and his officer, as well as their whole baggage and provisions. Later I learned that the prince intends to choose a location suited to agriculture, for the purpose of founding a German colony.

— Fr. Pierre-Jean DeSmet, S.J., 1851

A mother buried here, leaving five helpless little children, the youngest six weeks old.

— Phoebe G. Judson, 1853

There was a sickness on the plains, though 1853 was an exceptionally healthy one for immigrants. The measles started on the journey with us, but died for want of food. Of mountain fever we had some, accidents a few, colds a better supply than we cared for, sore eyes in abundance, and of sore mouths and lips a proposterously large supply. To wipe the fine dust from watery eyes with a rough coat sleeve or dirty apron was neither pleasant nor ornamental. But the very acme of petty torture and facial deformity was to lick a circle around a pair of raw lips.

To be sick at home in a cool, well ventilated, room, with fresh bedding, cooling drinks and tempting delicacies, the family physician within call, the drug store and neighbors within reach, is unpleasant and the sick couch is disagreeable. What, then, must it have been for the invalid confined in a traveling wagon wandering through a strange land, beset and being consumed by a strange disease, dependant on a stranger for doctor, the sun beating with "malignant rentlessness" on the thin wagon sheet but a few feet above his enfevered head, the dust sifting upon him in stifling clouds at every jar of

Wagon Ruts, Ash Hollow

the trundling, springless wagon, the chug-chug as the wagon wheels fell into holes, or strike with stunning jar upon rock or bone, the steep hill-side road that rolls his aching body with painful lurch against the lower side of the wagon bed, the steep down-hills that almost stand him on his feet and sends him, catching at wagon bows, to the front end of the wagon to the great disturbance of the children, the steep up hill that almost stands him on his head and fills him with a hopeful dread lest he slide out behind and be left as food for the wolves, and be at rest. We had no deaths in our train, though there were many newly made graves by the road side.

— *George B. Currey, 1853*

When we got to the going down place [descent to Ash Hollow], we certainly felt that we were 'between the Devil and the deep sea', had it been possible to avoid this, the place would have been thought impassable. In the past, wagons were let down with ropes, the places are still plainly marked — some more venturesome ones — or perhaps ones who had no ropes left their tracks in the sand and like a band of sheep the rest followed, only one yoke of cattle was left to each wagons, and all four of the wheels were locked. Besides being dreadfully steep, the road was badly cut up and the dust and sand so deep that the chuck holes could not be seen (but were plainly felt) — and any way the air was so full of dust that much of the time the oxen were barely visible — 'My kingdom' for a breath of fresh air.

— *Helen M. Carpenter, 1856*

I was bitterly disappointed . . . these Hollows have always been associated with dread in my mind, lurking savages, skulking cyotes and deeds of crime that made my blood chill. I was surprised to find them . . . a scene with which no one could connect a remembrance of the murders said to have been committed here. After supper we visited Mr. Carney's [Gen. W. S. Harney's] fortifications which were thrown up in haste to protect them [in 1855] against the Sioux Indians. The river had caved in and taken with it part of the wall while the rest are fast tumbling to decay.

— *Martha Missouri Moore, 1859*

It is described as a pretty bit in a barren land, about twenty acres, surrounded by high bluffs, well timbered with ash and cedar, and rich in clematis and other wild flowers.

— *Richard Burton, 1860*

Court House Rock

We encamped to-day in the neighborhood of a great natural curiosity, which, for the sake of a name, I shall call the old castle. It is situated up on the south side of the Platte, on a plain, some miles distant from any elevated land, and covers more than an acre of ground; and is more than fifty feet high. It has, at the distance of the width of the river, all the appearance of an old enormous building, somewhat dilapidated; but still you see the standing walls, the roof, the turrets, embrasures, the dome, and almost the very windows; and large guard-houses, standing some rods in front of the main building.

— *Rev. Samuel Parker, 1835*

In Chimney Rock's immediate neighborhood are formations not less singular, to which the Trappers have given names, indicative of their approach in form to different structures in civilized life; for instance; — the "Court House."

— *Alfred J. Miller, 1837*

The Chimney is not the only remarkable mound to be met with in this vast solitude. One is called "The [Court] House," another "The Castle," a third "The Fort," etc. And, in fact, if a traveler were not convinced that he is journeying through a desert where no other dwellings exist . . . he would be induced to believe them so many ancient fortresses or Gothic Castles, and with a little imagination, based upon some historical knowledge, he might think himself transported amid the ancient mansions of knight errantry . . . . but instead of all these magnificent remains of antiquity we find only barren mounds on all sides filled with cliffs formed by the falling of the waters and serving as dens to an infinite number of rattlesnakes and other venomous reptiles.

— *Fr. Pierre-Jean DeSmet, S.J., 1841*

June 18. We met a company of mountaineers from Fort Laramie who had started for the settlements early in the season, with flat-boats loaded with buffalo robes, and other articles of Indian traffic. The river became so low, that they were obliged to lay by: part of the company had returned to the Fort for teams; others were at the boat landing, while fifteen of the party were footing their way (back) to the states. They were a jolly set of fellows. Four wagons joined us from one of the other divisions . . .

June 19 . . . we encamped opposite the Solitary Tower [Court House Rock]. This singular natural object is a stupendous pile of sand and clay . . . . I conceive it to be about seven miles distant from the mouth of the Creek . . . the height of this tower is somewhere between

95

Trough of Oregon Trail, Near Jail Rock (left) and Court House Rock

six hundred and eight hundred feet from the level of the river. Viewed from the road, the beholder might easily imagine he was gazing upon some ancient structure of the old world . . . near by stands another pile of materials, similar to that composing the tower, but neither so large nor so high. The bluffs in this vicinity appear to be of the same material. Between this tower and the river stretches out a rolling plain, barren and desolate enough.

— *Joel Palmer, 1845*

At the summit it is about 20 by 10 feet broad and it is ascended by holes dug in the sides which other emigrants have made . . . .

We spent about an hour on the summit writing. Our heads became dizzy, we began to hunt the base and had a hard time to overtake our wagons which we could only see by the dust they raised; and being nearly fifteen miles off we traveled hard but did not overtake them until they camped for the night. We had left camp without a gun, pistol or knife, which we ought to have had as the wolves and bears became unusually thick before we got in.

— *Walter G. Pigman, 1850*

Saturday, 18th. Neglected my book for four days. Traveled over sand, and rough roads without much comfort, but heat.

Passed Courthouse Rock today. It looks much like a Courthouse from a distance. It is five or six miles from the road.

— *Agnes Stewart, 1853*

After a twelve miles' drive we fronted the Court-house, the remarkable portal of a new region, and this new region teeming with wonders will now extend about 100 miles. It is the *mauvaises terres*, or Bad lands, a tract about 60 miles wide and 150 long . . . .

The Court-house, which had lately suffered from heavy rain, resembled anything more than a court-house; that it did so in former days we may gather from the tales of many travellers, old Canadian voyageurs, who unanimously accounted it a fit place for Indian spooks, ghosts, and hobgoblins to meet in pow-wow, and to "count their coups" delivered in the flesh. The Court-house lies about eight miles from the river, and three from the road; in circumference it may be half a mile, in height 300 feet; it is, however, gradually degrading, and the rains and snows of not many years will lay it level . . . .

96

In books it is described as resembling a gigantic ruin, with a huge rotunda in front, windows in the sides, and remains of roofs and stages in its flanks: verily potent is the eye of imagination! To me it appeared in the shape of an irregular pyramid . . . in fact, it resembled the rugged earthworks of Sakkara . . . . According to the driver the summit is a plane upon which a wagon can turn . . . . perhaps, in the old days of romance and Colonel Bonneville, it served as a refuge for the harried fur-hunter.

— *Richard Burton, 1860*

27th . . . . Passed Convent Rock [Court House]. The Iowa City boys drove on faster than we wanted to; we let them go.

— *E. S. McComas, 1862*

Court House Rock, Jail Rock (near Bridgeport, Nebraska)

Chimney Rock

We reached "Nose Mountain," [Chimney Rock,] which appears . . . like the limbless trunk of a gigantic tree.

— *Warren A. Ferris, 1830*

Arrived [June 9] at the Chimney or Elk Brick the Indian name [of] this singular object . . . it looks like a work of art.

— *Nathaniel J. Wyeth, 1832*

June 10 — We saw ahead of us a big castle on a small mountain. As we approached it, it appeared like a big tower of sandstone standing alone. It was called the "Chimney Rock," and is probably three hundred feet high. On the south side of the Platte were immense herds of buffalo.

— *John Ball, 1832*

Opposite to the camp at this place was a singular phenomenon [Chimney Rock], which is among the curiosities of the country.

— *Capt. Benjamin Bonneville, 1832*

We are now in sight of . . . Chimney Rock . . . which can be seen at the distance of thirty miles. It is two miles from the river, . . . and from its peculiar form and entire isolation, is one of the most notorious objects on our mountain march.

— *William Marshall Anderson, 1834*

The bluffs on the southern shore of the Platte are, at this point, exceedingly rugged, and often quite picturesque; the formation appears to be simple clay . . . . There is also a kind of obelisk, standing at a considerable distance from the bluffs . . . known to the hunters and trappers . . . by the name of the "Chimney".

— *John K. Townsend, 1834*

Encamped at noon, near another of nature's wonders. It has been called the chimney; but I should say, it ought to be called beacon hill, from its resemblance to what was beacon hill in Boston.

— *Rev. Samuel Parker, 1835*

Late Evening Near Chimney Rock

Chimney Rock (near Bayard, Nebraska)

[June 10] . . . . Traveled all day in sight of the Chimney . . . . Above this spar of hard earth or rock there appeared one of the grandest scenes I ever beheld.

— *Asahel Munger, 1839*

. . . the bluffs of our side . . . gradually diminished until they were lost in the prairie. But behind them reddish cliffs arose, steeper and more imposing than we had yet seen . . . the first cliff in the first chain, perhaps eight miles from the river, presented quite the appearance of an old castle or citadel. More remarkable still is the last cliff of the same chain. Its tower-like top is seen from a distance of thirty or forty miles, for which it has been called the Chimney.

Near the Platte I saw . . . a so-called prairie-dog village . . . here we had a whole colony before us . . . this animal digs itself holes underground . . . such dwellings, at moderate space from each other, can be spread over an area of several acres, or even miles . . . . At a man's approach they raise a fiercer cry, wagging their short tails withal, as if prepared for serious combat . . . . He is found rather plentifully on either side of the Rocky Mountains . . . . The owls and rattlesnakes seem to do most damage to the prairie dogs.

— *Frederick A. Wislizenus, M.D., 1839*

On the 31st of *May* we camped two miles and a half from one of the most remarkable curiosities of this savage region. It is a cone-shaped eminence of not far from a league in circumference, gashed by many ravines and standing upon a smooth plain . . . . It seems to be the remnant of a lofty mountain.

In the neighborhood of this wonder, *all the hills present a singular aspect; some have the appearance of towers, castles and fortified cities.* From a little distance one can hardly persuade himself that art is not mingled in them with the *fantasies of nature.*

— *Fr. Pierre-Jean DeSmet, S.J., 1840*

A grand and imposing spectacle, truly; — a wonderful display of the eccentricity of Nature.

— *Rufus B. Sage, 1841*

The chimney was strikingly like the contemplated Washington Monument.

— *Elijah White, M.D., 1842*

July 9 (Saturday) . . . This afternoon we sighted at a distance the so-called Chimney Rock . . . nothing new otherwise. . . . Today a cow was killed . . . all meat was

saved and cut up in very thin slices. They are hung around the cart to dry and look like red curtains in the windows of a tavern. Oh, if there were a tavern here!
July 10 (Sunday). Today we again met several white people . . . . Toward evening we reached Chimney Rock and camped opposite it . . . . The whole chain of dirt hills certainly form strange figures here. Too bad that it is not granite.

— *Charles Preuss, 1842*

In the course of the day we passed the famous Chimney Rock . . . . I had already seen it, in 1840 and 1841, in my first visit to the Rocky Mountains . . . . I found it considerably diminished in height.

— *Fr. Pierre-Jean DeSmet, S.J., 1843*

I had quite an adventure while gathering "buffalo chips". Several of us were out from camp [near Chimney Rock] some little distance, picking them up and throwing them into piles. Our party had a pile and other parties had their piles, and as we were not far apart, it seems that we had to guard against trespassers. We were working hard and had become considerably excited, when I remembered a boy about my size with yellow sun-burnt hair and freckled face . . . came over into our district and attempted to get away with a large chip but I caught him in the act and threw another into his face with such violence as to knock off a scab and make the blood come . . . .

. . . . matches were not in use when we crossed the plains . . . to get fire at times a man would rub a cotton rag in powder and shoot it out of a musket or put it in the pan of a flint lock gun, and explode the powder in the pan; often a flint steel and punk was used.

— *Jesse Applegate, 1843*

Sunday, July 9 . . . Came in sight of Chimney (Rock) about noon. I mount sergeant of the guard and have some sport. Gave two members of the old guard a tour by way of punishment for sleeping on post the night before. Found one of my men sleeping at post and took his gun away.

[Three days later] . . . sold a gun at camp this morning, belonging to Isaac Williams, for having gone to sleep on post last night.

— *James Willis Nesmith, 1843*

[July] 27th. A clear cool morning the Ladies pleasant animated and in fine Spriits which make a fine contrer part to the morning Early we came in sight of the noted chimney rock at the supposed distance of 30 miles. It rises perpendicular and alone and looked like an old dry stub not larger in appearance than your finger 4 or 5 miles from our nooning raises a bank of clay & rock

[July] 28. Sunday Fine and dry not a drop of dew fell last night which circumstance is not uncommon in the region of country we are now approaching all our sick of old cronic disorder begin to ware a healthy appearance & active elastick movement nooned opposite the chimny rock Scotts Bluffs in full vieu ahead on the whole the vieu in all directions Singular and Picturesque emmence level plains east the river a mile wide meandring along but your eye can not tell at a short distance which way the water runs

— *James Clyman, 1844*

. . . after encampment, one of the company expressed his intention of going out in search of deer; . . . A sufficient length of time having elapsed for his return, we became anxious for his safety and five of us started to look for him, when to our horror we found his lifeless body on the ground divested of clothing and scalp. It was impossible to track the Indians to avenge his death, and in the morning we interred his body as decently as possible, and shedding a tear over the grave of one of our little community, we . . . resumed our journey.

. . . encamped close by this beacon of the plain, when adjusting matters in camp, some of us visited this curiosity and were highly gratified . . . on this huge pillar we found inscribed the names of many who proceeded us the year before.

— *Samuel Hancock, 1845*

June 20. Traveling fourteen miles, we halted in the neighborhood of the Chimney Rock. This is a sharp pointed rock . . . it is visible at a distance of thirty miles and has the unpoetical appearance of a hay stack with a pole running far above its top.

— *Joel Palmer, 1845*

On the left, the square bluffs were like the Hudson Palisades, with here and there a pilaster of silvery white; right in front, stood the lofty white Chimney Rock, like the pharos of a prairie sea.

— *Lt. Col. Phillip St. George Cooke, 1845*

. . . Chimney Rock in sight.

A Sioux received a present from another, who expected to get his favorite mule in return. The Sioux gave it accordingly, which so aggrieved the sqaw who had been accustomed to ride it . . . that the two women fell to fighting. The Sioux flogged them both, but being unable to separate them, and exceedingly exasperated at losing the mule, he grew so furious that he went out and vented his passion by killing seven of his horses. What a bump of destructiveness! This is the sort of passion that often drives an Indian to his exploits of desperate courage.

— *Francis Parkman, 1846*

The chimney might pass for one of the foundries in St. Louis, were it blackened by burning stone coal.

— *Virgil K. Pringle, 1846*

Saturday 22nd [May] . . . At the distance I should judge of about twenty miles, I could see Chimney Rock very plainly with the naked eye, which from here very much resembles the large factory chimneys in England . . . . Elder Orson Pratt is taking an observation to ascertain the height of Chimney Rock . . . .

Wednesday 26th . . . arrived at a point directly north of Chimney Rock which we ascertained by compass, having traveled since it was first discovered 41½ miles . . . . Elder Pratt found that Chimney Rock is 260 feet high from its base to its summit and the distance from our road at the nearest point three miles.

— *William Clayton, 1847*

After crossing the South Fork and entering Ash Hollow, you start up the south bank of the North Fork. Twenty miles up you will see Court House rock resembling a Missouri court house so much as to deceive many on their first trip. Father was once passing with a colored lad driving his vehicle. He had heard of this rock, and when opposite, the boy called father's attention to the rock saying, "Court must be in session, there are many horses hitched near the house." There were cedar shrubs growing at the front. This is not a rock but a hard, dry hill with little or no grass on it.

Fifteen miles above is Chimney Rock which was seen thirty miles back. This is not rock but a part of the hills south of the river, cut off the main hill by wind, water and time. The space between it and the main hill is near 300 yards. It is a square column perhaps 100 feet on its sides and somewhat more in height.

Twenty feet from the top is a white clay rock completely exposed and corresponding to a similar ledge in the main hill, confirming the supposition that the hill and Chimney Rock were once connected. The wagon road passing it is near the river opposite the Chimney, due south.

— *Lewis Bissell Dougherty, 1848*

I climbed up as far as anybody ever did and took a view of the country which was simply splendid all around the bottom was covered with camps among was Uncle Sam's trains.

— *Lucius Fairchild, 1849*

We headed toward this tapering rock, called by roamers of the prairie "Chimney Rock," though, to my eye,

Wildcat Range (near Bayard, Nebraska)

Prairie Storm Clouds

there is not a single lineament in its outline to warrant the christening. The Wellington Testimonial, in the Phoenix Park, elevated on a Danish Fort, would give a much more correct idea.

— *William Kelly, 1849*

It is the opinion of Mr. [Jim] Bridger that it was reduced to its present height by lightning, or some other sudden catastrophe, as he found it broken on his return from one of his trips to St. Louis.

— *Capt. Howard Stansbury, 1849*

On getting within a quarter of a mile of it I took a drawing of that wonderful natural monument. After which I clambered up the Chimney on the south side to the first and only bench above the top of the base or cone, which was a high as any mortal could climb it, for the stem of the Chimney runs perpendicularly about

200 feet higher. There I engraved my name and the name of my wife. There were several Ladies and Gentlemen on the rock with me; and after I had completed my name I looked to my left and there stood a young lady who had cut foot and handholes in the soft rock busily engaged in inscribing her name about 2 feet higher than my own!

— *James W. Evans, 1850*

It is cald rock but is nothing but sand and dirt.

— *A. C. Sponsler, 1850*

A few dary and foolhardy adventurers however, have, by cutting foot and hand-holds in the soft rock, raised themselves a few feet, in order to incribe their names the highest.

— *W. Wadsworth, 1852*

103

Sabbath, 19. Passed Chimney Rock. It looks more like it at a distance than it does when nearing it. A long sultry day with a storm in the evening . . . .

Fred and his man quarreled about striking some loose cattle. [Fred] struck him with his hand, and then knocked him down with his whip stock. A mean low dirty trick of his. I feel so mortified about it.

— *Agnes Stewart, 1853*

Late at night I again had a quarrel with my wife on account of the tailor, and I beat him so his eyes were blackened and his right arm lamed.

— *Hans P. E. Hoth, 1854*

Some years ago lightning is supposed to have struck this hill . . . . The Indians and mountaineers who beheld this catastrophe aver that masses of rock and earth were hurled to the distance of two or three miles.

— *Cornelius Conway, 1857*

. . . viewed from the southeast it is not unlike a giant jack boot based upon a high pyramidal mound, which, disposed in the natural slope, rests upon the plain . . . again the weather served us; nothing could be more picturesque than this lone pillar of pale rock lying against a huge black cloud, with the forked lightning playing over its devoted head.

— *Richard Burton, 1860*

Scott's Bluff

[May] 29th — We camp tonight a little below Scott's Bluff . . . . This place bears the name of an old mountaineer, who died here from sickness and starvation. The desertion and abandonment of this poor man, by his leader and employer, was an act of the most cruel and heartless inhumanity . . . . His death has left here a traveler's land-mark, which will be known when the name of the canting hypocrite and scoundrel who deserted him, will be forgotten, and remembered only

Gap at Scott's Bluff, Looking West

Scott's Bluff (near Gering, Nebraska)

in hell. Two of his companions remained with him for several days, bearing him along as his weakness increased, and only left him when compelled by the want of food. The unburied corpse of poor Scott was found at this spot, having crawled more than two miles towards his father's cabin, and his mother's home.

The only witness, the only watcher in his death-agony, was the dark raven and the hungry wolf, and keen, sharp and eager was his watch. I know the name of the soulless villain, and so does God and the devil. I leave him to the mercy of the One and the justice of ————. Had such a being a father? I know not; for the sake of humanity, let us hope that he never had a mother, but "dropped from the tail of a dung-cart."

This evening, about 5 o'clock, I felled a mighty bison to the earth. I placed my foot upon his neck of strength and looked around, but in vain, for some witness of my first great "coup." I thought myself larger then a dozen men. I tied little Blackhawk to his horns, and danced upon his body, and made a fool of myself to my heart's content, then cut out his tongue and sat down to rest and moralize.

Nothing can be more revolting, more terrific, than a front view of an old bull buffalo. His huge hump, covered with long wool, rising eighteen or twenty inches above his spine; a dense mat of black hair, padding a bullet-proof head; a dirty drunkard beard, almost sweeping the ground, and his thick, dark horns and sparkling eyes, give him altogether, the appearance and expression of some four-legged devil, fresh from———— Halifax. But nevertheless, and notwithstanding all this, his meat is good eating. Bosse, hump-ribs, side ribs, tongue and marrow-bones. "Sufficient for the day," is the fatigue and rest thereof.

— *William Marshall Anderson, 1834*

. . . struck the Platte again . . . . Here one of our men caught a young antelope . . . in a few days became so tame as to remain with the camp without being tied, and to drink, from a tin cup, the milk which our good missionaries spared from their own scanty meals. The men christened it "ZIP COON" and it soon became familiar with its name, running to them when called, and exhibiting many evidences of affection and attachment.

— *John K. Townsend, 1834*

[June 10] . . . . About 7 or 8 miles from us is what is called Scotch [Scott's] Bluff. It looks like an old castle with a rounding top, back from this from the river there are several others similar in line like a number of very large buildings. From them there was a towering bluff with here and there a cluster of black cedar shrubs.

— *Asahel Munger, 1839*

105

On Friday evening the company had a terrible alarm. One of our hunters, who was in the rear, was robbed of all he had by the Indians. They struck him with their ram-rods, and he ran away from them. Soon a war party of the Sioux Indians appeared in view. We soon collected together in order of battle, to be ready in case of an attack. The Indians stood awhile and looked at us, and probably thinking that "the better part of valor is descretion," they soon showed signs of peace.

Captain Fitzpatrick then went to them, and talked with them, for he was acquainted with them. Then they gave back all that they had taken from the young man and our men gave them some tobacco, and they smoked the pipe of peace.

— *Rev. Joseph Williams, 1841*

[July] 29. Keen claps of thunder with a profusion of Electrick fluid playin in all directions in a dry clear sky set the dry grass on fire in several places in sight of our traveling caravan which was soon extinguished by the rain Just mentioned.

supped on a most dlecious piece of venison from the loin of a fat Black taild Buck and I must not omit to mention that I took my rifle [and] walked out in the deep ravin to guard a Beautifull covey of young Laides & misses while they gathered wild currants & choke chirries which grow in great perfusion in this region and of the finerst kind.

— *James Clyman, 1844*

I directed my [eastward] course toward "the springs," situated about fourteen miles distant, in the vicinity of Robidoux' trading-house, for Colonel Mitchell had named this as the rendezvous for all those who proposed going directly to the United States. On the 24th, before sunrise, we set out in good and numerous company. I visited, in my way, two trading-houses, in order to baptize five half-blood children.

— *Fr. Pierre-Jean DeSmet, S.J., 1851*

During the afternoon some member of the train would ride ahead and select a camp for the evening, or often the guide-book was relied upon. Often several trains would camp at the same watering place, so that the camp would be an ephemeral village of several hundred people, and a thousand or more cattle. Stock was guarded during the night, sometimes near camp, and at others from one to two miles away. The men and larger boys took their turns in guarding the cattle and camp. Each day repeated its yesterday until the end of the journey. Our route extended for several hundred miles up the north bank of the Platte river, through an almost continuous meadow of wild grass, with billowy sand hills on the right and the yellow waters of the river on our left. On this part of our journey camp gossiping was indulged in and often protracted too far into the night, and as a consequence the people would be drowsy the following day.

I have seen representations of immigrant trains moving in close order, under mounted officers, the men on foot with shot pouch and powder horn at their sides, long rifles on their shoulders, pistols and formidable knives in their belts. In coming up the Platte our people were too sleepy for such wise precaution or pantomimic war. After the first few miles in the cooler morning scarce a woman or a child would be seen outside of the wagons, and as the sun beat hotter, the landscape lost its charms to the men, and they, too, sought the friendly cover of the wagons. The drivers stalked limberly and lonesomely by the sides of their ruminating teams, but as the sun beat upon that tireless plain, bathing the sweltering landscape with glimmering heat, the crack of the whip became less frequent and the drivers would crowd between the oxen's heels and the wagon wheel and take a sidewise seat on the wagon tongue, and nodding, drive. At intervals the driver would wave his long whip and drowsily drawl out "Get up thar," and relapse into silence. There was sort of a rhythmical sequence in these somniferous "Get ups," which at regular times welled out from that slow line of dusty teams and sleepy drivers. Like the answering calls of farm yard fowls, when one driver would call out "Get up," "Go along," each companion would repeat the admonition to his sluggish charge. Thus in sleepy dreaminess the train would wend along for hours.

The approach to a spring or running brook was the occasion for life and activity. The cups, coffee pots, cans and kegs were hurriedly sought amid the confused upper deck of the wagon, to the discomfort of the sleeping children, and a general excapade would take place from the wagon toward the water. All seemed indifferent as to toilet, but intent on getting a drink. You who have never breakfasted on fat bacon, coffee and camp-cooked bread and slept and dreamed of desert and thirst in an immigrant wagon, cannot understand why the immigrant would drink at every spring or creek. Nor can you, who have never stood by a bubbling spring, in a strange, wild land, with the thought that it may be miles and miles to another drinking place, comprehend the satisfaction afforded by the full-mouthed swallows from its cooling wealth.

— *George B. Currey, 1853*

There ought to be a Heaven for all ox that perish under the yoke, where they could roam in the fields of sweet clover and timothy.

— *Kirk Anderson, 1858*

West from Summit of Robidoux Pass, Adam's Needle (a Yucca) in Foreground

Scott's Bluff . . . . from a distance of a day's march it appears in the shape of a large blue mound . . . . As you approach within four or five miles, a massive medieval city gradually defines itself, clustering with a wonderful fullness of detail, round a colossal fortress, and crowned with a royal castle. Buttress and barbicon, bastion, demilune and guardhouse, tower, turret, and donjon-keep, all are there . . . . quaint figures develop themselves; guards and sentinels in dark armour keep watch and ward upon the slopes.

Presently we dashed over Little Kiowa Creek, forded the Horse Creek, and enveloped in a cloud of villainous mosquitoes, entered at 8:30 P.M. the station in which we were to pass the night. It was tenanted by one Reynal, a French creole — the son of an old soldier of the Grand Armee, who had settled at St. Louis — a companionable man, but an extortionate; he charged us a florin for every "drink" of his well-watered whiskey. The house boasted of the usual squaw, a wrinkled old dame, who at once began to prepare the supper . . . . These hard-working but sorely ill-favoured beings, are accused of various horrors in cookery . . . .

Our breakfast was prepared in the usual prairie style. First the coffee — three parts burnt beans — was placed on the stove to simmer until every noxious principle was duly extracted from it. Then the rusty bacon, cut into thick slices, was thrown into the fry-pan. Thirdly, antelope steak, cut off a corpse suspended for the benefit of flies.

— *Richard Burton, 1860*

Fort Laramie

June 12. We arrived at the Laramie Fork of the Platte. It was high, cold, and rapid, and comes from the mountains of the same name. The bank of this stream were covered with willows. Here we made a halt to make "bull boats" and rafts to carry ourselves and goods across . . . .

June 15. We came to the Black Hills [Laramie Range], so called because of the thick growth of cedar. Here, also, we found red sandstone. It was a region of rattlesnakes and large fierce bears.

— *John Ball, 1832*

[May] 31. — This evening we arrived at the mouth of Laramee's Fork, where Capt. [William L.] Sublette intends to erect a trader's fort. This is a bright and rapid stream of water, running out of the Black hills from the South . . . . The Black hills are spurs of the great Rocky mountain range, and derive their name from the dark shadows which the cedar and pine growing upon their sides, forcibly suggest.

June 1st . . . . This day we laid the foundation log of a fort, on Laramee's fork, and a friendly dispute arose between our leader and myself, as to the name. He proposed to call it Fort Anderson, I insisted upon baptising it Fort Sublette, and holding the trump card in my hand (a bottle of champagne), was about to claim the trick. Sublette stood by, cup reversed, still objecting, when [William] Patton offered a compromise which was accepted, and the foam flew, in honor of Fort William,

"Fort Laramie," 1849, by James F. Wilkins

which contained the triad prenames of clerk, leader and friend . . . .

Leaving Patton and fourteen men to finish the job, we started upwards. From the top of of the Black hills I got my first view of the Rocky Mountains — the snow covered mountains. My eyes have been fastened upon them all day, and at night I am not sobered . . . .

I saw, today, the tracks of a grizzly bear, and the Irishman's remark about his game cock (the duck), came to my mind: "Jasus, what a fut! but all hell couldn't up trup him."

— *William Marshall Anderson, 1834*

On the 1st of June, we arrived at Laramie's fork [site and origin of Fort Laramie, first known as Fort William, then Fort John, and, in 1846, moved a mile farther upstream and named Fort Laramie; it became a government post in 1849]. Here two of our "free trappers" left us for a summer "hunt" in the rugged Black Hills.

These men joined our party at Independence and have been traveling to this point with us for the benefit of our escort. Trading companies usually encourage these free trappers to join them, both for the strength which they add to the band, and . . . their generally good hunting qualities. Thus both parties accommodated, and no obligation is felt on either side.

— *John K. Townsend, 1834*

. . . the Ogallallah Indians [near Fort Laramie] had a buffalo and dog dance . . . . In the buffalo dance, a large number of young men dressed with the skins of the neck and head of buffalos with their horns on, moved round in a dancing march. They shook their heads, imitated the low bellowing of the buffalo, wheeled and jumped at the same time men and women sung a song, accompanied with the beating of a . . . drum. I cannot say I was amused to see how well they could imitate brute beasts . . . rational men imitating beasts, and old greyheaded men marshalling the dance and enlightened white men encouraging it by giving them intoxicating spirits, as a reward for their good performance . . . . The women are graceful, and their voices are soft and expressive. I was agreeably surprised to see tall young chiefs, well dressed, walking arm in arm with their ladies.

— *Rev. Samuel Parker, 1835*

[June 14th] we left camp in good humor, for the crotchety master of human crotchets, I mean the weather, smiled upon us and the vicinity of Fort Laramie, but sixteen miles, distant . . . .

At a distance it resembles a great block house; and lies in a narrow valley, enclosed by grassy hills, near by the left bank of the Laramie, which empties into the North Platte about a mile below . . . .

The distance from the boundary of Missouri and Fort Laramie, according to our daily reckoning, amounts to 755 miles, and was made by us in six weeks . . . . [We] found our average rate to be three miles an hour.

— *Frederick A. Wislizenus, M.D., 1839*

We found [near Fort Laramie] some forty lodges of the Cheyennes . . . . the head chiefs of this village invited me to a feast . . . . The chief embraced me and greeted me, saying, "Black robe, my heart was very glad when I learned who you were . . . . Be welcome, I have had my three best dogs killed in your honor, they were very fat."

. . . . This is their great feast, and that flesh of the wild dog is very delicate and extremely good; it much resembles that of a young pig . . . . Finally I learned that one may get rid of his dish by passing it to another guest, with a present of tobacco.

— *Fr. Pierre-Jean DeSmet, S.J., 1840*

The night of our arrival [in November] at Fort Platte [a rival fur post near Fort Laramie] was the signal for a grand jollification to all hands . . . who soon got most gloriously drunk . . . . Yelling, screeching, fireing, shouting, fighting, swearing, drinking and such like interesting performances, were kept up without intermission . . . . The scene was prolonged till near sundown the next, and several made their egress from this beastly carousal, minus shirts and coats — with swollen eyes, bloody noses, and empty pockets . . . . liquor, in this country, is sold for four dollars per pint.

— *Rufus B. Sage, 1841*

There are two Forts here, about one mile apart, and another about one hundred and fifty miles south. I tried to preach twice to these people, but with little effect. Some of them said they had not heard preaching for twelve years.

— *Rev. Joseph Williams, 1841*

August 27 . . . . We reached Laramie fort [eastbound] . . . after an absence of forty-two days . . . . the quick eyes of the Indians, who were on the lookout for us, discovered our flag as we wound among the hills . . . .

The emigrants to Oregon and Mr. [Jim] Bridger's party met here, a few days before our arrival. Division and misunderstandings had grown up among them; they were already somewhat disheartened by the fatigue of their long and wearisome journey . . . . They were told that the country was entirely swept of grass, and that few or no buffalo were to be found on their line of route; and, with their weakened animals, it would be impossible for them to transport their heavy wagons over the mountain. Under these circumstances, they disposed of their wagons and cattle at the forts; selling them at the prices they had paid in the states, and taking in exchange coffee and sugar at one dollar a pound, and miserable worn-out horses, which died before they reached the mountains . . . . Mr. [Tom] Fitzpatrick . . . had reached Laramie in company with Mr. Bridger; and the emigrants were fortunate enough to obtain his services to guide them as far as the British post of Fort Hall, about two hundred and fifty miles beyond the South Pass of the mountains.

— *Brevet-Capt. John C. Frémont, 1842*

September 14 (Wednesday evening) . . . . I am looking forward to great comfort tomorrow morning. De Conteau asked me for two shirts to be washed. They are drying now . . . . I should have discarded these dirty, ugly rags and gone without a shirt. Since I got married I am more particular and delicate in such matters — that is what comes with good habits, and this is due to a good, attentive housewife. Of course I don't know whether we can call it particular and delicate if one just dislikes to wear <u>one</u> shirt for twenty days and as many nights. At home <u>I</u> should have worn nine . . . and three nightshirts for the same period in ordinary, moderately warm weather.

Evening at the fire . . . . At night, after we had supper, I was very hungry. But the meat was so raw and tough that I either had to go to bed hungry or else let it roast on a stick a little longer. I did the latter. I thereby insulted de Conteau, who is rather sensitive as a cook, and since then he doesn't give a damn for me or my dirty shirts.

— *Charles Preuss, 1842*

One crossing where we forded . . . the water was so deep in places that it ran into the wagon boxes and a single team and wagon would have been swept away, so they formed the entire train in single file, and attached the teams and wagons to a chain extending through the entire length of the train. The crossing here severely tried the courage and endurance of the men, for they waded the river alongside their oxen, at times clinging to the ox yokes, and swimming.

— *Jesse Applegate, 1843*

We continued up the North Fork, and on the 13th came to Lauramie Fork, opposite Fort Lauramie. Finding it full, we were obliged to ferry, and for this purpose we procured two small boats from the Forts, lashed them together, and covered them with a platform made of wagon beds, which we had taken to pieces for the purpose. Upon this platform, we placed the loaded wagons by hand, and although the stream was very rapid, all succeeded in crossing without much difficulty . . . .

The fort is built of Dobies [adobe bricks]. A wall of six feet in thickness and fifteen in height, encloses an area of one hundred and fifty feet square. Within and around the wall, are the buildings . . . . These are a Trading House, Ware Houses for storing goods and skins, Shops and Dwellings for the Traders and Men . . . . A portion of the enclosed space is cut off by a partition wall, forming a carell [corral] for the animals belonging to the Fort. About one mile below Fort Lauramie, is Fort Platte; which is built of the same materials and in the same manner, and belongs to a private Trading Company.

— *Overton Johnson and W. H. Winter, 1843*

[August] 2nd . . . . Remained in camp to day trading and waiting for Blacksmith and other repairs went down to the fort [Laramie] after writeing to my Friend Starr of the Milwaukie Sentinell and found no prospect of his recieving my communication verry soon . . . . I purchased a dressed deer skin for 2.50 cents and returned to camp satisfied that money was allmost useless while all kinds of grocerys & Liquors ware exorbitantly high for instance sugar 1.50 cents per pint or cupfull and other things in proportion Flour Superfine 1.00 dollars per pint or 40 dollars per Barrel Spannish 30 no dried Buffaloe meat could be had at any price so our stores of provisions did not increase

— *James Clyman, 1844*

June 25. Our camp is stationary today; part of the emigrants are shoeing their horses and oxen; others are trading at the fort and with the Indians. Flour, sugar, coffee, tea, tobacco, powder and lead, sell readily at high prices. In the afternoon we gave the Indians a feast, and held a long talk with them. Each family . . . contributed a portion of bread, meat, coffee or sugar, which being cooked, a table was set by spreading buffalo skins upon the ground, and arranging the provisions upon them . . . . Having filled themselves, the Indians retired, taking with them all that they were unable to eat.

— *Joel Palmer, 1845*

. . . we came up to an encampment of Indians who proved to be a war party of two hundred or more of the Crow Tribe, and equipped for battle. They asked us through an interpreter, whether we had seen any of the Sioux Tribe . . . . This conversation took place between a deputation of five of our company and the Indians, which was done to prevent their coming too near us, and frightening our cattle . . . . Notwithstanding all this, an Indian approached a wagon in the rear, having a mule team attached, which became frightened and rushed forward, causing all the other teams to start also, and the whole train of forty wagons dashed across the plains, the drivers having no control over the frantic animals, and the women and children who were inmates of the wagons, screaming with all their voices, some of the wagons upset . . . and it was some time before we could . . . stop them; when we finally did, it was ascertained that we had sustained considerable injury, some of our wagons lying on one side and teams detached from them in some instances, other with the wheels broken, and the contents strewn promiscuously around, while some of our company were lying out with broken legs, and other seriously injured, the whole scene presenting a most disastrous appearance. The Indians having witnessed the entire affair, were hastening to us . . . but we, entertaining no very kind feeling for them just then, sent a guard of twenty men to intercept them and request they should advance no nearer . . . . Fortunately there was a grove of cotton wood in this vicinity where we could obtain wood for heating our wheel tires, and after a two days' delay we again started westward. In the evening we encamped at Fort Laramie.

— *Samuel Hancock, 1845*

June 19th — Gifts pass here as freely as the winds. Visit a trader, and his last cup of coffee and sugar, his last pound of flour, are brought out for your entertain-

Oregon Trail Ruts (near Guernsey, Wyoming)

ment; and if you admire anything that he has, he gives it to you. Little thanks expected or given on either side....

June 20th — Old smoke had a fat puppy killed and put into the kettle for us this morning. It was excellent.

June 26 — Emigrants crossing the river, and thronging into the fort — part of Russel[l]'s company, has split into a half dozen pieces. Passed along the line of waggons, conversing with the women, etc. These people are very ignorant, and suspicious for this reason — no wonder — they are grossly imposed on at the store.... The emigrants had a ball in the fort ... the other night. Such belles! One woman, of more than suspected chastity, is left at the Fort; and Bordeaux is fool enough to receive her.

— Francis Parkman, 1846

Yesterday [May 30] being a rainy day and most trains laying by having nothing else to do, a general destruction and devastation appeared to take Place — in almost every train — I thought I had seen destruction of property but this morning beat anything I had ever seen.... Trunks, clothes, Matrasses, Quilts, Beef, Bacon, Rice, Augers, Handsaws, planes, Shoes, Hats, Thread, Spools, Boss [?] Soap, mowing sythes etc. These were thrown out yesterday by one train in order to make their loads lighter.

....We found a number of emigrants here [at Fort Laramie] — many with broken down teams, some preparing to pack, others turning back, not being able to procure the necessaries for packing, and less able to proceed farther with their present teams. This appears

Register Rocks (near Guernsey, Wyoming)

to be a place of general renovating amongst travellers. Most stay a day or two for the double purpose of resting their mules and repacking their loads — Good waggons here bring from 4 to 30 dollars. Mules from 100 to 150 dollars . . . . Everything you buy cost four times as much as it is worth and every thing you sell bring perhaps one tenth its value.

— *Dr. T., 1849*

[May] My glowing fancy vanished before the wreched reality — a miserable, cracked, dilapidated, adobe, quadrangular enclosure, with a wall about twelve feet high, three sides of which were shedded down as stores and workshops, the fourth, or front, having a two-story erection, with a projecting balcony, for hurling projectiles or hot water on the foe, propped all around on the outside with beams of timber, which an enemy had only to kick away and down would come the whole structure.

— *William Kelly, 1849*

My Dearest Mother [Mary Dougherty], ... We reached this place on the 22nd [June] the day before yesterday & are to leave tomorrow morning. Our animals are a good deal wearied & it is for this that the command is delayed here . . . the dust . . . is insufferable. The road for 4 or 5 days back of this place is nothing but sand, most of the time nearly a foot deep.

Detail, Register Rocks

This has worn down the mules, more than all the march previous. We were just 3 weeks in making this place. The fort [Laramie] itself is the gloomiest most desolate looking place I ever saw. It looks exactly like a Penitentiary except there are no windows on the outside. The new fort is not to be established here but about 50 miles or more above. There is neither fire wood or any soil which will produce Hay. Major Sanderson & Mr. Woodbury have been above in search of a suitable spot for the Fort & will proceed with the command to the spot. We crossed the Platte without any trouble the waggons doubled teams & we had two good strong mules hitched to the tongue of the Carriage in front of the horses. The water just ran into the carriage. The river was more than a mile wide at this crossing. The Supply Train lost only two mules. Tomorrow we cross Laramie River. The water is much deeper than the Platte tho narrow. There has been considerable Cholera among the men & several deaths, always however owing to their own neglect in not making known the first symptoms. There is not a single officer who has had it. Our dear little ones have been very well indeed. So have Charlie & I. Maggie I think has improved very much she learns to talk very fast indeed can say almost everything by single words. Here sits she now by my side with her pa's shaving brush, which she has taken off the table & rubbing the leather all over her face looking as pleased as Punch — She calls you often & says, "Gam-ma come". Bless her heart she will forget you but Mary, she will not, she . . . often says, "I wonder what my Grandma's doing now. I spec she's thinken about me". I heard from Pa by Mr. Woodbury. He was getting well fast he wrote & how very anxious we were about him. Charlie [husband] is now in command of this 2nd Squadron owing to the continuous drunkness of Major Crittenden. Charlie complained to Col. [W. W.] Loring who had him arrested which placed Charlie in command . . . .

Pa has told you of the arrangement Charlie made with an Emigrant Family to cook & wash for us. We are very well pleased & satisfied so far. The woman is smart, managing & obliging. She cooks well, too. The man does nothing for us sometimes he waits on his wife, but generally Charlie has a soldier to bring & cut wood etc.

We find the whole Family & pay the woman $1 per week. They have four children. Indeed I think it is a blessing for them, for they would never have got through with this man, he is the slowest moving, laziest man, I ever saw. We churn, have plenty of milk & Mrs. Kelly sold milk to the amount of $20 . . . besides making all our bread with milk. We have the best bread in the whole command. Some use nothing but crackers . . . . We expect to reach Ft. Hall in a month from this. The animals are all being shod preparitory to climbing the Black Hills. This is the only Squadron

in which there is more than one Lady . . . . We are beginning to witness some of the suffering on these Plains. The other day we picked up a crazy man. His party had desserted him & left a note on the grave, near which he was found, stating he had gone crazy on his mother's death. A day or two afterwards we overtook a widow with 4 children. She had lost her husband & 2 children from cholera & all the rest were ill with it but one. Her party had deserted her. The colonel and quarter master rendered her every assistance, sent medical aid and men to get her cattle together & she proved her gratitude by bribing two teamsters to desert the command & join her & share her property with her. She has 40 head of cattle. Yesterday a family was found near here, the man lying in his waggon with his leg broken, his wife and little children there & no one else near. They were left by their party. Another a mile distant very sick & his cattle gone, no one to look after them. Assistance was sent to each. I fear this is only a beginning of the misery before us.

. . . . Do write me often Ma. You don't know what a pleasure it will give me to hear from your own hand. How do the boys get on? I hope they improve. Tell them to write to me. Give my love to them & tell them not to forget their sister & to be good boys. Give my best love to dearest and best of Fathers. Tell him to write to us both. Remember me to all the neighbors & to the blacks.

Charlie says you must enquire at the Post Office in Liberty [Missouri] how to direct letters to Oregon City in Oregon & direct our letter accordingly. He sends his best love to you & the boys & will write to Pa.

— A. [Ann Dougherty Ruff], 1849

I carried a little motherless babe five hundred miles, whose mother had died, and when we would camp I would go from camp to camp in search of some good, kind motherly women to let it nurse, and no one ever refused when I presented it to them.

— Margaret W. Inman, 1852

26th . . . . went to the Fort and had an "adventure."

— E. S. McComas, 1862

Warm Springs

The road [on the return trip east] led over an interesting plateau between the North fork of the Platte on the right, and Laramie river on the left. At the distance of ten miles from the fort, we entered the sandy bed of a creek . . . where, on the left bank, a very large spring gushes with considerable noise and force out of the

Warm Springs (Platte County, Wyoming)

limestone rock. It is called "the Warm Spring," and furnishes to the hitherto dry bed of the creek a considerable rivulet.

— *Brevet-Capt. John C. Frémont, 1842*

August 20 (Saturday). It was bloody cold last night [on Frémont's return trip east] and when I got up before five o'clock, I saw the grass white with hoarfrost. In Baltimore you are probably perspiring at this time . . . .

Kit [Carson] has just shot a fat cow. Two bulls ran right through our midst. God knows how many shots were fired at them; they paid no attention. Some hunters! Thank God, the Indians left us in peace. I believe we are safe now . . . . it is apparent that these mountains cannot be compared to our Alps. Yet they are hardly less remarkable in their way . . . . Here everything is wild.

— *Charles Preuss, 1842*

On the morning of the 16th, we left the Forts, and after having traveled ten miles, we came to the Black Hills, and encamped at a large Spring, the water of which was quite warm. The road through these hills is, of necessity, very circuitous; winding about as it must, to avoid the steeps, ravines, and rocks. They are very barren and some of them are high.

— *Overton Johnson and W. H. Winter, 1843*

[August] 3. dry parched hills which make a verry Singular appearance dotted all over with Shrubby Junts of dark looking Pine and cedars . . . . but feew Springs and no brooks as the water rises and Sinks occasionly along their gravelly beds . . . .

[August] 5 Shortly after dark their came on a thunder Shower with such a Squall of wind that allmost all our Tents ware fluttering on the ground in a moment the large cold drops of rain pelting us furiously all over & not even sparing the delicate Ladies & small children which ran helter skeltter in all directions seeking for shelter . . . .

. . . turning your head to S. W. & W. an extensive view of the roughest & most raged mountain [Laramie Peak] in all this rough region mellowed down by the distance into smoothe sharp pinecles with others rising in the back ground to a great hight.

— *James Clyman, 1844*

Leaving the valley of the Warm Spring Branch . . . we passed today the nearly consumed fragments of about a dozen wagons that had been broken up and burned by their owners: and near them was piled up, in one heap, from six to eight hundred weight of bacon, thrown away for want of means to transport it further. Boxes, bonnets, trunks, wagon wheels, whole wagon bodies, cooking utensils, and, in fact, almost every article of household furniture, were found.

— *Capt. Howard Stansbury, 1852*

Hembree Death

[July 18] A very bad road. Joel J. Hembree's son Joel fel off the waggon & both wheels run over him.

[July 19] Lay Buy. Joel Hambree departed this life about 2 o'clock.

[July 20] We buried the youth & in graved his name on the head stone.

— *William T. Newby, 1843*

July 20. We buried a small boy this morning that died from a waggon having passed over the abdomen.

— *Marcus Whitman, M.D., 1843*

Thursday, July 20. — I came on ahead with Captain Gantt and an advance guard, passed over some very rough road, and at noon came up to a fresh grave with stones piled over it, and a note tied on a stick informing us that it was the grave of Joe Hembree, child of Joe J. Hembree, aged 6 years, and was killed by a wagon running over its body.... The grave is on the left hand side of the trail close to Sqaw Creek Butte.

— *James Willis Nesmith, 1843*

But one death ... occurred ... far out under the mountains. Here the loose riders of our moving camp gathered one morning to examine a rude pyramid of stones by the roadside. The stones had been planted firmly in the earth, and those on top were substantially placed, so that the wolves, whose marks were evident about the pile, had not been able to disinter the dead. On one stone, larger than the rest, and with a flat side, was rudely engraved: J. Hembree — and we place it here, as perhaps the only memento those who knew him in the States may ever receive of him. How he [Joel Hembree] died we cannot of course surmise, but there he sleeps among the rocks of the West, as soundly as though chiseled marble was built above his bones.

— *Matthew C. Field, 1843*

Laramie Peak

Jun 4. — Our direction [from Laramie Fork] is a little north of west, and we have, perhaps, made the distance of twenty-five miles. We are still short of the Red Buttes, the usual crossing place, where the Platte is left for the Sweetwater, one of its tributaries. We have now a change, and that change the odd variety of roses, rattlesnakes and snow-covered mountains.

— *William Marshall Anderson, 1834*

The black Hills [Laramie Range] do not derive their name from anything peculiar in the color of the soil and rocks of which they are composed, but are so called from being covered with shrubby cedars, which give them a dark appearance when seen at a distance .... At this place the [fur] caravan halted, and ... the men were allowed a "day of indulgence," in which they drink

J. Hembree Grave

ardent spirits as much do they please, and conduct as they choose. Not unfrequently the day terminates with a catastrophe of some kind, and to-day one of the company shot another . . . the ball entered the back and came out at the side. The wounded man exclaimed, "I am a dead man." After a pause, said, "No, I am not hurt."

The other immediately seized a rifle to finish the work, but was prevented by the bystanders, who wrested it from him and discharged it into the air. The next day a quiet day.

— *Rev. Samuel Parker, 1835*

[June 15th], we left Fort Laramie to journey again in westerly direction through the wilderness. Our way led over the Black Hills . . . leaving the Laramie River to our left, and ascending the [Platte] North Fork at a moderate distance from it . . . . For four days we camped on little streams that flow into the North Fork . . . . The road was growing daily more difficult . . . . We were visibly ascending.

— *Frederick A. Wislizenus, M.D., 1839*

July 25 (Monday) . . . Today we pitched camp at noon in order to dry meat since there are great numbers of buffalo here.

A barometer, not the best one though, has gone wrong. The bad road between here and Laramie killed it. We left the large chronometer in Laramie; Fremont succeeded in making it run again, and he was jubilant when he heard again the ticking and the tick-tocking. In comparing we found, however, that every twenty-four hours it went wrong by about an hour. Oh, you American blockheads!

— *Charles Preuss, 1842*

Early in the morning we fired several rounds, and made as much noise as possible in honor of the day of Independence. We started in the morning and soon passed an encampment where we had the pleasure of beholding the "Star Spangled Banner" floating in the cool breeze. We traveled a few miles farther and passed another camp with two large American flags waving above it.

— *Reuben Cole Shaw, 1849*

July 4 — [Black Hills] . . . stopped to get a Fourth of July dinner and to celebrate our nation's birthday . . . . A storm arose, blew over all the tents but two, capsized our stove with its delicious viands, set one wagon on fire and for a while produced not a little confusion in the camp . . . . After the storm was over we put up the stove, straightened up the tent, and got as nice a dinner as we had upon the "Glorious Fourth" in Boston last year. We then took care of our game, consisting of 5

black-tailed deer, 1 antelope and three buffalo . . . . I will give you a description of my dress: a red calico frock, made for the purpose in the wagons; a pair of mockasins, made of black buffalo hide, ornamented with silk instead of beads, as I had none of the latter and a hat braided, of bullrushes, and trimmed with white, red and pink ribbon and white paper. I think I came near looking like a squaw.

— *Elizabeth Wood, 1851*

Horace Dolly . . . killed Charles Botsford yesterday by shooting . . . for which the company killed said Dolly today, by hanging. Said Dolly had a wife and two children.

— *John E. Dalton, 1852*

July 27 . . . . Today we find additional and melancholy evidence of the difficulties by those [emigrants] who are ahead of us. Before halting to noon, we passed eleven wagons that had been broken up, the spokes of the wheels taken to make pack-saddles, and the rest burned or otherwise destroyed; the road [near Red Buttes] has been literally strewn with articles that have been thrown away. Bar-iron and steel, large blacksmith's anvils and bellows, crowbars, drills, augers, gold washers, chisels, axes, lead, trunks, spades, ploughs, large grindstones, baking ovens, cooking-stoves . . . kegs, barrels, harness, clothing, bacon, and beans, were found along the road . . . . The carcasses of eight oxen, lying in one heap by the roadside this morning, explained a part of the trouble. I recognised the trunks of some of the passengers who had accompanied me from St. Louis to Kansas, on the Missouri, and who had here thrown away their wagons and everything they could not pack.

— *Capt. Howard Stansbury, 1852*

Wednesday, 29 . . . . We had the worst roads yesterday. We had dreadful places to come down, ugly places to go up, and . . . . Oh, dear, I wish we were in Oregon, or even out of these Black Hills. I am tired of them; they are so dismal looking.

Thursday, 30. Oh, dear, we have to stay here two or three days and it will appear two or three weeks. I want to go on and never stop at all if it could be helped, but the oxen's feet are all tender . . . . We must stop and let them get well again.

— *Agnes Stewart, 1853*

Friday, July 4th . . . . Passed Larramie Peak . . . . went hunting, killed one sage hen and crippled a wolf. "played hell". Layed bye, washed, and baked . . . . rained which stopped the mosquitoes.

— *E. S. McComas, 1862*

Laramie Peak (Wyoming)

Sweetwater Road

Upper Platte Crossing

July 4th. This brings to mind hurry and bustle, preparations for pleasure excursions throughout the union. Scarcely any person but what is going to have, or expects to have, a little more than usual today, while we are going on our weary journey. Crossed the North Platte yesterday . . . . The sand was so heavy that it was hard to haul the wagons down hill.

We paid five dollars [ferriage] for each wagon, and four yoke of oxen, and 12½ cents per head for the rest of the cattle, and the same for each man except one driver for each team. The ladies went across free for their dear little feet would not wear out the bridge . . . .

. . . . They are playing the fiddles and dancing, and I can shut my eyes and think I am at some gathering . . . just like I used to be. It recalls old times to me.

Tuesday, 5th. Such a warm day. Everyone is worn out and tired with the heat. We finished the Fourth of July by dancing. After Helen and I sitting on the hill and moralizing so serious we came down and cut capers like a parcel of fools.

— *Agnes Stewart, 1853*

Ridge on Avenue of Rocks (Natrona County, Wyoming)

Oregon Trail, Approaching Avenue of Rocks

Willow Springs

We came to the Willow Springs, where we found a beautiful Spring, of very clear cold water, rising in a little green valley, through which its waters flow about one mile, and sink in the sand. We also found here, an abundance of Willow wood . . . . The great scarcity of the Buffalo, through this country . . . was attributable . . . to the presence of Sir William Stewart, with his pleasure party, and fifty or sixty fine horses for the chase; who, while we were passing through the Buffalo country, constantly kept several days ahead of us running, killing and driving the game out of reach. It was cheap sport to them, but dear to us.

— Overton Johnson and W. H. Winter, 1843

The trail passes between considerable alkali lagoons, close to the smaller one on our left, and perhaps 2 miles from the larger one — on the right. They remind one strongly of ponds of ice — dazzling white in the snow. Sal eratus encrusts all the mud and grass near them; and the main surface of it is about the consistenci and appearance of imperfectly frozen milk.

— William Clayton, 1847

We arrived at Willow Springs where we had intended camping. It has been a noted camping place on account of the water, fuel and grass. We found the grass all pasteured out, the willows all consumed, and teams and people enough here to use the water about as fast as it came from its fountain.

— Henry Allyn, 1853

Came 25 m. through awful sand and bad hills. Had to let our wagon down with ropes. Came 10 m. and stopped where masquitoes were thicker than any person . . . could imagine.

— E. S. McComas, 1862

Willow Springs (near Casper, Wyoming)

121

Sweetwater River, Seminoe Mountains (Wyoming)

Independence Rock

June 23 — We reached the Sweetwater, traveling through a naked, bleak country, the bare granite rocks lifting their craggy heads above the sea of sand and sandstone . . . . At noon we reached "Independence Rock." It is like a big bowl turned upside down; in size about equal to two meeting houses of old New England style.

— *John Ball, 1832*

We have breakfasted this morning at the base of Rock Independence. There are few places better known or more interesting to the mountaineer than this huge boulder . . . . On the side of the rock names, dates and messages, written in buffalo-grease and powder, are read and re-read with as much eagerness as if they were letters . . . from long absent friends . . . being a place of advertisement, or kind of trappers' post office . . . . It is a large, egg-shaped mass of granite, entirely separate and apart from all . . . ranges of hills. One mile in circumference, about six or seven hundred feet high, without a particle of vegetation . . . .

Some years ago, a party of buffalo killers and beaver skinners celebrated here our national jubilee on the great Fourth of July. What noise, what roar of powder and pomp of patriotism surrounded and echoed from this eternal monument my informant did not say, nor can I imagine. I shall suppose the immortal Declaration was talked over, Washington toasted, and Rock Independence baptised.

— *William Marshall Anderson, 1834*

. . . on the 9th, encamped at noon on the banks of the Sweetwater. Here we found a large rounded mass of granite about fifty feet high, called Rock Independence.

122

Like the Red Butte, this rock is also a rather remarkable point in the route . . . . we see carved the names of most of the mountain bourgeois. We observed those of the two Sublettes, Captain Bonneville, Serre, Fontinella . . . .

— *John K. Townsend, 1834*

[Ahead] the Mountains are indeed Rocky Mountains. They are rocks heaped upon rocks, with no vegetation, excepting a few cedars growing out of the crevices near their base. Their tops are covered with perpetual snow, which are seen on our left and before us . . . [the next four days past Independence Rock] cold winds were felt. The passage through these mountains is in a valley.

— *Rev. Samuel Parker, 1835*

[June 14th] We crossed over a high ridge to the Sweet water, so called from the great purity of its waters. The most remarkable spot upon this river is the famous Independence Rock . . . . It is the great register of the desert; the names of all the travelers who have passed by are there to be read, written in coarse characters; mine figures among them.

— *Fr. Pierre-Jean DeSmet, S.J., 1840*

[June 28-29.] The first rock which we saw, and which truly deserves the name, was the famous Independence Rock . . . . At first I was led to believe that it received this pompous name from its isolated situation and the solidity of its base, but I was told that it was called so because the first travelers arrived at it on the very day when the people of the United States celebrate the anniversary of their emancipation from Great Britain . . . .

I called this rock on my first journey "The Great Record of the Desert."

— *Fr. Pierre-Jean DeSmet, S.J., 1841*

This night we have the sound of the violin but not much dancing. 'Woe unto the wicked; for they shall have their reward.' Our company is composed mostly of Universalists and deists.

— *Rev. Joseph Williams, 1841*

August 22 — There was such a hurry this morning that Fremont became angry when my horse urinated. He whipped his tail when it had only half-relieved nature.

. . . Tomorrow morning the boat will be inflated, and we shall try to sail to the Platte . . . What a miserable rock is this Independence Rock compared to the rocks we saw in the mountains. And what a name! Many a human wretch, too, bears a high-sounding name.

— *Charles Preuss, 1842*

August 23 . . . we reached our encampment at Rock Independence where I took some astronomical observations. Here, not unmindful of the custom of early travelers and explorers in our country, I engraved on this rock of the Far West a symbol of the Christian faith . . . .

Sweetwater Hills, Saleratus Lake

Independence Rock (Natrona County, Wyoming)

One George Weymouth was sent out to Maine by the Earl of Southampton, Lord Arundel . . . and in the narrative of their discoveries, he says: "The next day, we ascended in our pinnace [boat] that part of the river which lies more to the Westward, carrying with us a cross — a thing never omitted by any Christian traveler — which we erected at the ultimate end of our route."

This was in the year 1605, and in 1842 I obeyed the feelings of early travellers, and left the impression of the cross deeply engraved on the vast rock one thousand miles beyond the Mississippi.

— *Brevet-Capt. John C. Frémont, 1842*

Thursday, [July] 27th . . . After partaking of a pot of glourious buffalo soup, cut our meat to dry and then started out to take a view of the scenery, and climbed Independence Rock . . . . on one side is an extended plain with a small stream meandering through it; while in view, at three encampments, consisting of 120 wagons, with their 700 or 800 animals feeding, and in the distance of the wild buffalo, feeding at their leisure.

— *John Boardman, 1843*

Sunday, July, 30 . . . After breakfast, myself, with some other young men, had the pleasure of waiting on five or six young ladies to pay a visit to Independence Rock. I had the satisfaction of putting the names of Miss Mary Zachary and Miss Jane Mills on the Southeast point of the rock, near the road, on a high point. Facing the road, in all spendor of gun powder, tar and buffalo greese, may be seen the name of J. W. Nesmith, from Maine, with an anchor . . . .

Monday, July 31 . . . Came up to Martin's Company about 2:00 o'clock, and found some very sick men in the Company . . . . We have in company thirteen wagons and thirty-one men, a small band indeed, but all seemed determined to go on through.

We camped on Sweet Water, with a high range of mountains on the right, or Northwest . . . . Applegate and Childs ahead. Old Zachary, a man fond of rows, has been excluded from Martin's Company for defrauding a young man by the name of Matney and of his provisions, and throwing him off in the wilderness. The old rogue, with the two oteys [Oto Indians] encamped about a mile ahead, alone; a small camp, but a big rascal.

— *James Willis Nesmith, 1843*

Independence Rock, Northeast Side

On the 20th, we encamped on Sweet Water, one of the tributaries of the [Platte] North Fork, near the Independence Rock; which is a huge isolated mass of coarse granite . . . . It was called Independence Rock, by Mr. Wm. Sublet [Sublette], an old Indian Trader; who, several years ago, celebrated here, the 4th of July.

— *Overton Johnson and W. H. Winter, 1843*

[August] 16 Moved on up the creek Saw the notable rock Independance with the names of its numerious visitors most of which are nearly obliterated by the weather & ravages of time amongst which I observed the names of two of my old friends the notable mountaneers Tho. Fitzpatrick & W. L. Sublette as likewise one of our noblest politicians Henry Clay coupled in division with that of Martin Van Buren a few miles furthe[r] up the creek pases through the South point of a most ruged & solid looking granite rock by a verry narrow pass [Devil's Gate] after passing which we entered a valy Surounded by low ruged mountains . . . .

— *James Clyman, 1844*

July 12 . . . we arrived at Independence Rock . . . a solitary pole of gray granite . . . portions of it are covered with inscriptions . . . some carved, some in black paint, and others in red.

— *Joel Palmer, 1845*

We encamped near Independence Rock, which . . . occupies an area of two or three acres and is about a hundred and fifty feet high . . . . It is situated near Sweet Water River, a tributary of the Great Platte, upon whose banks we have traveled so far, and to which we bade adieu . . . . I may here say this Sweet Water River is justly entitled to the name it bears, for the water is truly sweet, coming directly out of the Rocky Mountains pure and sparkling.

— *Samuel Hancock, 1845*

July 7th. On top of Independence Rock. How often I have read and thought about it, and now I am on top of it. The wind blows very hard. That is the reason it is so unpleasant for those wearing skirts. It is quite easy to ascend, but I think it will be more difficult to descend.

— *Agnes Stewart, 1853*

126

Though much of the writing has been washed away by rain, 40,000 — 50,000 souls are calculated to have left their dates and marks from the caping of the wall to the loose stone below this huge signpost. There is, however, some reason in the proceeding; it does not in these lands begin and end with a silly purpose, as among climbers of the Pyramids, and fouilleurs of the sarcophagi of Apis, to bequeath one's few poor letters to a little athanasia prairie travelers, and emigrants expect to be followed by their friends, and leave, in their vermillion outfit, or their white house paint, or their brownish-black tar — a useful article for wagons — a homely but hearty word of love or direction upon any conspicuous object.

— *Richard Burton, 1860*

Independence Rock

Here is the body of Caroline Todd
Whose soul has lately gone to God;
E're redemption was too late,
She was redeemed at Devil's Gate.

— *On a grave board, 1862*

Devil's Gate

These [hills] are the termination of a high range of land running from south to north. They are very near the river Sweetwater, high and abrupt, and . . . there is a pass [Devil's Gate] through the range a short distance back from the river, the width of a common road, with perpendicular sides of two to three hundred feet high.

— *Rev. Samuel Parker, 1835*

[June] . . . . Travelers have named this spot the Devils Entrance [Devil's Gate]. In my opinion they should have rather called it Heaven's Avenue.

— *Fr. Pierre-Jean DeSmet, S.J., 1841*

August 2. — Five miles above Rock Independence we came to a place called the Devil's Gate, where the Sweet Water cuts through the point of a granite ridge. The length of the passage is about three hundred yards, and the width thirty-five yards. The walls of rock are vertical, and about four hundred feet in height; and the stream in the gate is almost entirely choked up by masses which have fallen from above.

— *Brevet-Capt. John C. Frémont, 1842*

Fremont is roaming through the mountains collecting rocks and is keeping us waiting for lunch. I am hungry as a wolf. That fellow knows nothing about mineralogy

or botany. Yet he collects every trifle in order to have it interpreted later in Washington and brag about it in his report. Let him collect as much as he wants — if he would only not make us wait for our meal.

Today he said the air up here is too thin; that is the reason for his daguerreotype was a failure. Old boy, you don't understand the thing, that is it.

. . . As I said, these Rocky Mountains are no Swiss Alps. But it is true that they are magnificent, strangely shaped rocks. In a few days I shall be able to say more about them.

Our fare is getting worse and worse. No thought of bread any longer. Ham and bacon are likewise gone. Dried buffalo meat, hard as wood, and antelope prepared in buffalo fat — that is all. How glad we would be if we only had the pork which we buried at the Platte.

— *Charles Preuss, 1842*

July 31 . . . . Through this romantic pass the river brawls and frets over broken masses of rock that obstructs its passage.

— *Capt. Howard Stansbury, 1852*

Many people complain that Ash Hollow is the entrance to hell and Devil's Gate its exit. But I maintain that Devils Gate is the entrance.

— *William Keil, 1855*

Bones, Near Sweetwater River (Wyoming)

Granite Slabs, Rattlesnake Hills (Wyoming)

A condition of distress here met my eyes that I never saw before or since. The [Mormon] train was strung out for two or three miles. There were old men pulling and tugging their carts, sometimes loaded with a sick wife or children, women pulling along sick husbands, little children six to eight years old struggling through the mud and snow. As night came on the mud would freeze on their clothes and feet. We gathered on to some of the most helpless with our riatas tied to the carts, and helped as many as we could into camp . . . . Such assistance as we could give was rendered to all until they finally arrived at Devil's Gate fort, about the first of November. There were some 1200 in all, about one-half with hand-carts and the other half with teams.

The winter storms had now set in in all their severity. The provisions we took amounted to almost nothing among so many people, many of them now on very short rations, some almost starving. Many were dying daily from exposure and want of food.

— *Daniel W. Jones, 1856*

Rattlesnake Hills

For several days now we had on our right a chain [Rattlesnake Hills] of those naked rocks, so properly called Rocky Mountains. They are nothing but rocks heaped upon rocks.

— *Fr. Pierre-Jean DeSmet, S.J., 1840*

[August] 17. Smokey But the sun rose over the Eastern Mountains in its usual majesty Some recent Signs of a war party of Indians ware discovered yestarddy which caused some uneasiness . . . . roled up the Stream on the South side arange of the most ruged bare granite rocks lay along the North side [Rattlesnake Hills] close to the water . . . . saw some fine herds of Ibex or wild sheep some of which ware taken and & found to be verry fine eating . . . .

This region seems to be the refuses of the world thrown up in the utmost confusion.

— *James Clyman, 1844*

Wednesday, August 1 . . . . Frost during the night; morning clear, calm, and very beautiful. The road passing occasionally through deep, heavy sand, continued up the right bank of the Sweetwater . . . . The valley is here nearly two miles wide, with rolling hills between the two mountain ranges, which . . . form its limits.

About a dozen burnt wagons and nineteen dead oxen were passed to-day along the road; but the destruction has been by no means as great as upon the North Fork of the Platte and the crossing over to the Sweetwater.

— *Capt. Howard Stansbury, 1852*

From the granite range [Rattlesnake Hills] five or six miles to a parallel mountain ridge at the south, is called the "Valley," of the Sweet Water . . . . we stopped in the opening of a romantic pass . . . . Two hunters, who had been sent after buffalo, joined us . . . with the uneasy haste of a retreat: they had found a grizzly bear with three cubs, and had managed to kill one and had taken a second alive . . . . the live one, exhausted by the chase and the excessive heat, seemed dead, and they laid it in the edge of the water . . . when suddenly the little beast assumed vigorous life with so fierce a growl, as to disperse his spectators like a boombshell.

— *Lt. Col. Phillip St. George Cooke, 1857*

Sweetwater River

This stream [Sweetwater] is one of the most beautiful tributaries of the Platte. It owes its name to the purity of its waters.

— *Fr. Pierre-Jean DeSmet, S.J., 1842*

Oregon Trail Ruts and Split Rock, Rattlesnake Range

Oregon Trail Ruts, East of Split Rock (Wyoming)

Sweetwater River (Wyoming)

In about three miles, we reached the the entrance of a kanyon where the Sweet Water issues upon the more open valley we had passed over . . . . The usual road passes to the right of this place; but we wound . . . our way up the narrow valley for hours. Wildness and disorder were the character of the scenery . . . . Here were many old traces of beaver on the streams.

— *Brevet-Capt. John C. Frémont, 1842*

I fancied that when we got to that river [Sweetwater] I would have all the sweet water I could drink. When we came to the river . . . I ran down to the water's edge and, bending over, resting my hands, took a drink of the water, but . . . the water was very common indeed, and not sweet.

— *Jesse Applegate, 1843*

. . . we had among us the prince of cranks.

He was a chronic grumbler and nothing ever met his approval. He was always hungry and thirsty, forever tired and sleepy, too indolent to carry wood or water, and too lazy to wash himself or bathe the saddle galls on his mules. He would lie, cheat, and steal, shirk guard duty whenever he could frame an excuse, and was a regular all-around nuisance. He . . . had no eye for the beautiful unless it was cooked, he never saw a grand old mountain until he had thumped his head against it, and then cursed because it was in his way . . . .

On one occasion as we were about to encamp on the bank of a stream, in alighting from his mule he sprained an ankle. Seating himself on a rock he called the Doctor, who gave the foot a glance and said, "wash it," and then pressed on. After washing his foot the Doctor was again consulted, who ordered him to wash the other foot. He obeyed the order, after which his hurt was properly cared for.

— *Reuben Cole Shaw, 1849*

Monday, July 12 .... Since I wrote we have passed the Devil's Gate, crossed the Sweetwater five times, and now ascending the Rocky Mountains and in two days we will get our first sight of Oregon [Territory] .... Mary lost one of her oxen, one of the best. It could ill be spared.

— *Agnes Stewart, 1853*

Ice Slough

We gathered [at Ice Slough] several buckets of ice, from which we had Mint Juleps in abundance.

— *Dr. T., 1848*

July 14 .... I saw on the borders of the marsh a great quantity of this never ending alkali .... [Everyone] who could stop at the ice bed, did so, and furnished himself with as much as he could conveniently carry.

— *Maj. Osborne Cross, 1849*

... we dug down about eighteen inches and came to a bed of solid clear ice. We dug up enough to put into water-kegs and enjoyed the luxury of ice-water all that hot day, while we traveled through the famous SOUTH PASS of the Rocky Mountains.

— *Granville Stuart, 1852*

It is asserted that ice can be found on this marsh at any season of summer by digging two feet beneath the surface; we tried it in a number of places, and in two of them found a substance resembling ice in appearance; we obtained a good specimen, and have it yet, so conclude it's not ice, but know it to be a mixture of salt and soda.

— *W. Wadsworth, 1858*

Ice Slough

Rocky Ridge Near South Pass (Fremont County, Wyoming)

Approaching South Pass

Next-the Columbia

[During and after 1843 the Oregon Trail crossed the Continental Divide and headed toward the Whitman Mission at Walla Walla near the Columbia. From South Pass the emigrants traveled to the Big Sandy and the Bear or Fort Bridger. Here in the valley of the Green had been a center of the fur trade, a place known to the early explorers — Stuart and Hunt, Wyeth and Sublette, Smith and the mountain men — and to the early missionaries — the Whitmans and Lees, the Spaldings and Walkers, Parker and Fr. DeSmet. From here the original trail turned northwest toward Walla Walla and the Columbia, via Soda Springs, Fort Hall, the Snake, Fort Boise, Grand Ronde Valley, and over the Blue Mountains to the Whitman Mission, then by raft and boat and portage to The Dalles and Fort Vancouver and the Willamette Valley. In 1844 and '45, most emigrants went a more direct route, driving from Grand Ronde over the Blues and across the Umatilla to The Dalles. In later years the Barlow Road took them from The Dalles overland across the Cascades to the Land of Milk and Honey.]

South Pass

June 27 — We encamped on the southeast foothills of the Wind River Mountains, and the last branch of the Sweetwater, and June 28 found us on the great watershed between the Atlantic and Pacific oceans . . . . This is the celebrated South Pass, and from it the waters flow into the Gulf of Mexico and Gulf of California. On this extensive prairie buffalo are feeding by the hundred thousands.

— *John Ball, 1832*

. . . this evening, with the sun, we passed from the Eastern to Western America . . . . Yesterday, from a scarcely preceptible elevation, we could distinctly see waters flowing east and west . . . . The face of the country from the Red Buttes on the Platte to the Sweetwater, and from thence to the main Colorado . . . is sand and nothing but sand. In fact, except the bottoms . . . from the Kaw west there is no soil visible. It is one immense desert, a true American "Sahara."

— *William Marshall Anderson, 1834*

July 4th Crossed a ridge of land called the divide . . . . A number of Nez Percé . . . came out to meet us, and have camped with us tonight. They appear to be gratefied to see us actually on our way to their country.

— *Narcissa Prentiss Whitman, 1834*

Hail to Oregon!

The passage through these mountains is in a valley, so gradual in the ascent and descent, that I should not have known that we were passing them, had it not been that . . . the atmosphere gradually became cooler . . . . This valley was not discovered until some years since [by Robert Stuart, 1814]. Mr. Hunt and his party, more than twenty years ago, went near but did not find it . . . . Though there are some elevations and depressions in this valley . . . . [there] would be no difficulty in the way of constructing a rail road from the Atlantic to the Pacific ocean; and probably the time may not be very far distant, when trips will be made across the continent, as they have been made to the Niagara Falls, to see nature's wonders.

— *Rev. Samuel Parker, 1835*

June 24] . . . we passed [South Pass] from the waters] tributary to the Missouri to those of the Colorado . . . . The pass across the mountains is almost imperceptible; it is five to twenty-five miles in width, and eighty in length.

— *Fr. Pierre-Jean DeSmet, S.J., 1840*

The ascent had been so gradual . . . we were obliged to watch very closely to find the place at which we had reached the culminating point. This was between two low hills, rising on either hand fifty or sixty feet. When I looked back at them . . . I should compare the elevation which we surmounted immediately at the Pass, to the ascent of the Capitol hill from the avenue, at Washington . . . . Approaching it [South Pass] from the mouth of the Sweet Water, a sandy plain, one hundred and twenty miles long, conducts, by a gradual and regular ascent, to the summit, about seven thousand feet above the sea; and the traveller . . . suddenly finds himself on the waters which flow to the Pacific ocean . . . . the distance from Fort Laramie is 320 miles.

[Artemesias] . . . grow everywhere — on the hills, and over the river bottoms, in tough, twisted, wiry clumps . . . and the whole air is strongly impregnated and saturated with the odor of camphor and spirits of turpentine which belongs to the plant.

— *Brevet-Capt. John C. Frémont, 1842*

Lewiston (saleratus) Lakes

"Cadaver of an Ox," 1866, by Frank Buchser

Sweetwater River, Ninth Crossing

Monday, August 7. Left Sweet Water this morning, it being the last water of the Atlantic that we see. Crossed the Divide . . . . across a plain of sand and sage, and encamped on [the Little] Sandy . . . . We now consider ourselves in Oregon Territory and we consider this part of it a poor sample of the El Darado.

— *James Willis Nesmith, 1843*

. . . our pilot said, "Now for seven miles to the divide, where the water runs west to the Pacific." . . .

Here we saw a grand sight . . . . Away down the mountain side ahead of us, was an Indian village of three hundred tepees, . . . Of a sudden we came into their view. There was a quick yell to their horse guards and their ponies were rapidly brought into the village. Men and squaws and children . . . tore down the wigwams. They ran to their ponies, the squaws lashed the tent-poles to them, leaving the ends dragging on the ground. Tepees, buffalo robes, cooking utensils, provisions, and everything pertaining to the village were gathered up in an incredibly short space of time, and . . . before we were down the hillside, they were off for the hills that lay to the right. "Pegleg" Smith and another mountaineer came out from the village, telling us that they had tried to quell the Indians' fears, but it was all in vain. They were afraid of our "walking lodges."

— *Edward Henry Lenox, 1843*

Here, then [at the top of South Pass], we hailed Oregon!

— *Joel Palmer, 1845*

From the South Pass the nature of our journeying changed, and assumed the character of a retreat, a disastrous, ruinous retreat. Oxen and horses began to parish in large numbers; often falling dead in their yokes in the road. The heat-dried wagon, striking on rocks or banks, would fall to pieces. As the beasts of burden grew weaker . . . teams began to be doubled and wagons abandoned. The approaching storms of autumn, which . . . meant impassable snow, admitted of no delay. Whatever of strength remained of the jaded cattle must be forced out. Every thing of weight not absolutely necessary must be abandoned.

— *George B. Currey, 1853*

137

South Pass, Continental Divide, Wind River Range (Fremont County, Wyoming)

Pacific Springs

... I thought of mother's bread & butter many times as any hungry child would, but did not find it on the way. I fancy pork & potatoes would relish extremely well. Have been living on fresh meat for two months exclusively. Am cloged with it. I do not know how I shall endure this part of the journey [west of South Pass].

— *Narcissa Prentiss Whitman, 1834*

I witnessed [August 6] at Pacific Springs an instance of no little engenuity on the part of an emigrant. Immediately along the road was what purported to be a grave ... having a headboard, on which was painted the name and age of the deceased, the time of his death, and the part of the country from which he came. I afterward ascertained that ... the grave, instead of containing the mortal remains of a human being, had been made a safe receptacle for divers casks of brandy, which the owner, could carry no further.

— *Capt. Howard Stansbury, 1850*

Wind River Range, South Pass

Pacific Creek, West Slope of South Pass

Wind River Range

. . . although the mountains are spotted with snow, yet the plains are very hot and sultry . . . we saw some white grizzly bears, and killed some mountain sheep, the horns of which are as thick as a man's leg, and about two feet long.

— *Rev. Joseph Williams, 1841*

. . . the air at sunrise is clear and pure . . . . A fog, just risen . . . lies along the base of the mountain . . . the scenery becomes more interesting and grand, and the view here is truly magnificent; but indeed, it needs something to repay the long prairie journey of a thousand miles.

— *Brevet-Capt. John C. Frémont, 1842*

[July 18] . . . . The Wind River Mountains are on our right, about twenty miles distant. They presented a most grand appearance. Huge masses of ice and snow piled peak upon peak, with large bodies of timber covering

Wind River Range (Fremont County, Wyoming)

Plume Rock, Wind River Range

portions of the mountains. We viewed the southern termination of this range; but they extend to the north further than the eye can penetrate.

— Jesse Applegate, 1843

We are 7640 feet above the level of the sea, our guide books say, and almost to the line of perpetual snow. The Wind River range of mountains, abutting on our right, loom out almost over our trail . . . .

We have passed over, perhaps, the highest point of unbroken surface on the continent . . . the cold chilling air, and the difficulty of weak lungs to breath when little wearied, indicate our situation.

— S. H. Taylor, 1853

Little Sandy

. . . we camp at Little Sandy Creek, the first water which takes its course to the west, toward the Pacific Ocean. It is a small arm of the Green River . . . .

Yesterday we passed an old beaver colony. How those fellows can work! It is nothing for them to saw with their teeth through trees one to one and one-half feet in diameter . . . . The poor fellows are so pursued that one finds them only sporadically in this region . . . .

For several days now I feel dizzy when I bend down and want to straighten up again. Could it be caused by eating meat without bread? . . .

This noon we camp at Big Sandy.

— Charles Preuss, 1842

Here we are much annoyed by the Army crickets, the whole surface of the ground being covered with these insects, about an inch and a half long, and without wings.

— Samuel Hancock, 1845

Trail Split/Sublette's Cut-off

[Sublette's Cut-off, sometimes called the Dry Drive, on the Little Sandy, because of the scarcity of water on the route, crossed directly to the Bear River and bypassed Fort Bridger. The regular or old Oregon Trail went down the Big Sandy, forded the Green River near its forks, and then proceeded to Fort Bridger. It joined the cut-off near the mouth of Smith's Fork, at Cokeville, Wyoming.]

Strangely, Whitman did not direct the train [to Bear River] over Sublette Road [from Big Sandy]. Rather they went by way of Bridger [to Bear River] from Pacific Springs.

— Jesse Applegate, 1843

Saleratus Deposits, Little Sandy River (Sublette County, Wyoming)

The left hand trail [to Fort Bridger], which we took, twelve miles from the Little Sandy strikes the Big Sandy, follows down it and strikes Green River above the mouth of Big Sandy.

— *Joel Palmer, 1845*

Monday, July 2, 1849. Leaving the Sweet Water River went through what is called the South Pass . . . . Road's good . . . . Had fine view of [Wind River] mountains at our right. Camped west of Pacific Springs . . . .

3rd, Tuesday. Nooned on Dry Sandy 11 miles from our last night's encampment . . . . Reached Little Sandy about 6 P. M. . . .

July 5th, Thursday. We went to Big Sandy, this we forded and went up the opposite bank about three miles . . . . Distance from Little Sandy to Big Sandy is six miles.

July 6, Friday. We rested here until half-past three o'clock when we commenced our long march on Sublette's Cut-Off . . . . 41 miles without water . . . . Traveled on until sunrise, July 7th. Halted again and let cattle graze, after which we continued our march reaching Green River a little before night . . . . Had traveled more than 24 hours. Men and animals nearly worn out. Roads good . . . .

— *Henry W. Burto, 1849*

Big Sandy

Monday 16 . . . . Encamped on Big Sandy. Got my horse in the mire; not hurt any. Felt well: picked gooseberries at noon. In the afternoon rode 35 miles without stopping . . . . But come to get off my horse almost fainted. Laid as still as I could till after tea; then felt revived. Washed my dishes, made my bed, and rested well. In the morning spent an hour washing, rubbing and dressing. Feel quite well again. But 45 miles to ride in one day is hard.

— *Mary Richardson Walker, 1838*

In the vicinity of . . . [Big Sandy] as the Captain had mistaken our road for another, the caravan wandered for three days at random . . . . I thought myself entirely lost . . . . On the 20th of July we seriously thought of continuing our journey . . . . We were compelled to clear a passage, sometimes in the middle of a ravine, sometimes on the declevity of a rock and frequently through bushes. We traveled in this manner for ten days, to reach Bear river, which flows through a wide and beautiful valley, surrounded by lofty mountains.

— *Fr. Pierre-Jean DeSmet, S.J., 1841*

Parting of the Ways: Sublette Cut-off

Oregon Trail Ruts (Big Sandy, Wyoming)

Big Sandy River

Haystack Butte (Sweetwater County, Wyoming)

3rd Sunday.... We will now cook our grub with nothing but a frying pan to cook in but that is enough for two certainly.... This afternoon Baldwin lost a fine stallion with a disease which appears to kill almost all the horses that die on the roads. They get stupid and commence swelling, generally in the breast, and die in a verry short time.

— *E. S. McComas, 1862*

Green River

We are now at the place we started for when we left St. Louis.... I should not put it down at more than thirteen hundred miles.

This evening we were visited by six trappers from Drips and Fontenelle's camp. They were extremely glad to see us. We gave them the news in broken doses; beginning with matters three years old. This was delightful, fresher by several years than they had heard. Then we brought them up by degrees to the intelligence of the present day... these men have been in the mountains for the last twelve years without a visit to the settlements....

14th. — Have I, or have I not, immortalized myself today? I have raised [on Green River] with my own hands, our glorious flag, "the star-spangled banner," the badge of freedom and Union — on the brow of our great northern Andes. The first ever displayed on these unmeasurable heights. It had scarcely smoothed out its wrinkles and began to dance its joyous measures in the breeze, than four men were seen darting like Cossacks over the plains....

Into the tent they rushed. Somehow I learned their names. They were [Lewis] Vasquez, the long lost Vasquez, [Thomas] Fitzpatrick, [John] Gray, and the Little Chief. Vasquez and [William] Sublette are shaking hands with their right and smacking and pushing each other with the left. They both ask questions and neither answer, I sat by a listener and looker on. Three camps are now within fifty or sixty miles of each other. In a few days I shall know what a mountain rendezvous means....

16th. — Mr. Sublette has just returned from Fitzpatrick's camp, bringing with him the Little Chief, Insillah, which signifies in English the War Eagle's plume.... This amiable little fellow was looking intently at my white hair which Sublette observing, pronounced Gen. [William] Clark's Flathead name, Red Head Chief, and putting the first fingers of his right hand on his tongue, intimated that we were relatives.... He immediately pressed me to his side, and rapidly related his boy-hood recollections of the Clark and Lewis expedition.

17th. — We have moved our camp a few miles up the river where we were joined by Fitzpatrick, of the Rocky Mountain Fur Company. We are a motley set. Whites, French, Yankee, Nez Perces, Flatheads, and Snakes, or Shoshones.

Whilst dining in our tent today, I heard the simultaneous cry from English, French and Indian mouths, of a bull, un caiac, trodlum, and oh, Spirit of Nimrod, what a spectacle! A huge buffalo bull, booming through the camp, like a steamboat, followed by an Indian yelling and shaking his robe. Loud shouts of "Hurrah

144

Kentuck," "Oka-hey trodulum," "go ahead bull," and whiz, whiz, went a dozen arrows, bang, bang, as many guns, and poor Jean Baptist [the buffalo] leaped from the bank and floated, broad side up, down the the rapid current of Green River. This wonderful exhibition of skill, perseverence and daring, was performed by the Bull's Head in fulfillment of a promise, made the night before, to Capt. Sublette, that he would drive an old bull through the camp to please Hi-hi-seeks-tooah, his Little White Brother. And he did both.

18. — Capt. [Nathaniel J.] Wyeth, of Boston, who left the settlements ten days before us, came into camp this evening. He is on his way to the mouth of the Columbia river, where he expects a vessel, freighted with merchandise, to be exchanged for furs, salmon, &c. I have declined an invitation to accompany him, although his return trip, by way of the Sandwich Islands, is a strong temptation. I think I am far enough from home for this time.

Mr. Edward Christy, of St. Louis, has just arrived from Fort Vancouver, bringing with him a considerable number of Snakes [Indians] and Nez Perces. Yells, songs and oaths are heard all day and all night long. Like flies on a sugar barrel, or niggers at corn shucking, the red-skins are flocking to the trading tents. We have now perhaps not less than fifteen hundred around us.

— *William Marshall Anderson, 1834*

Although we were emerging from the mountains . . . peaks covered with perpetual snow were seen in almost every direction, and the temperature of the air was uncomfortably cold.

. . . The American Fur Company have between two and three hundred men constantly in and about the mountains, engaged in trading, hunting and trapping. These all assemble at rendezvous upon the arrival of the caravan, bring in their furs, and take new supplies for the coming year, of clothing, ammunition, and goods for trade with the Indians. But few of these men ever return to their country and friends. Most of them are constantly in debt to the company, and are unwilling to return without a fortune; and year after year passes away, while they are hoping in vain for better success.

— *Rev. Samuel Parker, 1835*

Green River (Sweetwater County)

There are [June 15] about 40 French men that came thare in A. D. 1814 they ware drove from canida they keep a ferry [across Green River] which we had to pay $3.00 for Each Wagon, they live in Indian stile with the Squaws for Wives & many half Bloods children & the hansomest horses I ever Saw, they handle a large quantity of money, & Manage the Indians to Suit themselves.

— *David Cosad, 1839*

July 8, Sunday. The [Green] River was not fordable . . . . We had to wait our turn at the ferry. Everyone enjoying himself as well as he could . . . . At nine o'clock our wagons were drawn up to the ferry for 50 cents per wagon. The last one was over about 4 o'clock . . . .

July 9, Five miles from our camp came to a beautiful valley . . . . Fontenelle Creek.

July 10, Tuesday. Our course today lay in high mountains with little spring-streams coming out on our path every little ways. Traveled about 18 miles . . . . Camped on Ham's Fork. Grass good.

— *Henry W. Burto, 1849*

We adopted the trapper's system [of washing clothes] . . . . when camping on rapid streams of clear water . . . . We first secured a pole the length of a fishing rod . . . then securely tied the loose ends . . . to the corners of a blanket . . . and as many shirts or other garments as we cared to wash . . . . [and this] outfit was placed in the current.

Under favorable conditions a washing of this kind was completed in one or two hours, though we had no facilities for giving our shirts a laundry finish, no Chinaman could more thoroughly wash them.

— *Reuben Cole Shaw, 1849*

Our road today lay [southwestward] along the right bank of Big Sandy, until we reached Green River, which we crossed above the junction, and encamped a couple of miles below. The increased altitude, and the consequent dryness of the atmosphere, had so shrunk the woodwork of many of our wagon-wheels, that various expedients had to be resorted to, in order to prevent them from falling to pieces.

— *Capt. Howard Stansbury, 1849*

August 21 . . . . I am weary of this journey, weary of myself and all around me. I long for the quiet of home where I can be at peace once more . . . . Passed a graveyard with ten graves in it. They lie side by side as peaceful as if the Church bells of their native village tolled over them.

— *Agnes Stewart, 1853*

Emerging from the [Green] river plain we entered upon another "mauvaise terre" [of Black's Fork], with knobs and elevations of clay and green gault, striped and banded with lines of stone and pebbles; it was a barren desolate spot, between the Green River and its western influent, the shallow and somewhat sluggish Black's Fork [near Fort Bridger].

— *Richard Burton, 1862*

Ham's Fork (near Granger, Wyoming)

"Fort Bridger," 1849, by James F. Wilkins

Ham's Fork

August 1st . . . . At night [on Ham's Fork, near Soda Springs] I tried to preach to the deists and swearers. Some of them seemed angry, but I thought I cleared my conscience . . . the next day I felt weak from living on dry buffalo meat, without bread. Employment is still fishing and hunting, and such swearing I never heard in my life before.

— *Rev. Joseph Williams, 1841*

Our course is up the Big Muddy [Ham's Fork], and nearly north . . . . This is limestone country. [Next day.] Emigrants would do well to push on up to near the head of this creek, as the grass is good, and there are excellent springs.

— *Joel Palmer, 1846*

Fort Bridger

[Dec. 10.] Pierre Chotau[:] I have established a small fort, with blacksmith shop and a supply of iron, in the road of the immigrants on Black Fork and Green River, which promises fairly. In coming out here they are generally well supplied with money, but by the time they get here they are in need of all kinds of supplies, horses, provisions, smith-work, etc. They bring ready cash from the States, and should I receive the goods ordered will have considerable business in that way with them, and establish trade with the Indians in the neighborhood, who have a good number of beaver among them. The fort is a beautiful location . . . receiving fine, fresh water from the snow on the Uintah range. The streams are alive with mountain trout.

— *James Bridger, 1843*

July 3rd [?] Reached Bridger's Fort. Company had left for the United States about thirty days before, and we saw nothing there but three little, starved dogs. We saw the grave of an Indian woman, who had been killed by the Shiennes [Cheyenne]. From here we could see the mountain tops spotted with snow.

— *Rev. Joseph Williams, 1843*

Sunday, August 13th . . . Arrived at Bridger and Vasquez's fort expecting to stay 10 or 15 days to make meat, but what our disappointment to learn that the Sioux and Cheyenne's had been here, run off all the buffalo, killed 3 Snake Indians, and stolen 60 horses.

— *John Boardman, 1843*

August 30. We lay over for the day at Fort Bridger, and I become somewhat unsettled. My clothing was now beginning to show worse for the wear, and I mentioned this to Mrs. Morrison, who is gathering up articles to wash. She says, "Yes, John; and if you can trade anything at the Fort here, and get some deerskins, I'll fix your pants for you." Seeing me look a little bewildered, she went on, "that means sewing buckskin over a pair of old pants before and behind . . . ."

The best of new warm clothing was the only suit I had ever bought for myself. Miner's wives and mothers about Newcastle-on-Tyne [England] did all that kind of business for their families . . . . Looking over the things I might have to trade I concluded to try if I could get a few dressed deerskins for my double-barreled gun; though the piece was now somewhat impaired . . . . Jim Bridger was doing his own trading — a powerful man . . . quick and sharp at a bargain he said, as soon as I had shown him the gun and stated that I wanted deerskins for it. "Young man, I can't do it, we get few deerskins here. I'll give you ten goat [antelope] skins; that's the best I can do." . . . . I started to camp satisfied with my purchase.

. . . in the evening I asked Captain Morrison if he could now dispense with my assistance, telling him that I felt inclined to try a year or two of this trapper's life. He said; "John . . . I suppose I could do without you from this on but I would advise you not to stop here — these men you see here are a little account either to themselves or their country, they will do you no good, and the time you stay here will be lost out of your life, if you do not lose life itself. I wouldn't stop if I was you."

My father could not have bettered this counsel.

— *John Minto, 1843*

It [Fort Bridger] is built of poles and daubed with mud; it is a shabby concern. Here are about twenty-five lodges of Indians, or rather white trappers' lodges, occupied by their Indian wives. They have a good supply of skins, coats, pants, moccasins and other Indian fixins, which they trade for flour, pork, powder, lead, blankets, butcher-knives, spirits, hats, ready made clothes, coffee, sugar, &c. They ask for a horse from twenty-five to fifty dollars, in trade . . . . They generally abandon this fort during the winter months.

— *Joel Palmer, 1846*

Saturday, August 11 . . . We crossed Ham's Fork and Black's Fork three times, brought us to Fort Bridger — an Indian trading post, situated on Black's Fork, which here branches into three principal channels, forming several extensive islands, upon one of which [the westernmost] the fort is placed. It is built in the usual form, of pickets, with the lodging apartments and offices opening into a hollow square, protected from attack from without by a strong gate of timber . . . . Major Bridger courtesly placing his black-smith shop at my service. . . . [He] has been engaged in the Indian trade, here, and upon the head waters of the Missouri and Columbia, for the last thirty years.

— *Capt. Howard Stansbury, 1852*

He [Jim Bridger] had had, within four years, two quivers-full of arrows in his body. Being asked if the wounds had been long supparating, he answered humorously 'in the Mountains meat never spoils'.

— *Fr. Pierre-Jean DeSmet, S.J., 1852*

148

Thursday, Sept. 5 . . . This [Fort Bridger] is the trading post much frequented by the Shoshones, Utahs, and Uintah Indians . . . . The emigrant road forks here, one branch leading to Fort Hall, by the Soda Springs, and the other, pursuing a more southerly course leads to the City of the Salt Lake.

— *Capt. Howard Stansbury, 1852*

Uinta Mountains (near Fort Bridger)

Bear River

Rocky Mountains, July 16, 1826
Dear and Respected Brother, . . . We [in the Ashley expedition] had a very good traveling over an inconsiderable ridge, we fell on a considerable river, called Bear River, which rises to the S. in the Utaw Mountains, bears N. 80 or 90 miles, when it turns short to the S. W. and S. and after passing the mountains, discharge itself into the Great Salt Lake. On this river and . . . adjacent country, we have taken beaver with great success. Since the autmn of 1824, you have no doubt heard, and will hear by public prints, of the furs brought in by Gen. Ashl[e]y . . . .

I have been on the very eve of returning this summer, but owing to this unexplored country, which I have a great curiosity to see, I have concluded to remain one or two years. We celebrated the 4th of July, by firing three rounds of small arms, and partook of a most excellent dinner, after which a number of political toasts were drunk.

— *Daniel T. Potts, 1826*

. . . we are still in a dangerous country but our company is large enough for safety. Our cattle endure the journey remarkably well. They . . . . supply us with sufficient milk for our tea & coffee which is indeed a luxury . . . .

Feel to pity the poor Indian women who are continually traveling in this manner during their lives & know no other comfort. They do all the work, such as getting the wood, preparing food, picking their lodges, packing & driving their animals, the complete slaves of their husbands.

— *Narcissa Prentiss Whitman, 1836*

July 18. We came on two miles [in Bear River valley] to the sumit. Here we caught up with a widow woman who had buried her husband back on the Platte River. She had four or five little helpless children to care for. All the rest of the Company had gone on, leaving her alone with her team and little ones to get over the mountains the best she could . . . .

After the [wagon] wheel was repaired Mr. Burns offered to drive the team and help her . . . but she very kindly declined the offer, picked up her whip, gave it a whirl and a crack, and started on down the mountain.

We did not see or hear anything more of her after leaving the sumit, that company should have seen to it . . . to take her safely through to her journey's end.

— *Enoch W. Conyers, 1852*

July 20, Sabbath. Oh, my patience . . . . We have come up and down til I forget most of what I wanted to write.

We are in Bear River Valley now. How dreary everything looks to me . . . . We do not know what is to be our lot in life, nor do we know what is before us in the world.

— *Agnes Stewart, 1853*

Emigrant Crossing Near Thomas Fork (Bear Lake County, Idaho)

Soda Springs (Idaho)

Smith's Fork

[July 18] . . . Husband [Marcus] has had a tedious time with the wagon to-day. It got stuck in the creek [Smith's Fork] this morning when crossing, and he was obliged to wade considerably in getting it out. After that, in going between the mountains . . . so steep that it was difficult for horses to pass, the wagon was upset twice; did not wonder at this at all; it was a greater wonder that it was not turning sumersaults continually. It is not very graceful to my feelings to see him wearing out with such excessive fatigue, as I am obliged to. He is not as fleshy as he was last winter. All the most difficult part of the way he has walked, in laborious attempts to take the wagon. Ma knows what my feelings are.

— *Narcissa Prentiss Whitman, 1836*

August 21-22 . . . We continued our road down the [Bear] river, and at night encamped [near Smith's Fork] with a family of emigrants — two men, women, and several children — who appeared to be bringing up the rear of the great caravan . . . .

It was strange to see one small family traveling along . . . so remote from civilization. Some nine years since, such a security might have been a fatal one; but since their disastrous defeats . . . a little north, the Blackfeet have ceased to visit these waters.

— *Brevet-Capt. John C. Frémont, 1843*

Soda Springs

The most noted curiosity . . . of this singular region is the Bear Spring, of which trappers give wonderful accounts . . . . Captain Bonneville describes it as having the taste of beer. His men drank it with avidity, and in copious draughts . . . . The Indians, however, refuse to taste it . . . .

We have heard this also called the Soda Spring.

— *Washington Irving, 1832*

A few yards from our camp is a curious spring called the Soda Spring. There are several places where it boils up . . . and though large quantities are thrown up it does not run off upon the surface but finds its way to the river underground where you can see it bubbling up in various places. The boiling in one place resembles very much the rapid boiling of water in a large chaldron.

— *Rev. Jason Lee, 1834*

Went today [July 30] ten miles off our route with Husband Mr. McLeod & a few others, to visit Soda Springs. Was much delighted . . . . The first object of curiosity . . . were several white mounds on the top of which were small springs of soda. These mounds were covered with a crustation made from the evaporation of the water . . . . On some rocks a little below in the

151

opening were dead flies & birds in abundance which had approached so near the crater, as to be choked with the gas which it constantly emits. On putting the face down, the breath is stoped instantly & a low rumbling noise like the roaring of fire is heard beneath.

— *Narcissa Prentiss Whitman, 1836*

We found [July 16] the waters a luxury indeed, as good soda as I ever drank boiling up out of the earth . . . . The mother spring of all is said to be 10 or 12 feet across, and no bottom has ever yet been found . . . . The water is clear and has a smart taste like small beer, though it has more of the sting to it than any beer I ever drank. I drank freely of it. It had a very good effect . . . . The whole surface of the earth about this place . . . presents every proof of having been a volcano, the lava covers the whole surface of the earth . . . . There is a bed of white clay . . . . This is used by the Indians in all parts of the mountains for whitening skins &c.

— *Asahel Munger, 1839*

Some places on Bear river exhibit great natural curiosities. A square plain of a few acres in extent presents an even surface of fuller's earth of pure whiteness, like that of marble, and resembling a field covered with dazzling snow. Some of them have a slight taste of soda . . . perhaps they are not inferior to the celebrated waters of the Spa, or of the lime Springs in Belgium.

— *Fr. Pierre-Jean DeSmet, S.J., 1841*

July 9th . . . . These Springs seem to boil like a pot of water; but there is no heat in them . . . . There is something like lava that has been thrown out of a hole, and lies some inches thick on the ground.

— *Rev. Joseph Williams, 1841*

At noon [September 7] in a cedar grove, came to the famous Soda Spring. The water boils up in numerous places, and has no visible outlet. The water much superior to that manufactured in the States; it is very pleasant and I took my fill. The stones . . . resemble pumice stones, except heavier. The country for miles is full of fissures, very deep, where the rock are rent and thrown in many shapes. Forty rods from the soda Spring, immediately on Bear River, is a hot spring; it rumbles, roars, and gushes up water, much like in appearance, the puff of a high pressure steamboat. The water tastes much of copper.

— *John Boardman, 1843*

. . . we reached the Soda Springs [September 7]. They are on the East side of Bear River, and are scattered over a level space, about equal . . . to one square mile; with a slight inclination to the River, and elevated above it some fifteen feet. A large portion of this level space is covered with a stinted growth of Pine and Cedar. The earth is of various colors. In some places it is almost perfectly white, and in others, quite red, etc. Above, below, and on the opposite side of the River, the valley is rich, and covered with fine grass.

— *Overton Johnson and W. H. Winter, 1843*

We camped very near [Soda Spring] and nearly a quarter of a mile from Bear River . . . . Here we met Fremont, with his party . . . Fremont's men were having a high time drinking soda water. Fremont had a cannon; the first I had ever seen, a six-pounder, they said, and made of bright shining brass. It was resting on a low carriage.

— *Jesse Applegate, 1843*

[September] 7 . . . . the Strongest Spring is about ½ a mile North from the river which is so highly charged that it almost takes your Breath to drink acup of it Quick from the Srping But the most Singular one is below near the river Spouting [Steamboat] as much as 6 feet high & a heavy collumn I had not more than one hour to make my examination I regrett much that I was so hurried.

— *James Clyman, 1844*

August 4 . . . . the size of these mounds continually increases, as the water oozes out at different points, and produces a crust which becomes quite hard. The rocks, for miles around, are of the soda formation.

— *Joel Palmer, 1845*

Arriving at Bear River we camped and met there with a party of Indians and three Frenchmen, living with them, and . . . these people were busily engaged in catching the Army crickets by sticking the ends of sticks in the ground, in rows so thick that crickets could not pass through them, and terminating the rows in points like the letter V with an opening at the end where they placed a basket to receive the crickets they drove into the traps; in an incredibly brief time the basket would be filled and they would place another, continuing this all day; they thus caught immense quantities which were dried on a stone kiln and then removed to a mortar . . . where with a pestle they reduced these singular insects to meal or flour which seemed to be regarded as a staple and delicate article of food among them, which they eat heartily and grow fat upon.

In preparing it for food, this meal is stirred into a kettle of boiling water until rendered thick mush, when an inch of grease remains on top; they say that this meal

"The Scouting Party," by William T. Ranney, c. 1851

will keep for a year, upon hearing which I could but voluntarily exclaim that it would last in my possession much longer . . . encamped in the evening at a natural soda spring . . . we used this water in making our bread and found it answered all the purposes of yeast, so we carried a quantity away as a substitute for it.

— *Samuel Hancock, 1845*

July 22 . . . . One of our company, R. L. Boyle, made a wager that he could stop the flow of water from this [Soda] spring by setting on the crevice. He waited until the water began to recede, then took off his pants and seated himself on the crevice . . . . Doyle soon began bobbing up and down at a fearful rate.

At this stage of the fun several of the boys took hold of Doyle and tried to hold him on the crevice, but in this they failed, for the more weight they added to Doyle the more power the spring seemed to have, and Doyle kept on bobbing up and down like a cork. Finally Doyle cried out, 'Boys there's no use trying to hold the Devil down. It can't be did. I am now, pounded into a beefsteak'.

— *Enoch W. Conyers, 1852*

About 11 o'clock [July 25] we arrived at the far famed Soda-Springs . . . . Placing the face near the surface, the vapor has the same effect which the inhaling of hartshorn [ammonia water] produces.

— *Celinda K. Hines, 1853*

At Soda Springs on Bear river, we received word from the trains ahead of us indicating that increased trouble might be expected from the Snake Indians, whose country we were about to enter . . . . The means of communication with the trains in front was the "Bone Express." The road up the Platte was strewn with bones, mostly buffaloes . . . . From the Black Hills . . . the whitened bones of the perished cattle of previous immigrations, were strewn thick along the route. On these white bones the passing pilgrim would pencil his message, and place it in a conspicuous place by the roadside, an open letter for all to read . . . . Sometimes the lack-luster skull would inform John and Mary was all right, or a sholderblade would inform Polly that James was going to take the California road, assuring her that wood and water were better on that route, and hoping she would follow directions for crossing streams and gullies, or to find grass and water one mile or more off the road, were sometimes found on the ever-present bone. Information about the Indians was also conveyed, or rather fixed by means of the "Bone Express."

— *George B. Currey, 1853*

Steamboat Springs

We were traveling at a serious disadvantage, ours being the last train of the season of 1848 bound for Oregon, which was detrimental to our stock, for we found in making a camp at the end of a day's journey, from 20 to 25 miles, we would have to drive a mile or two out of our way to get good grass . . . .

Steamboat Springs was quite a noted place, a general camping ground for emigrants . . . . It would spout up four or five feet in height and quit for 15 to 20 seconds. Some of our party thought it would be good water to wash their hands and face in, but it did not turn out as they expected. There was a substance in it of a tarry nature, which made it quite difficult to comb the hair, for it matted the hair together. About 1½ miles from this camp there were several soda springs, so we had all the soda water we could drink, free of cost.

— *James D. Miller, 1848*

. . . 'Soda Springs,' — by some called 'Beer Springs.' We arrived here at day break [July 11] and corralled. The teams that we had been with for several days, expressed very great surprise . . . to find us before them & snugly & pleasantly layed up in this delightful spot . . . .

The whole valley, however, is the most interesting spot of earth that I ever beheld. Here is a grand field for the geologist, minerologist, naturalist, & any other kind of 'ist' that you can conceive. The road crosses here a little creek which empties, 200 yds. from the crossing, into Bear River . . . .

. . . . The greatest curiosity of all, however, is . . . 'The Steamboat Spring.' This is situated upon the edge of the river, half a mile from the first spring. Out of solid rock, with a hole 1 foot in diameter, gushes forth the water, foaming, whizzing, sizzling, blowing, splashing & spraying. It throws it up from two to three

feet high. There is a little intermission of a few seconds every now & then . . . . A few feet from this large one are two smaller ones, which are phizzing away all the time . . . . This large one has also a suction power. Some one around reached a cup into it, when it was immediately drawn from his hand into the hole. He, however, delved down for it, & found it the length of his arm in, & required a considerable jerk to get it out.

— *Wakeman Bryarly, 1849*

Sheep Rock

September, Wednesday, 9th. [On way east to St. Louis] . . . discovered an extensive Plain [Bear River valley] lying before us — through this we steered due east and in 18 miles struck a River [Bear] running through an apparently level country in about a south direction . . . . This river is a 100 yards wide, and is here confined between a high rocky Bluff bank and a Hill [Sheep Rock] . . . . The prairies being here burnt smooth, we are obliged [at evening] to proceed 10 miles farther, camped on right bank of Bear River, on west outskirts of Soda Springs, ere we could find grass enough to satisfy our hungry horses for the night.

— *Robert Stuart, 1812*

[September] 26 . . . our stock of provisions had again become extremely low; we had only dried meat sufficient for one meal, and our supply of flour and other comforts was entirely exhausted. I then immediately dispatched one of the party, Henry Lee, with a note to [Kit] Carson, at Fort Hall, directing him to load a pack-horse with whatever could be obtained there in the way of provisions, and endeavor to overtake me on the [Bear] river . . . .

In sweeping around the point of the mountain which runs down into the bend, the river here passes between perpendicular walls of basalt . . . the mountain, which is rugged and steep, and, by our measurement, 1400 feet above the river directly opposite the place of our halt, is called the Sheep Rock . . . .

I ate here for the first time, the Kooyah, or tobacco root [*Valeriana edulis*], the principal edible root among the Indians who inhabit the upper waters of the streams on the western side of the mountains . . . It was characterized by Mr. Preuss [Fremont's cartographer] as the most horrid food he had ever put in his mouth; and, when in the evening, one of the chiefs sent his wife to me with a portion which she had prepared as a delicacy to regale us, the odor immediately drove him out of the lodge . . . To others the taste is rather an agreeable one, and I was afterwards always glad when it formed an addition to our scanty meals.

— *Brevet-Capt. John C. Frémont, 1842*

Saturday, August 26 ... Kit Carson, of Freemont's company, camped with us [near Soda Springs], on his return from Fort Hall.

— *James Willis Nesmith, 1843*

September 7 .... Five miles below [north] the river makes an acute angle about a bold and lofty point, called the sheep rock, running away to the South West .... Formerly the Blackfeet Indians frequented this country; and, at this rock, they had repeated battles with the Mountaineers, and with other tribes of Indians; and here the effects of their deadly encounters may still be seen, in bleached skulls and scattered bones.

— *Overton Johnson and W. H. Winter, 1843*

We passed on the way a party of emigrants numbering 359 souls and driving 39 wagons. They were commanded by the patriarch of Mormondom, otherwise Captain John Smith .... His followers accepted gratefully some provisions with which we could afford to part.

— *Richard Burton, 1860*

Toward the Snake

2nd Had an unusual long ride today [after Soda Springs]. Heat excessive. Truly I thought "the Heavens over us were brass, & the earth iron under our feet." Our route for two or three days past has been quite level. But the same scenery prevails, rocks & sandy plains covered with a species of wormwood called sage of a pale green, offensive both to the sight & smell. We meet with frequent fertile spots however, often enough to furnish us & our animals with a comfortable Inn for the night. Had a feast of service berries today the first ripe ones we have seen .... which rested me much, & answered the place of a dinner very well.

— *Marcus Whitman, M.D., 1836*

The [Bear] river resembles in its course the form of a horseshoe, and falls into the Great Salt Lake, which is about 300 miles in circumference, and has no communication with the sea.

— *Fr. Pierre-Jean DeSmet, S.J., 1841*

Sheep Rock (Soda Point), Wasatch Range (Caribou County, Idaho)

There was some division and strife among us about going; some who set out for California changed their minds to go to the Columbia. Those who went to California . . . were much perplexed about getting through, as they had no regular guide . . . .

We turned off from Bear River, and struck on [northwest] to the waters of the Snake River.

— *Rev. Joseph Williams, 1841*

Pursuing our journey the next morning, we discovered Indians on the hills not far off . . . . The Indians were lurking around all night howling in imitation of wolves, to deceive us, and enable them to approach and occasionally the guard would fire in the direction of one of those noisy visitors, to keep them at a safe distance. As soon as it was light enough we turned the cattle out to feed, and found . . . many of them pierced by arrows, whereupon twenty of us armed with rifles charged the thicket close by and five Indians retreated to the hills adjacent.

Upon our return to camp we ascertained a number of the enemy's shot had penetrated our wagon beds, fortunately doing no other damage, although the families had taken refuge in the wagons during the skirmish.

— *Samuel Hancock, 1845*

August 3, 1846. We made an early start from the springs, intending to go to the Port Neuf River, but was stopped by an awful calamity in 3½ miles. Mr. Collin's son, George, about 6 years old, fell from the wagon and the wheels ran over his head . . . . The remainder of the day occupied in burying at the place where we leave the river [near Sheep Rock].

— *Virgil K. Pringle, 1846*

Portneuf Plain

[July 28]. One of the axle-trees of the wagon broke to-day; was a little rejoiced; for we were in hopes they would leave it, and have no more trouble with it. Our rejoicing was in vain, for they are making a cart of the back wheels this afternoon.

— *Narcissa Prentiss Whitman, 1836*

On the 14th of August our wagons . . . arrived at the outlet of a defile which seemed to us the end of the world. On our right and left were frightful mountains . . . our beasts of burthen were, for the first time, exhausted. Murmurs arose against the Captain [John Bartleson], who, however, was imperturbable . . . . for we had traversed the highest chain of the Rocky Mountains

and were nearly in sight of Fort Hall . . . the next morning we . . . arrived on a plain watered by the Portnuef River, one of the tributaries of Snake. We trotted or galloped over fifty miles . . . the whole way presented evident remains of volcanic eruptions.

— *Fr. Pierre-Jean DeSmet, S.J., 1841*

July 14, 1849 . . . I have been in musquitoe country but confess I never saw them in their glory. [At Spring Creek, near Fort Hall.] They were so thick you could reach out and get a handful . . . . Our animals were very near stampeding from them and our guards were so busy saving their own eyes that it was almost impossible for them to watch the animals.

— *Wakeman Bryarly, 1849*

Five miles to the north, Fort Hall, with its whitewashed walls, is plainly in view. The "Three Buttes" rise in the distance, while the Port Neuf, with its bright, sparkling waters, flows at our feet. The scene was one of surprising beauty, and richly repaid us, for our dreary ride across the desert plain of sage. The Port Neuf is a clear bold stream . . . The plain between it and Snake River presents a level bottom . . . reposing on sandy loam and gravel, numerous springs . . . . Passing over this delightful plain, we leave Fort Hall on our left; and five miles beyond it terminated our journey at Cantonment Laring, our point of destination . . . . The result of this exploration has been to demonstrate the entire practicability of obtaining an excellent wagon road from Fort Hall to the Mormon settlement upon the Great Salt Lake.

— *Capt. Howard Stansbury, 1852*

Grasses at Fort Hall (Bingham County, Idaho)

Fort Hall

Sunday July 27. Mr. M'Coy [Thomas McKay], a gentleman in the employ of the Hudson's Bay Company, after which [Rev.] Jason Lee, by his request, held a meeting [at future site of Fort Hall] . . . . At the time appointed, about thirty Indians, and as many whites, came together to hear the word of the Lord. Brother Lee opened the meeting by reading the fifteenth Psalm, and singing the hymn beginning, "The Lord of sabbath let us praise," Prayer and an address followed by J. Lee. The congregation gave the most profound and solumn attention . . . being the first season of public worship.

— *Cyrus Shepard, 1833*

[July 14] . . . . We are now on a stream which pours its waters directly into the Columbia, and we can form some idea of the Great Oregon river by the beauty and magnitude of its tributary. Soon after we stopped Captain W. [Wyeth], Richardson, and two others left us to seek for a suitable spot for building a fort [Fort Hall, named for Henry Hall, a senior member of Wyeth's financial backers] . . . . Most of the men were immediately put to work, felling trees, making horse-pens, and preparing the various requisite materials for the building . . . . Our camp is a beautiful one. A rich and open plain of luxuriant grass, doted with buffalo in all directions, a high picturesque hill in front, and a lovely stream of cold mountain water flowing at our feet . . . .

At the fort (July 26), affairs look prosperous: the stockade is finished; two bastions have been erected, and the work is singularly good, considering the scarcity of proper building tools. The house will now soon be habitable, and the structure can then be completed at leisure by men who will be left in charge, while the party travels on to its destination, the Columbia.

Mr. Lee is a great favorite with the men, deservedly so . . . . I have often been amused and pleased by Mr. L.'s manner of reproving them for the coarseness and profanity of expression which is so universal amongst them. The reproof . . . clear, and strong, is always characterized by the mildness and affectionate manner peculiar to the man . . . .

August 5th. — At sunrise this morning, the "star-spangled banner" was raised on the flag-staff at the fort, and a salute fired by the men . . . . All in camp were then allowed the free and uncontrolled use of liquor, and, as usual, the consequence was a scene of rioting, noise, and fighting, during the whole day; some became so drunk that their senses fled them entirely . . . . We had "gouging," biting, fisticuffing, and "stamping" in the most "scientific" perfection; some even fired guns and pistols at each other . . . . Such scenes I hope never to witness again; they are absolutely sickening.

— *John K. Townsend, 1834*

To Leond. Jarvis, ESQ., Oct. 6th

Dear Uncle . . . . We manufactured a magnificent flag from some unbleached sheeting a little red flannel and a few blue patches, saluted it with damaged powder and wet it in vil[l]a[in]ous alchohal, and after all it makes, I do assure you, a very respectable appearance amid the dry and desolate regions of central America. Its bastions stand a terror to the skulking Indian and a beacon of safty to the fugitive hunter . . . . After building this fort I sent messengers to the neighboring nations to induce them to come to it and trade . . . .

I am yrs. & c. N. J. W.
— *Nathaniel J. Wyeth, 1834*

On the 18th 1834 we [Wyeth's trappers] commenced the actual construction of the Fort which was a stockade eighty feet square, built of cotton-wood trees set on end, sunk two and one half feet in the ground and standing about fifteen feet above with two bastions eight feet square at the opposite angles.

— *Osborne Russell, 1834*

[August] 3d. Came to Fort Hall . . . . A cool breeze made our ride very pleasant. Husband & myself were alone entirely behind the dust of camp & enjoyed a sweet repast in conversing about home & dear friends . . . . Was much cheered with a view of the Fort at a considerable distance. Any thing that looks like a house makes us glad. Called and were hospitably entertained by Capt Thing who keeps the Fort. It was built by Cap Wyeth a gentleman from Boston, whom we saw at [fur-trading] Rendezvous, on his way to the east. Our dinner consisted of dry buffalo meat, turnips & fried bread, which was a luxury. Mountain bread is simply course flour & water mixed & roasted or fried in buffalo grease. To one who has had nothing but meat for a long time this relishes very well. For tea we had the same with the addition of some stewed service berries.

4th Enjoyed the cool retreat of an uper room this morning while writing. The buildings of the Fort are made of hewed logs, roof covered with mud bricks, chimney & fireplaces also of the same . . . . Since dinner visited the garden & corn field. The turnips in the garden appear thrifty . . . . The peas looked well but had most of them been gathered by the mice. Saw a few onions that were going to seed . . . . This is their first attempt at cultivation. The building at Fort William on Larimys Fork of Platte, Black Hills, are made in the same way, but larger & more finished than here.

— *Narcissa Prentiss Whitman, 1836*

July 30. sister P's birthday. I have got most well again am going to washing in the room at the fort [Hall] which in form size and cleanliness resembles your hog sty.

— *Mary Richardson Walker, 1838*

Fort Hall lies on the left bank of the Snake River, between the mouths of the Blackfoot and Portneuf Creeks.... A small cannon is in the courtyard....

The Snake River has its source on the western slope of the main chain of the Rockies, and flows in northwesterly direction about eight hundred miles, when it unites with the Clarke River, coming from the northeast, to form the Columbia River.... The Snake River flows through a sandy plateau, in which there can be found almost no game and very little food for the animals. About one hundred miles from the Columbia, the Snake River pierces a spur of the Rockies, the Blue Mountains.... The broad Snake River valley is in the main sterile country. The climate there is moderately warm. The summers are remarkable for great dryness....

The only settlement made by citizens of the United States is now on the Wallamette.... Some New York Methodist missionaries have recently settled here and gathered around them a little colony of Americans,

Canadians and Indians. As they do not trade, but devote themselves only to agriculture and cattle raising, the Hudson's Bay Company has put no obstacles in their way, but, on the contrary, encourages them and takes supplies from them at fixed prices. For a bushel of wheat, for instance, the company usually gives fifty cents in goods, while it receives on its part one dollar and a half in money from the Russians in California.

— *Frederick A. Wislizenus, M.D., 1839*

At the time I took the wagons [as guide to Fort Walla Walla], I had no idea of undertaking to bring them into this country. I exchanged fat horses to those [three] missionaries [who accompanied the American Fur Trade Company's expedition as far as Green River, Wyoming, where they secured the services of Newell to pilot them to Fort Hall] for their animals, and after they had gone a month or more for Willamette and the American Fur Company had abandoned the country for good, I

concluded to hitch up and try the much dreaded job of bringing a wagon to Oregon [a pioneering route from Fort Hall across the Snake River plains and through the Blue Mountains] . . . .

On the 5th of August . . . we put out with the wagons. Joseph L. Meek drove my wagon . . . .

In a rather tough and reduced state, we arrived at the Whitman's Mission station in the Walla Walla Valley, where we were met by that hospitable man . . . . On hearing me regret that I had undertaken to bring wagons, the Doctor Whitman said, "O, you will never regret it. You have broken the ice and when others see that wagons have passed they too will pass, and in a few years the valley will be full of our people!"

The Doctor shook me heartily by the hand. Mrs. [Narcissa] Whitman too welcomed us, and the Indians walked around our wagons, or what they called "horse canoes," and seemed to give up.

— *Robert "Doc" Newell, 1840*

Horses Near Fort Hall

Monday [September] 11th. Fort Hall is situated in a large plain on Snake River; & built of square cakes of mud baked in the sun; it is inferior to Fort Laramie . . . . there was neither meat, flour nor rice to be had. Nothing but sugar and coffee at 50 cents per pint; rice worth 35 cents per pound where they have it, flour 25 cents per pint, though dry goods are cheaper than at any other of the posts, Laramie; calico worth $1.00 yard; shirting $1.00, tobacco $1.00 to $2.00; liquor $32 per gallon. They have cattle here but will not sell . . . . Fremont has sent in from the Salt Lake for provisions; is eating horse meat . . . .

— *John Boardman, 1843*

I visited the people in the fort [Hall] with Mother and other folks, and found [Indian] women and children living there . . . . Those women wore bracelets of gold or brass on their wrists, broad rings of gold or brass on their fingers, and a profusion of bright colored, mostly red, ribbons on their garments. Those bright colors I thought were in beautiful contrast with the brown skin and glossy black hair of the women . . . .

Though there was no scarcity of wild game, there was a very large and fat ox slaughtered here by the emigrants . . . we boys were at the place where the oxen had been killed, and found the stomach or paunch lying there on the ground: the weather being warm, it was swollen to the size of a large barrel . . . . The sport consisted in running and butting the head against the paunch and being bounced back . . . .

. . . . There was a boy by the name of Andy Baker, much taller than I was; He was slender, had a long neck, and his hair was cut very near to the scalp. This boy was ambitious to excel all the others, and . . . . [he] backed off much farther than anyone had before and then lowering his small head, charged the paunch at the top of his speed, and when within a couple of yards of the target, leaped from the ground, the boys yelling, "give her goss, Andy!" and came down like a pile driver against the paunch, but he did not bound back.

We gathered around to see what the matter was, and discovered Andy had thrust his head into the stomach, which had closed so tightly around his neck that he could not withdraw his head. We took hold of his legs and pulled him out, but the joke was on Andy, and "Give her goss, Andy," was a favorite joke among the boys long after.

— *Jesse Applegate, 1843*

Capt. Grant then in charge of the Hudson Bay Company at Fort Hall, endeavored to dissuade us from proceeding further with our wagons, and showed us the wagons that the emigrants of the preceeding year had abandoned, as an evidence of the impracticability of our determination.

Dr. Whitman was persistent in his assertions that wagons could proceed as far as the Grand Dalles of the Columbia river, from which point he asserted they could be taken down by rafts or batteaux to the Willamette valley, while our stock could be driven by an Indian trail over the Cascade mountains, near Mt. Hood.

— *James Willis Nesmith, 1843*

In coming down a hill my little brother five years old, fell over the front gate of my wagon to the ground. I picked him up fearing that he was killed, but his life was spared, as I have no doubt in answer to Grandfather Swan's prayer.... Sad to say, it happened otherwise with G. T. Naler's little boy who also fell over the front end of the wagon during our journey. In his case the great wheels rolled over the child's head, crushing it to pieces.

On arriving at Fort Hall, the commander of the Fort sent word that he wished to see our captain. Father mentioned at supper that he was to visit the commander ... and I was allowed to go with him. Arrived at the fort we found a stockade of logs twenty feet high. We climbed a stairway around a cupola to Captain Grant's room, where we found a large fat Scotchman. He said, "Is this Captain Lenox?" "Yes sir," was the answer. "I hear you are going through to the Columbia River this fall." "Yes sir." "But do not try that, you may lose all these women and children in the snow. You had better pack from here. I will trade you ponies for your cattle, as I did the forty-two emigrants last year." As proof to our eyes, there stood the nineteen wagons beside the fort, but father replied, "We are going to stay with the wagons until we are compelled to leave them." On returning to the camp we found Dr. [Marcus] Whitman at father's tent. "I have sad news, Captain Lenox," he said. "I have just received this letter from my wife, by the hand of an Indian. The Indians have burned my mill, and she is afraid they will murder her, and wishes me to hurry home, so I must leave you at five in the morning. Sit down with me here, while I write out a way bill for you to follow, with camping places marked, and I will send Stickas, a Christian chief, to meet you and pilot you across the Blue Mountains."

— *Edward Henry Lenox, 1843*

At Fort Hall, we fell in with some Cayuse and Nez Perce Indians returning from the buffalo country, and as it was necessary for Dr. [Marcus] Whitman to precede us to Walla Walla, he recommended to us a guide in the person of an old Cayuse Indian called "Sticcus." He was a faithful old fellow, perfectly familiar with all the trails and topography of the country from Fort Hall to The Dalles, and ... he succeeded by pantomine in taking us over the roughest wagon route I ever saw.

Sticcus was a member of Dr. Whitman's church, and the only Indian I ever saw that ... practiced the Christian religion. I met him afterward in the Cayuse war. He did not participate in the murder of Dr. Whitman and his family, and remained neutral during the war between his tribe and the whites, which grew out of the massacre.

I once dined with Sticcus, in his camp, upon what I supposed to be elk meat. I had arrived at that conclusion because, looking at the cooked meat and then at the old Indian interrogatively, he held up his hands in a manner that indicated elk horns; but, after dinner, seeing the ears, tail and hoofs of a mule near camp, I became satsified that what he meant to convey by his pantomine was "ears" not "horns".

— *James Willis Nesmith, 1843*

September 16 .... We started with fifteen pounds of buffalo pemmican, purchased from a Kanaka [Hawaiian] servant of the Hudson's Bay Company at Fort Hall. Mr. G. W. Bush, always watchful, followed us out from the wagon and said, ".... Take my advise: any thing you see as big as a black bird, kill it and eat it."

— *John Minto, 1844*

When we got to Fort Hall ... we laid by a day or two. Some of our company wanted to go to California and here was where the roads parted. But my father said he was going to drive his teams into the Willamette Valley. Superintendent Grant, of Fort Hall ... remarked, "Well, we have been here many years and we never have taken a pack train over those mountains yet, but if you say you will take your wagons over the mountains, you will do it. The darned Yankees will go anywhere they say they will."

— *William Barlow, 1845*

At Fort Hall we were met by an old man named Caleb Greenwood and his three sons; John 22, Britain 18, and Sam 16. Caleb Greenwood, who originally hailed from Novia Scotia, was an old mountain man and was ... employed by Captain Sutter to come to Fort Hall to divert the Oregon-bound emigrants to California .... He called the Oregon emigrants together the first evening we were in Fort Hall and made a talk. He said the road to Oregon was dangerous on account of Indians. He told us that while no emigrants had as yet gone to California, there was an easy grade and crossing the mountains would not be difficult. He said that Capt. Sutter would have ten Californians meet the emigrants who would go and that Sutter would supply them with plenty of potatoes, coffee and dried beef. He also said ... that to every head of a family who would settle near Sutter's Fort, Captain Sutter would give six sections of land of his Spanish land grant. After Greenwood had spoken the men of our party held a pow-wow which lasted nearly all night. Some wanted to go to California, while others were against it. [Samuel] Barlow, who was in charge of our train, said that he would forbid any man leaving the train and going to California. He told us we did not know what we were going into, that there was a great uncertainty about the land titles in California, that we were Americans and should not want to go to a country under another flag. Some argued that California would become American territory in time; others thought that Mexico would fight to hold it and that the Americans who went there would get into a mixup and probably get killed.

The meeting nearly broke up in a mutiny. Barlow finally appealed to the men to go to Oregon and make Oregon an American territory and not waste their time going to California to help promote Sutter's land schemes.

Next morning old Caleb Greenwood with his boys stepped out to one side and said: 'All you who want to go to California drive out from the main train and follow me. You will find there are no Indians to kill you, the roads are better, and you will be allowed to take up more land in California than in Oregon, the climate is better, there is plenty of hunting and fishing, and the rivers are full of salmon.'

My father, Jarvis Bonney, was the first one of the Oregon party to pull out of the Oregon train and head south . . . . There were eight wagons in all that rolled out from the main train to go to California with Caleb.

The last thing those remaining in the Barlow train said to us was, 'Good-bye, we will never see you again. Your bones will whiten in the desert or be gnawed by wild animals in the mountains.' [Bonney's family decided, at Sutter's fort, not to become "Spanish subjects" and in April 1847 went north to Oregon.]

— Benjamin Franklin Bonney, 1846

Our camp was located one mile to the southwest of the fort [Hall]; and as at all the other forts the (Snake) Indians swarmed about us . . . . in consequence of the continual wars which they have engaged in with the Sioux, Crows and Blackfeet, their numbers are rapidly diminishing.

— Joel Palmer, 1846

. . . the two crossings of Snake River and the crossing of the Columbia and other smaller streams were represented by those [Hudson's Bay Company employees] in charge of this fort [Hall] as . . . being attended with great danger; it was also said that no company hereto-fore attempting the passage of those streams succeeded but with the loss of men from the violence and rapidity of the currents . . . . In case we escaped destruction at the hands of the savages, we were told that a more fearful enemy, famine, would attend our march, as the distance was so great that winter would overtake us before making the Cascade Mountains. On the other hand, as an inducement to pursue the California route, we were informed of the shortness of the route, when compared with that to Oregon, as also of the many other superior advantages it possessed.

— Joel Palmer, 1846

American Falls

August 13 – We [in Wyeth's expedition] traveled west northwest over two ridges . . . and came in view of the Lewis River [Snake] at the American Falls. The course of the river is nearly west. Extensive plains stretched away to the north, and a far-off snow-clad mountain range was seen. Here I lost my pocket thermometer.

— John Ball, 1832

Fri. Aug. 1 [A few miles west of Fort Hall] . . . The American Falls are quite interesting and picturesque . . . . As soon as we had camped most of the males went in to bathe and the females soon followed but a little distance from there.

— Rev. Jason Lee, 1834

Of the country one general remark will apply to the whole from the American Falls which by the by I had like to forgotten to describe to you perhaps I had better leave them undiscribed as I think their Name like most of the names given to streames and places in this country disappoint the expectation of the beholder.

— Rev. W. H. Gray, 1838

[September] 12 About Sunrise we ware again on the trail and passed the [American] falls whose musick luled us to sleep last night these falls have but little perpendicular pitch but fall about 16 or 18 feet in a verry short distance . . .

— James Clyman, 1844

August 11 . . . . The country is extremely barren, being sandy, sage plains (These falls [American] derive their name from the following circumstance. A number of American trappers going down this stream in their canoes . . . were hurried along by the violence of the current; and passing over the falls, but one of the number survived.)

— Joel Palmer, 1846

The scene [at American Falls] was truly magnificent. Here was an entire change in the face of the country as well as the river. But a few miles back, we had looked on it running quietly through a wide, fertile valley, and winding around not more than 400 yards, and in a short distance was precipitated over huge rocks, to resume its course through a deep canon, the perpendicular walls of which were formed of basaltic rock . . . .

The road passed along the bluff, bending to the right, which soon caused us to lose sight of the falls. In this day's march we crossed many gorges, or deep ravines, that were very much broken, and very difficult to travel over.

— *Maj. Osborne Cross, 1849*

Hunt's Point

On 28th our journey [west to build Astoria, for John Jacob Astor] was less fortunate. After passing several rapids, we came to the entrance [Hunt's Point] of a Canyon. Mr. [Ramsay] Crooks canoe upset, one of his men was drowned, Many goods were lost.

— *Wilson Price Hunt, 1811*

[August] 29th [eastbound from Astoria to St. Louis] . . . 1 mile above [on Snake River, near Hunt's Point] is Clappins Rapid, a very long and bad Rapid, where a man of that name was drowned (last fall, in the partie's descent, 1811), when Mr. Crook's canoe split and upsett.

— *Robert Stuart, 1812*

Snake River, Below American Falls (Power County, Idaho)

Our camp to day was 30 miles we found water only once in that distance we reached Snake River [near Hunt's Point] almost exhausted with thirst and fatigue beeing on the way about 8 hours and traveling near 4 miles to the hour. course do West. You will beare in mind that the S. R. is verry crooked and in one course we only touched on it at several points and the grass along the River being poor we keped as far from it as possible its general course is however do West insted of N. W. as laid down on the Maps.

— *Rev. W. H. Gray, 1838*

Massacre Rocks

Towards the close of the evening we passed many ledges of rocks, which formed a complete valley, having an outlet so narrow that but one wagon could pass at a time [Massacre Rocks] . . . . The right bank of the river along here rises to the height of at least fifteen hundred feet, entirely of basaltic rock, and resembles very much the palisades on the Hudson river . . . .

After sundown, we came to what is called Fall creek, a rapid little stream . . . . On the opposite side of this little brook the hill was so steep as to require sometimes sixteen mules to a wagon, and as many men as could well get hold of a rope, to get it to the top; this will give you some faint idea of the very great detention . . . in crossing 166 wagons. It was, however, accomplished.

— *Maj. Osborne Cross, 1849*

Raft River/California Cut-off

[The Raft River, near its junction with the Snake, was where emigrants who decided on going to California left the Oregon Trail. Those like Benjamin Bonney's family followed the course of the Mary's River (renamed by Frémont as the Humboldt) to the Sink, Carson River, the Sierras and on into California. Bonney, however, decided against living under the Mexican flag and went the next year to Oregon.]

September 26 . . . the ridge in which Raft River heads is about 20 miles distant, rocky, and tolerably high.

September 27 — It was now no longer possible to travel regularly every day, and . . . the halting-places were now generally fixed along the road, by the nature of the country, at places where, with water, there was a little scanty grass. Since leaving American Falls the road had frequently been very bad. The many, short, steep ascents, exhausting the strength of our worn-out animals, requiring, always at such places the assistance of the men to get up each cart, one by one;

and our progress with twelve or fourteen wheeled carriages . . . in such a rocky country was extremely slow.

— *Brevet-Capt. John C. Frémont, 1842*

[September] 13. last night contrary to our expectations we came to a brook with a broad valley of fine grass this brook is called cassia & is the place whare Mr Hitchcock left our rout & went South with 13 wagons in company for callifornia [Raft River] this days Travel is the most Barren Sterril region we have yet passed nothing to disturb the monotony of the Eternal Sage plain which is covered with broken cynders much resembling Junks of pot mettal & Now & then a cliff of Black burned rock which looks like Distruction brooding over dispair found a filthy pond of water at noon . . .

— *James Clyman, 1844*

Here the California trail turns off [Cassia Creek, affluent of Raft River]. The road has been very dusty and heavy traveling Joseph Walker, guide, took to this route to California — the J. B. Chiles [1843].

About fifteen wagons had been fitted out, expressly for California; and, joined by the thirty-five ["diverted" by Greenwood], completed a train of fifty wagons; what the result of their expedition has been, I have not been able to learn.

— *Joel Palmer, 1845*

Snake River, Massacre Rocks Palisades (Power County, Idaho)

California Trail Leaves Oregon Trail, Near Raft River (Cassia County, Idaho)

30th . . . . We started by 6:00 O'clock drove back a mile to the ford and crossed Raft River. Ford three rods wide and three feet deep. Raft River is a very deep and rapid stream and runs north to Snake River. After leaving the river we ascended a hill and found ourselves on a strange plain which, I think, has been the scene of volcanic action.

— *Basil Nelson Longsworth, 1853*

Caldron Linn

Saturday 29th [August, eastward to St. Louis] . . . . The Indian path going by far too much to the south for our purpose, we on leaving Camp steered E by S for 20 miles over (what is in this Country) called a Prairie, but Forest of Wormwood (sage brush, Artemesia Tridentada) is more properly its name; we again struck the main river [Snake] at the Caldron Linn where one of the unfortunate Canoes was lodged among the rocks, but although we wished . . . to see in what state she was, the Bluffs intimated that to gratify our wish we

must risk our necks, so we of course declined it —

. . . nothing that walks the earth could possibly pass between . . . [the cliffs] and the water, which in such places is never more than 40 yards wide . . . . but its general width for the 30 miles in question is from 35 to 40 [yards] and in one place, at the Caldron Linn the whole body of the river is confined between 2 ledges of rock somewhat less than 40 [feet] apart and here indeed its terrific appearance beggars all description — Hecate's Caldron was never half so agitated when vomiting even the most diabolical spells, as is this Linn in . . . resemblance to that as something more infernal . . . more particularly as the tout ensemble of these 30 miles has been baptised the Devil's Scuttle Hole.

— *Robert Stuart, 1812*

[September] 14. Left our camp on the river & Steered S. of W. across a Barren Sage plain corssed one brook of water & Saw 2 Antelope the only animals seen in some days The earth is the driest I ever saw it & the dust rises in perfect clouds every particle of moistness &

adhsion is obliterated & lost & currents of dust is frequently seen rolling down the path & Spreading like hot embers that have been well Stirred came to the River to noon & grze the River running through cliffs of Black Volcanic Rocks which grew Steeper & higher as we decended down the River at length we left the Bluffs of the River being 1000 or more feet of Perpendicular Rock standing from the plain to the water & the river pressed to 20 or 30 feet in width

— *James Clyman, 1844*

[July] Monday 25th. Sage, sage, nothing but sage, seems one endless sage plains, here we camped, poor grass . . . . Myriads of grasshoppers . . .

— *David (or John) Dinwiddie, 1853*

4th. This day we made ten miles and camped on Snake River, our camp being on a high bluff with the river lying half a mile distant and six or eight hundred feet below us with very bluff banks . . . . This is a remarkably strange place. The ground is level to the very edge of the bluffs, which are two miles apart and perpendicular for two or three hundred feet and then slope at an angle of 45° and are covered with rocks above and tumbled down in wild confused masses. This range of rocks covers a height of three or four hundred feet, there is then a slope of land extending to the water which is quite steep and rocky. Through this the river flows with a rapid current and in places considerable falls.

— *Basil Nelson Longsworth, 1853*

[September] 8th . . . . Had to wait till noon to repair a broken waggon . . . . The country all the way down the Snake River is one of the most desolate and dreary waste in the world. Light soft ground with no soil on top, looking like an ash heap, dust six inch deep and as light as flour. When a man travells all day in it he looks like a miller. You can see nothing but his eyes and them look red. The dust is here so light that it sometimes raises 300 feet above the train. The ground is covered with two of the most detestable shrubs that grows, grease would [wood] and artemesia or wild sage.

— *E. S. McComas, 1862*

Falls at Caldron Linn, Snake River

Caldron Linn (Jerome County, Idaho)

Salmon Falls

Soon we met [November 11] two Chochonis.... We crossed a prairie, and arrived at a camp of his tribe. The women fled so precipitately that they had not time to take with them such of their children as could not walk. They had covered them with straw. When I lifted it to look at them, the poor little creatures were terror-stricken. The men trembled with fear as though I had been a ferocious animal. They gave us a small quantity of dried fish, which we found very good, and sold us a dog....

On the 12th, I visited some huts at which was a large quantity of salmon. These huts are of straw, are shaped like ricks of grain, and are warm and comfortable.... I bought two dogs. We ate one of them for breakfast.

— Wilson Price Hunt, 1811

... Salmon Falls, where we found about 100 lodges Shoshonies busily occupied in killing & drying Fish —...

Salmon ... become an easy prey — With the greatest facility prodigious quantities are slaughtered daily and it must have been from this place that the dead and wounded [fish] came which we saw picked up by the starving wretches below....

Their spears are a small straight piece of Elks Horn, out of which the pith is dug, deep enough to receive the end of a very long willow pole & on the point an artificial beard is made fast by a preparation of Twine and Gum

this point of Horn is about seven inches long and from a little below where the Pole enters a strong string of the same length is attached, which is fastened in a like manner to the handle so that when the Spearsman makes a sure blow the wicker catches, pulls off the point and leaves the salmon struggling with the string through his body.

— Robert Stuart, 1812

11th. Teaus & Wed. have been very tedious days, both for man and beast. Lengthy marches without water.... Had a present tonight of a fresh Salmon, also a plate of fried cakes from Mr McLeod (Girls if you wish to know how they taste, you can have the pleasure by taking a little flour & water & make some dough roll it thin, cut it into square blocks, then take some beaf fat & fry them. You need not put either salt or pearl ash in your dough.) Believe me I relish these as well as I ever did any made at home.

12 Frid. Raised camp this morn at Sunrise. Came two hours ride to the Salmon fishery. Found a few lodges of Diggers of the Snake tribe so called because they live on roots....

Friday eve. Dear Harriet the little trunk you gave me has come with me so far & now I must leave it here alone. Poor little trunk, I am sorry to leave thee. Thou must abide here alone & no more by thy presence remind me of my Dear Harriet. Twenty miles below the Falls on Snake River. This shall be thy place of rest. Farewell little Trunk.... The hills are so steep rocky that Husband thought it best to lighten the waggon as much as possible & take nothing but the wheels, leaving the box with my trunk.... If I were to make this journey again I would make quite different preparations.... Our books what few we have, have been wet several times. In going from Elmira to Williamsport this trunk fell in to the creek & wet all my books & Richards, too very much.... The custom of the

Snake River, Near Upper Salmon Falls (Gooding County, Idaho)

country is to possess nothing & then you will loose nothing while traveling farewell for the present.

— *Narcissa Prentiss Whitman, 1836*

11th On the moove 8¼ A. m go 11 miles and camp on little Cassis find plenty of grass stay all day hear we got fresh salmon beeing only 6 miles above Fishing falls.

12th Friday off 6 A m go to the falls and stop to breakfast on fresh salmon caught by the Indians who live on fish and roots in this region . . . .

— *Rev. W. H. Gray, 1838*

Mon. [August 17] after riding about one hour we came to the [Salmon] falls — here we got a supply of fish to last us to Ft Boysa [Boise] . . . . These are not perpendicular falls, but rapids where they [the Indians] catch fish (which run up into places made for the purpose, with stones) with their hands—Stopped for our breakfast on Snake river.

— *Asahel Munger, 1839*

The first sound that struck my ear seemed to jar the earth like distant thunder. As we approached, many Indians were seen, and long lines of something of a red color, which I thought were clothes hung out to dry . . . but as we came nearer I learned that those lines were salmon which the Indians were drying in the sun.

— *Jesse Applegate, 1843*

[September] These [Salmon] Falls are not perpendicular .... The great body of the water runs down an inclination of not more than twenty-five feet in three hundred yards on its point. When they spear the salmon the barb immediately comes off, but is attached by a cord to the lance and the fish is played about, until they can get near enough to kill, or throw it upon the shore ....

.... The surrounding country is very rough, broken, and entirely destitute of both grass and wood. The hills are, from the water in the River, about three hundred feet high. On the South side they are cut up by ravines; but on the North they come bold and unbroken up within a few hundred yards of the water. There is nothing very picturesque or wild about these Falls, compared with the world of waste and wreck around them. The Indians take immense quantities of Salmon here, which they cut into thick slices, dry in the Sun, and afterwards pack them up in grass cases.

The natives ... live principally upon fish and roots; and are the filthiest, most depraved, and degraded creatures, anywhere to found among the dregs of human nature. We have been told, that during the Salmon season, they become as fat as penned pigs; and in the winter, so poor and feeble, that they frequently die from actual starvation.

— *Overton Johnson and W. H. Winter, 1843*

Friday, September, 8 .... Went down to the falls and purchased some salmon. Had a fight in camp this evening. Old Zachary stabbed Mr. Wheeler with his knife.

— *James Willis Nesmith, 1843*

Our encampment [October 1] was about one mile below the Fishing falls ... fisheries from which the inhabitants of this barren region almost entirely derive a subsistence commence at this place. These appeared to be unusually gay savages, fond of loud laughter; and, in their apparent good nature and merry character, struck me as being entirely different from the Indians we had been accustomed to see ....

Oct. 2. Very many of them [Indians] ... were oddly and partially dressed in overcoats, shirt, waist coost [coats] or pantalons, or whatever article of clothing they had been able to procure from the emigrants; for we had now entirely quitted the country where hawk's bells, beads, and vermillion were current coin, and found here only useful articles, and chiefly clothing, were in great request.

— *Brevet-Capt. John C. Frémont, 1843*

These miserable Indians [October 2] are a happy, harmless people. Here too, only wealth makes them insolent and arrogant, as it does the Sioux with their long buffalo skins, their nice lodges, etc. These poor devils sew together twenty groundhog skins, and yet the garment does not reach to their knees. Their winter lodgment is made of reeds, and salmon is their only food, which, to be sure, is never exhausted. Below the falls the fish rise in such multitudes that the Indians can pierce them with their spears without looking. Now that we have butter and salt, this is a good dish ....

One hears nothing but the word *hagai*, "fish" ....

This Snake river is interesting, I must confess. The most beautiful little waterfalls, twenty to forty feet high. Then steep, volcanic, rocky shores .... The waters which come from the mountains disappear in the lava or rocky plain and come out again on the bank of the river [Thousand Springs].

— *Charles Preuss, 1843*

[September] 16 Pased down the Kenyon to the mouth of a Small river & over the ridge to the little or upper Salmon Falls whare we found a number of Indians encamped who offered us plenty of dried Salmon cheap ... these fall are Surrounded with high inaccessable Clay & rock Bluffs the vally norrow & Broken up with ravines Sandy without vegitation except Sage & some of the Same Kind of useless hardy plants .... an intire want of water except in the River [which] runs in such a precepice that only a few places can [be] desended even on foot & then to return to the summt is ½ a days hard labour about 10 A.M. we came to the ford or upper crossing of the river & saw a few Teams on the opposite side that had left Fort Hall 6 days before us. Soil since we left portnuff Slaked & unslaked lime volcanic rocks ...

— *James Clyman, 1844*

August 20 .... Here are eighteen or twenty Indian huts ... this place is a succession of cataracts for several miles, the highest of which does not exceed twelve feet.

— *Joel Palmer, 1845*

We soon came [August 16] to the Big Salmon falls .... large rocks are seen projecting above the surface of the water, against which it dashes in parts of the falls with great violence and forms in one place a perpendicular fall of six or eight feet. It was at these falls that we met a few Indians for the first time since leaving Fort Hall .... The men were good-looking, well formed and appear stouter than the generality of Indians farther north. They are thickset and well built, and there is nothing sullen about them, a quality you meet with among the northern tribes on the Mississippi [River]. On the contrary, [they] appear pleasant and fond of talking, and from what little I saw of them are a harmless and inoffensive race of people. The women whom I found at the lodges were in appearance inferior to the men. I saw none who possessed the least beauty. All [who] were there are principally the Root Diggers, who live in abject poverty compared with the balance of their nation. They are in fact nothing more than the degenerate portion of the Snake nation, Bonards [Bannocks] and Nez Perces, who prefer living among the neighboring hills and subsist by digging roots (from whence they take their name) [to] following a more noble occupation of catching beaver and hunting big game.

— Maj. Osborne Cross, 1849

Went to the ferry [August 10], a short distance. This family that were with us, Mr. Russel[l] lost an ox in the morning .... Saw at the ferry a horse that had been bitten by scorpions, dying. A short distance below the ferry is Salmon Falls.

They are perpendicular ... but not very high ... very scraggy and ... very pretty and interesting. Crossed the ferry, paying $6.00 per wagon. They paid $10.00 to some men for swimming the cattle over on account of the difficulty of doing so.

— Celinda K. Hines, 1853

Thousand Springs

Sunday, 24th September [near Thousand Springs] ... made good headway and camped at dark .... How seldom as this evening comes around do I think of the happy hours I have had on this day with those I live, and whose memory I hold most dear. And why, — the only, and good reason is — a person is thinking of the tedious and tiresome journey — of his animals as all depends on them, whether they may not be stolen or get away, perhaps turn their packs and lose part of the things, or break something; and when near camping time, he is all anxiety to get good grass, wood and water. As soon as camp is struck, then get wood, make fire, cook and eat, then mend pants, mocassins, packsaddles, cruppers, lash-rope, girths, &c, or alter his packs, as one too heavy and hurts the mule's back. Then comes making bed.

— John Boardman, 1843

September 30 .... We followed the trail of several wagons which had turned in towards Snake River, and encamped, as they had done, on the top of the escarpment. There was no grass here, the soil among the sage being entirely naked ....

Immediately opposite to us, a subterranean river burst and directly from the face of the escarpment, and

Thousand Springs (Gooding County, Idaho)

falls in white foam to the river below . . . . A melancholy and strange looking country — one of fracture and violence, and fire . . .

— *Brevet-Capt. John C. Frémont, 1843*

[September] 15. Left our camp on the brook & moved off west over a Sage plaine . . . . late in the afternoon we desended the main Kenyon on Snake River The Black battlement cliffs of this river remind one of the Fragments of a world distroyed or at least distroyed for all human purposes on the river we found a Small fishing party of Ponacks [Bannocks] who had plenty of small fish of the Sucker mouthed Kind Several Temendious Springs come Pouring out of the rocks oposite . . .

— *James Clyman, 1844*

Along the river for four miles there is a vast quantity of crystal spring water pouring down the rocky cliffs into the river. In many places it falls down from one to three hundred feet and nearly covers the rocks for hundreds of feet together, forming a most pleasing and sublime spectacle. The water falls in such large quantities that for miles along the river the water is perfectly clear for from thirty to sixty yards from the shore.

— *Basil Nelson Longsworth, 1853*

[August 9th.] Saw some very fine falls [at Thousand Springs] from streams on the north side of the river. The first was a perpendicular fall of many feet in height. Most of the others issued out of the banks of the river and falling several feet flowed into the river.

— *Celinda K. Hines, 1853*

Three Island Crossing

August 13, 1836 . . . We have come fiteen miles and have had the worst route in all the journey for the cart. We might have had a better one but for being misled by some of the company . . . .

. . . . The [Snake] river is divided by two islands into three branches, and is fordable. The packs are placed upon the tops of the highest horses and in this way we crossed without wetting. Two of the tallest horses were selected to carry Mrs. [Eliza] Spalding and myself over . . . . Husband [Marcus] had considerable difficulty in crossing the cart. Both cart and mules were turned upside down in the river and entangled in the harness . . . .

There is one manner of crossing which husband has tried but I have not, neither do I wish to. Take an elk skin and stretch it over you, spreading yourself out as much as possible, then let the Indian woman

Three Island Crossing (near Glenns Ferry, Idaho)

carefully put you on the water and with a cord in the mouth they will swim and draw you over . . . .

— *Narcissa Prentiss Whitman, 1836*

[September 11] We crawsed Snake Rive[r]. First we drove over a part of the river, one hundred yards wide on to a island; then we tide . . . wagons to gether by a chane in the ring of the leed cattles yoke & made fast to the waggon . . . . We carried as maney a [as] fifteen waggons at on time. We had to go up streeme. The water was ten inches up to the waggeo[n]s beds in the deepe placees. It was 900 hundred yards acraws.

— *William T. Newby, 1843*

Twenty-seven miles below the Salmon Falls we came to the crossing where the companies which preceded us had passed over to the North side [of the Snake] . . . . It is nothing else than a wild, rocky barren wilderness, of wrecked and ruined Nature, a vast field of volcanic desolation.

— *Overton Johnson and W. H. Winter, 1843*

October 3. — About 2 o'clock we arrived at the ford where the road crosses to the right [north] bank of Snake river. An Indian was hired to conduct us through the ford, which proved impracticable for us, the water sweeping away the howitzer and nearly drowning the mules . . . . The emigrants had passed by placing two of their heavy wagons abreast of each other, so as to oppose a considerable mass against the body of water . . . . we had a resource in the boat, which was filled with air and launched; and at seven o'clock we were safely encamped on the opposite bank, and the . . . carriage, howitzer, and baggage of the camp carried over in the boat.

— *Brevet-Capt. John C. Frémont, 1843*

August 23 . . . . Those crossing this stream can escape the deepest of the holes by having horsemen in the van and at each side.

— *Joel Palmer, 1845*

August 28th, we took up our daily travels, following a deep cut trail made by the pack animals, but without a pilot now. We soon came to the crooked, treacherous Snake River, where we lost two of our men, Ayres and Stringer . . . . Ayres, who was an old man about sixty, got into trouble with his mules in crossing the stream. Stringer, who was about thirty years of age went to his relief, and both of them were drowned in sight of their women folks whom they had ferried across. The bodies were never recovered.

— *Samuel Hancock, 1845*

September 14. Blocked up our wagon beds and forded Snake River which was wide, deep and swift.

September 15. Laid by. This morning our company moved on, except for one family. The woman got mad and wouldn't budge nor let the children go. Her husband had the cattle hitched on for three hours and coaxed her to go, but she wouldn't stir. I told my husband, so he and Adam Polk and Mr. Kimball each took a young one and crammed them in the wagon and the husband drove off and left her sitting. She took the back track and traveled out of sight. She cut across and overtook her husband. He had sent his boy back to camp after a horse that had been left. When she came up, her husband said 'Did you meet John?' 'Yes' she said, 'I picked up a stone and knocked out his brains.' Her husband went back to ascertain the truth of what she said and while he was gone, she set fire to the wagon that was loaded with their store goods. The cover burnt off and some valuable articles were burned. He saw the flames and came running up and put it out, and then mustered up spunk enough to give her a good flogging.

— *Elizabeth Geer, 1847*

We forded the Snake River [August 21] which runs so swift that the drivers (four to a team) had to hold on to the ox yokes to keep from being swept down by the current. The water came into the wagon boxes, and after making the island we raised the boxes on blocks . . . . The "Telegraph Company," as we call them, who passed us in such a hurry on the Platte, have left their goods and wagons scattered over the mountains. We find them every day. Their cattle have given out . . . . We drove too slow on the Platte, and the "Telegraph" hurried too fast, and . . . our cattle are comparatively strong . . . . We have met some "packers," and they inform us that we are too late to cross the Cascade mountains this season.

— *Elizabeth Wood, 1851*

8th. This morning by daylight our wagons were crossing the [Snake] river. We had to load and unload our wagons, row the skiff and then pay $4 per wagon and 50¢ a head for swimming cattle by the side of the boat. By 8:00 o'clock our wagons were all safely over . . . . but the wind was high and we did not swim our cattle until in the afternoon . . . . Three men whom we had employed swam to the island and drove our cattle across the remaining part of the river. They also swam three other lots of cattle, for which they received $2 per lot . . . . The Salmon Falls here are pretty and descend fifteen or twenty feet, forming many beautiful cascades, the . . . roaring of the waters can be heard for five or six miles.

— *Basil Nelson Longsworth, 1853*

Hot Springs at Base of Volcanic Hills (near Teapot, Elmore County, Idaho)

Hot Springs/Teapot

[August] 15th A m we stoped half an hour at the hot springs [six miles east of present-day Mountain Home] I put in some dry fish that we had it boiled tender in 10 minutes the water of this spring is verry hot I can hold my hand in boiling water nearly as long as in this spring it runs from the Mountain tastes brackish and hard is verry clear continually emits steam.

— *Rev. W. H. Gray, 1838*

Oct. 4 . . . . Leaving the [Snake] river . . . we ascended a long and rather steep hill to a plain 600 feet above the river . . . artemesia still covers the plains . . . .

Oct. 5. — In about nine miles the road brought us to a group of smoking hot springs, with a temperature of 164° . . . .

These springs are near the foot of the ridge [Teapot, a dark, rugged-looking mountain], in which some of the nearer rocks have a reddish appearance.

— *Brevet-Capt. John C. Frémont, 1843*

August 16 . . . . these springs rise nearly in a level plain at the foot of the mountain and are hot enough to boil meat perfectly done in a few minutes . . . . distance made today, eighteen miles.

— *Jesse Harritt, 1845*

August 13 — Friday. — We started at 6 a. m. and traveled two miles to Hot Springs . . . . Mrs. Burns

tried one of them by immersing her finger, but quickly removed it without being told, declaring it entirely too hot for washing dishes . . . . There is one cold stream of water issuing from this same rock. I sat down on this rock, putting my right hand in a cold spring of water and my left hand in a hot spring of water, the two springs being only five feet apart.

— *Enoch W. Conyers, 1852*

Beyond the Mountains, which rise on the South of this point, is the great Salt Lake. Eighty-eight miles below [west of Three Islands] the crossing of Snake River, we crossed two small branches of hot water. This region appears once to have been overflowed from the East by a vast flood of lava . . . . and the sandy base which composes the hills, seems to have given away to the actions of time, until these table hills are but the fragments of the vast wreck. In these deserts we found the Horned Toad.

— *Capt. Howard Stansbury, 1852*

17th. We drove up a long hill with many large columns of rock to our right . . . . Our grass was down the stream half a mile [near Hot Springs]. Just as we got the cattle to their feed I was attacked by very severe diarrhea pains. I felt some bad but . . . drank near a gill of brandy made thick with sugar which stopped the pains immediately but I still felt unwell for several days.

— *Basil Nelson Longsworth, 1853*

Rocky Pass/Big Rocks

15th. Yesterday Mr McLeod with most of his men left us wishing to hasten his arrival at Snake [Boise] Fort, leaving us a pilot & his weakest animals . . . . We passed the hot Springs just before noon which are quite a curiosity. Boiled a bit of dry Salmon in one of them in five minutes.

16th This evening found a plenty of berries called hawthorn . . . . They are as large as a cherry & taste much like a mealy sweet apple.

— *Narcissa Prentiss Whitman, 1836*

October 6. — . . . we found ourselves suddenly in granite country . . . the artemesia disappeared almost entirely . . . green short grass, like that of the early spring. This is the full or second growth, the dried grass having been burnt off by the Indians; and wherever the fire has passed, the bright-green color is universal . . . . The road at noon reached a broken ridge, on which were scattered many boulders or blocks of granite . . . . The Indians made a few unsuccessful attempts to steal horses from us . . . . The traveler is on perpetual watch.

— *Brevet-Capt. John C. Frémont, 1843*

. . . near the western side of this field of Slag rises a ruged steep and high mountain composed of rough greyish granite nearly Bear of vegitation and in many Places the field of Slag and the mountain approach so near that it was with great difficulty that our pack Horses could find sufficient room to pass and near this western side I observed a greate many large masses of this granite rock standing in all inclinations . . . . and had the appearance of having been afloat in the liquid mass the more weighty parts having sunk and shot up . . .

— *James Clyman, 1844*

Big Granite Rocks with Black Mica, Smoky Quartz, and Garnets

Sometimes for the distance of many miles the entire surface of the country was covered with a medium sized stone or boulder, just large enough to make it difficult to travel over them; the only way the teams could distinguish the route was by the bruised and broken boulders, occasioned by the wheels of the front wagons passing over them, and the blood from the feet of our poor animals . . . . frequently we were obliged to leave them lying upon the rocks.

— *Samuel Hancock, 1845*

The Indians along this road are expert in theft and roguery . . . . at night an Indian stole into the camp, unhobbled the horse, cut the rope, and took him off, leaving the young man undisturbed in his sleep. A few days there after, this Indian effected a sale of the horse to one of a party of emigrants traveling behind us.

— *Joel Palmer, 1845*

October 17. Cold, windy. Our cattle ran off in search of water. Camped without wood except a small shrub

Arid Nook in Granite Rocks

called greasewood. We found a hole of water 12 or 13 feet across. Had to water 150 head of cattle with pails. Had to stand out all night in the rain to keep the cattle from crowding in this hole and drowning each other.

— *Elizabeth Geer, 1847*

18th. This morning early we ascended a long hill and after driving three or four miles, one of us saw Boise River. One of our oxen was quite sick and would not eat. About 1:00 we struck the river which is a beautiful river forty or fifty yards in width. The water has a rapid current and is as clear as crystal and quite full of fish . . . .

20th. We left camp and drove until noon over a very dusty and sandy road which was covered with sage . . . and struck the river on the west side of the bluff, where we ate some dinner and then drove on until we reached the ford of Boise . . . . There is a very good soil along Boise River, the bottoms being from two to four miles wide and mostly covered with a heavy growth of grass. There might be thousands of tons of pretty fine hay made here.

— *Basil Nelson Longsworth, 1853*

Boise River

On the 20th November, the rain which had commenced to fall the previous night, gave us [traveling west to Astoria] a little water. This alleviation was timely, as several Canadians had begun to drink their urine . . . .

On the 21st. at sunrise, we saw before us a river [Boise] which flowed westerly. Its shores were fringed with cottonwoods and willows. Some indians had established a camp there. They had many horses, and were better clad than those we had seen previously. They informed us that beaver are common further up in this small river . . . .

On the 22nd, we met some indians. From my observations and the few words I could understand, the distance from this place to the Big River [Columbia] was very considerable; but the indians told me nothing of the route I must follow. We obtained some fish, seven dogs and two horses.

— *Wilson Price Hunt, 1811*

September 17 — We had some fresh fish boiled in baskets, the water being kept boiling by hot stones. For a day [near Boise] we went up a creek from the southwest trapping. Our horses were cut loose at night by the Indians, and my camlet cloak was stolen. As a general rule, the Indians were kind and freindly, and would make us presents of food, but they could forego the attempt to steal our horses of which we had two to each man any more than a negro can leave a hen roost alone.

— *John Ball, 1832*

In trading for some salmon, an Indian attempted to sna[t]ch a paper of fish hook from me but he did not make out returned to camp and sent two men to trap for beaver they left their horses and went into the

willows to look [for] the sign during which time the Indians none of whom were in sight stole a cloack from Mr. Ball.

— *Nathaniel J. Wyeth, 1832*

August 21st . . . . Our [new wagon] Captain, Armington, is one of the most liberal, freehearted men in this country. He has shown us a great deal of kindness, though far from being a religious man . . . .

[Next day] we reached Fort Bois. Here we rested two days. Our Captain Armington is a very profane man, which seems to give fresh spring to our swearers.

The first night we staid at Fort Bois I lay on the bank of the river, where I could scarcely sleep for the Indians, who sung all night in a very curious manner. This is their practice when they are gambling . . . . The salmon also kept a great noise, jumping and splashing about in the water.

— *Rev. Joseph Williams, 1841*

October 7. — The day was bright, clear, and pleasant, with a temperature of 45°; and we breakfasted at sunrise, the birds singing in the trees as merrily as if we were in the midst of summer. On the upper edge of the hills on the opposite side of the creek, the black volcanic rock reappears; hills swept in such a manner as to give it the appearance of an old crater . . . . The road was occasionally enlivened by meeting Indians, and the day was extremely beautiful and pleasant . . . .

When we had about 8 miles, we were nearly opposite to the highest portions of the mountains on the left side of the Snake river valley; and continuing on a few miles beyond we came suddenly in sight of the broad green line of the valley of the Riviere Boisee [Boise River and valley], black near the gorge where it debouches into the Plains, with high precipices of basalt, between walls of which it passes, on emerging from the mountains.

. . . . At the time of the first occupation of this region by parties engaged in the fur trade, a small party of men under the command of ——— Reid [John Reed], constituting all the garrison of a little fort on this river, were surprised and massacred by the Indians; and to this event the stream owes its occasional name of Reid's river [Boise].

— *Brevet-Capt. John C. Frémont, 1843*

September 19 . . . encamped at the first possible chance we found to descent to the River Gross Boise or Bigwood [Boise] which here comes rushing out of the most uneven Ruged Mountain I had yet seen & passes rapidly down through a Steep Kenyon which cannot [be] assended or descended even on foot except in a few places this is a rapid Stream about 40 yards wide & is fine for Salmon . . .

[September 20]. Set down the river west the moun-tains to our right and the perpendicular rock Bank to the left both receding & deminishing a fine valley opened to our view & we pased down through the dust which was almost past endureance but not much wose than it had been for Several day past . . . . ourselves & animals are completey tired out with dust & burned Prairies.

— *James Clyman, 1844*

Near Fort Boise, a young Indian signed for us to stop and go with him into the timber; and led the way to a camp under cottonwood trees. He moved away the fire and live coals, then began to carefully remove the sandy soil, uncovering a fair-sized salmon baked in the hot sand. Putting this carefully aside, he dug down further and unearthed a beaver skin, which he wished to sell . . . .

We made Fort Boise that evening, and mustered among us enough money to purchase twenty pounds of Oregon flour. The trader in charge refused to sell a little dried elk meat. It was "for the master," he said.

[Later.] Our Oregon friends gave us rice and tea and sugar, and things looked generally pleasant as the result of our trust in Providence. To complete our satisfaction, a cavalcade of Indian women now came along with horses loaded with camas roots.

We purchased some fresh roots to boil with our game; but the sqaws knowing better than we how to use Camas, brought out some cakes of camas bread they had left over from their lunch. These cakes were eight to ten inches broad and one and a quarter thick, of brown color, and texture like new cheese, but more glutinous, with a sweet and agreeable taste; undoubtedly a very nutritious food. We bought all the women had, fishhooks being our money.

— *John Minto, 1844*

We continued on down this river . . . . to old Fort Boise where it emptied in the Snake River . . . . before crossing it the first time, and in the early morning when all the men and boys of the train were out after the cattle and the women folk were preparing breakfast, about 40 dirty, war-painted Snake Indians drove their ponies right into camp, among the wagons and fires, which caused quite a commotion for a short time. We soon hurried in and got out guns, those who did not have guns with them. We fully expected trouble, and we did not show any white feather or fear of the red devils. They had scared the women and children. They were more than saucy before we got to camp, riding around among the camp fires, pulling back the front end or back end of our wagon sheets. But when we showed fight, they then wanted bread or something to eat, which we gave to the skunks, and in a short time they left us.

— *James D. Miller, 1848*

Fort Boise

Thomas McKay, established a fort which became Fort Boise, 1834. He loved the Snake River plains and during the course of a visit to Missionary Jason Lee's on August 16, 1834 McKay informed Lee of his intention to remain on the river to trap and trade with the Indians. Although it seems that McKay built his fort, records indicate that Hudson's Bay Company supervised, and later became manager of McKay's Snake Fort — Fort Boise. McKay being an enterprising and trustworthy, it is not strange to learn that "he envisioned the day when Fort Boise would be connected with the Oregon settlement."

— Nathaniel J. Wyeth, 1836

15th. Wed. Have at last arrived at Boise. Travelled hard all day. We are all tired, yes, very tired . . . but we are now almost at our journey's end, only 200 miles further to go . . . .

16th. Thursday. Find it good to rest. Have baked a pie & biscuits today. The good people at the Fort kindly supplied us with milk, pumpkins & turnips . . . .

20th Sat. Last night I put my cloths in water & this morning finished washing before breakfast. I find it not very agreable to do such work in the middle of the day when I have no shelter to protect me from the suns schorching rays. This is the third time I have washed since I left the states, or home . . . . Once at Fort Williams [Laramie] & at Rendezvous [Green River].

— Narcissa Prentiss Whitman, 1836

Saturday, September 30th . . . . All felt elated when they came in sight of the Fort, supposing they would get plenty of provisions; but how soon were all our hopes dampened when we learned the Oregon company had bought all that could be spared . . . .

Sunday, Oct. 1st . . . . Some have talked of little else than getting something to eat, and getting where it was plenty . . . at home — Missouri, Illinois, or almost any place . . . . So far we have got nothing. Tallow 33¢ per pound, none. Salt 50¢; coffee 50¢, sugar 50¢ per pint; none of either. Monday, October 2d. The company got a beef at 7¢, and divided equally to those going to California, and half rations to rice, Winter & Johnson going to Oregon.

— John Boardman, 1843

When we arrived at Boise . . . we were again with a considerable company. The river we found to be about a hundred yards wide, quite rapid, and too deep to ford . . . . while camping in the neighborhood of this fort . . . we children were much surprised and delighted to find beads, generally small and white in color, in ant hills . . . . while searching for more presently came to a place where the ground was white with them, and looking up discovered that we were under a broad platform raised on posts seven or eight feet high, and that the platform . . . was thickly strewn with the decayed corpses of dead Indians . . . . Many of the bodies were yet rolled up in blankets and robes. Some had been torn into fragments by carrion crows . . . and skulls and other bony parts of the body lay bleaching

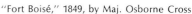

"Fort Boisé," 1849, by Maj. Osborne Cross

Snake River, Near Fort Boise; Mount Mitchell

Cottonwood Trees, Near Fort Boise (Canyon County, Idaho)

in the sun; a few had fallen to the ground. After this ghastly find we did not tarry long, for the shades of evening were now creeping along the ground.

— *Jesse Applegate, 1843*

Pa, . . . rode a horse, as he had not done before, and assisted in driving them [cattle]. By some cause or other he went too far down the [Boise] river, his horse reared with him, and saying, "I must take care of myself," he got off. He endeavored to get hold of the horse as he let go of the bridle, but being on the lower side, the current took him down and the horse swam out of his reach. He tried to go to an island, but finding the current too strong turned to the shore. He soon sank. Most of the men were near but none of them dared to go in, the danger was too great.

— *Celinda K. Hines, 1853*

Malheur River

[September] 22 Left our camp 2 miles above Fort Boise & passed the mud walld Fort of Boise & the cleark was kind enough to make us out a Sketch of the rout to walla walla . . . found the ford good & Smoothe but rather deep for wagons . . . Snake River running N. The Trail carried us over another Sage plain 14 miles to Malure [Malheur] River a dirty deep Stream running to the N.E. with a fine large vally . . . .

180

[September] 23 . . . the entire country covered with sage which for some cause or other is nearly all dead . . . . encamped on Snake River which here comes out of a rough looking mountain to the east & makeing a Short curve goes off into mountains again to the North our camp is verry poor for grass . . . . this evening we raised our bread with saleratus picked up a few miles east of independenc rock on sweet water [River] . . .

— *James Clyman, 1844*

September 3. We traveled fifteen miles, to Malheur, or Malore, as it is sometimes called; here is a good camp. This is a stream of about ten yards in width, having its source in a range of mountains to the South-west, and pursuing its meanderings . . . until it arrives at Snake River, into which it empties.

[Earlier this day] a few miles below Fort Bois . . . . we met Dr. [Elijah] White, as sub-Indian agent, accompanied by three others, on their way from Oregon to the states [bearing a memorial from the provisional government of Oregon, requesting Congress to extend the sovereignty and laws of the United States over the Oregon settlements].

— *Joel Palmer, 1845*

Had an unusual allowance of dust to the mile today [near the Malheur River], but got the most of it off before night . . . . The girls have as dirty faces as anybody . . . . Thanks be to the rewarder of troubles, 460

miles more will get us dirty-faced boys and girls out of this dirty faced kingdom.

— *John T. Kerns, 1852*

September 8. We parted our company yesterday, the Stevensons and Buckenhams taking the old road, and the Loves and Stewarts taking the new road going south from the old one. Some say it is much nearer, and some say not. We will soon find out. We came twelve miles over very dusty roads to the Malheur River again, crossing one valley with no water. Camped beside the river, and cooked and ate under the willows. It was a beautiful spot, to me at least. Pack up and go again like a band of gypsies. I feel very lost without the rest of the company.

September 9 . . . . fifteen miles up the Malheur, passed several bluffs and forded the river six times. Lost father and found him again.

— *Agnes Stewart, 1853*

12th. Crossed the Malhue . . . through an alkali valley which might properly be termed Carron Valley from the great number of dead cattle which are here . . . . it looks slightly like freezing to death, verry much like being blowed away in a hurricane and a good prospect of being killed by Indians to say nothing of dicing for want of tobacco. Through all these fiery ordeals we expect to come out all O. K. [The next day] . . . I counted twenty seven head of dead cattle along the road.

— *E. S. McComas, 1862*

Malheur River, Beyond High Ridges (near Vale, Oregon)

Farewell Bend

[August] Friday 19th, Three miles to Snake River, here [on the Malheur] we stopped and grazed, here the river turns to the right, and we bid farewell to Snake River, as we see it no more . . . . [Farewell Bend.]

— David (or John) Dinwiddie, 1853

27th. We remained until noon in camp. This morning we gave an Indian Chief and his son their breakfast. They ate with a degree of refinement which was amusing to me . . . .

. . . . Started early and passed up the creek four miles and then came to a long hill.

Here we passed a man who was lying at the point of death. He had been opening an ox that had died of mortification and had received a portion of the same in a sore on his hand, which mortified and produced sudden death. We were informed that he died a few hours after we left.

— Basil Nelson Longsworth, 1853

Burnt River

[August] 25. We continue our course up Brula or Burnt River 11 miles . . . our trail beeing along the sides of the Mountain and only wide enough for a single animal to pass winding around and along steep presipisses and among the rocks which scarcely permits the foot of man or beast to secure a firme foot hold, while passing along.

— Rev. W. H. Gray, 1838

[Burnt River] . . . . The trail here led down a steep hill. I stopped on the brink and looked down, and asked anxiously, "Have we to go down that awful place?" "Yes," said father, "there is no other way, son." Other drivers said, "Take off three yoke, Eddie." "Well, I must prospect the bottom first," I replied. We had to turn square up stream. The water was deep and swift; I went back and said: "Now I will rough-lock both hind wheels, and then six men stand on it and I will try it." The plan worked finely. At the water's edge

Snake River—Farewell Bend

I turned the leaders up stream, making the short turn all right. The next teamster's wagon upset in the swift water with Mrs. Athey. She was pulled out from underneath the wagon with nothing worse than a soaking.

— *Edward Henry Lenox, 1843*

Only traveled ten miles, over the roughest roads we have yet encountered on the journey, being up and down the sideling mountains, into the brush and across the creek every 200 or 300 yards, and over places enough to hide all despairing sinners. Weather warm and the country possessed of some handsome scenery.

— *John T. Kerns, 1852*

September 10. Came twenty miles today, hard on man and beast. Very warm. Nothing but hills and hollows and rocks. Oh dear, if we were only in the Willamette Valley or wherever we are going, for I am tired of this . . . .

September 11. Traveled eight miles yesterday over very rough stony roads, came to water in four miles, and again in four miles more. The water came up in sight several places and sank again. Began to ascend the Burnt River Mountains, or the Blue Mountains, I don't know which, but one thing I do know, they are very serious hills to come up with.

— *Agnes Stewart, 1853*

[September] Sunday, 14th. We are just four months from home today and four months it has been too of dust, hard work and hard fare....We encamped in the long dreaded Burnt River Canyon near a pile of skulls of a train that were massacreed in '52 here [in the Cayuse War]. After we had come over four hundred miles together to come through this canyon united, our Captain resigned and we are now going it every fellow for himself. I traded my shot gun today for a double barrelled rifle.

— *E. S. McComas, 1862*

Powder River

[September] 26 . . . . Saw to our left mountains clothed with pine and other evergreen timber a few houis brought us to another detested sage plain . . . . the day verry Smokey & I begin to daubt M^r. Espy^s theory of produceeing rain by any phisical means as the whole country has been on fire for a month past & no rain yet . . .

— *James Clyman, 1844*

Burnt River Canyon (Baker County, Oregon)

[August 30] Camped on the Powder creek. This valley is the most handsome that we have seen since leaving Bear river. The valley is several miles wide, covered with a heavy coat of grass.

On the west is a high range of mountains, called the Blue Mountains, which are covered with forests of pine, fir, etc. and the whole country abounds with game, such as bear, deer, prairie chickens, etc., besides numbers of wolves, panthers, etc.

— *John T. Kerns, 1852*

From about this time there began to be organized what was termed "Walkers' train;" that is, young men who had no family connections in the train, would take a small allowance of provisions, a bed quilt or blanket, and push ahead for the end of the journey. The general pretext was to save provisions and leave more for the women and children, but I always doubted the genuine chivalry of the move, but rather deemed it a route in which the consideration of the actors was purely personal. As we reached the Powder river plain one automn afternoon [not far from present-day Baker City], the dark billow of the Blue Mountains rolled athwart our pathway and as we stood gazing at its shadowy but formidable hights, from the lofty roll to the left of the Meacham [Oregon] Station [Lee's Encampment], there shot up to the sky a stately column of smoke; all eyes caught it. I heard some of the women say "Signal Fire." The men said nothing, but looked, first at the dark ascending pillar of smoke, and then at the groups of women and children. What were their thoughts I never knew. At night extra precaution as to surprise was taken, and as provisions were now quite low, an immigrant yearling was slaughtered for food. It was neither rare nor jucy, yet it was an improvement on nothing.

— *George B. Currey, 1853*

Grande Ronde

October 12 — Having nothing to eat [in Grande Ronde valley], we killed an old horse, and as hungry as we were, we did not relish it. We vowed if we killed another we would take a young one. The meat of a good horse tastes like venison.

October 13 — Captain Wyeth took four men and the best horses and started ahead for Walla Walla . . . .

October 14 — . . . Here I noticed in the western horizon something stationary, although it looked like a cloud in the bright sky. It proved (I afterwards found) the grand and snowy Mount Hood. I called the attention of the men to it. This we hailed as a discovery, and the grandest sight we had yet seen.

— *John Ball, 1832*

28th This morn lingered with Husband on the top of the hill that overlooks Grand Round [Grande Ronde], for berries, untill we were some distance behind camp. Have no distressing apprehensions now the moment we are out of sight of camp for we have entirely passed the dangerous country. Always enjoy riding alone with him, especially when we talk about home friends. It is then the tedious hours are sweetly decoyed away . . . .

"The Trappers," by William T. Ranney, c. 1850

Grand Round is indeed a beautiful place. It is a circular plain, surrounded with lofty mountains & has a beautiful stream coursing through it in some places is delightful, & the soil rich, in other places we find the white sand & sage as usual so peculiar to this country. We nooned upon Grand Round River. The Cammas [camas, a bulbous plant with blue flowers] grows here in abundance & it is the principal resort of the Cayouses & many other tribes.... It resembles an onion in shape & color, when cooked is very sweet, tastes like a fig.

Their manner of baking them is very curious. They dig a hole in the ground, throw in a heap of stones, heat them to a red heat cover them with green grass, upon which they put the Cammas & cover the whole with earth, when taken out it is black. This is the chief food of many tribes during winter. After dinner we left the plains & ascended the Blue Mountains.

— Narcissa Prentiss Whitman, 1836

The 28th Sabbath go 14 miles stop to noon at the South West end of the Grand Round [Grande Ronde] this Valley is appropriately named is surrounded on every side with high Mountains to appearance it is about 15 miles in diameter with a beautiful streame running along the East end on eastern side of it and another entering on the South side and running along the Western end Both sides of the circle running through the Mountains out of the Valley on the N. Eastern part of the ring .... The tops of the Mountains around are also covered with beautifull Pines Spruce and the Fir Balsom making truly a Grand Round.

— Rev. W. H. Gray, 1836

We now started for Wallawalla, over hills and rough roads.

8th. We came to Gunpowder River, a small stream.

[9th] ... we staid on a pleasant plain where beautiful springs come down from the spurs of the Blue Mountains. We staid on the Grand Round, a beautiful plain, about twenty miles long and ten broad. It is well calculated for farming, and is well watered.

— Rev. Joseph Williams, 1841

[On the Grande Ronde Falls] ... we were joined by Stickas, the promised pilot, who came holding out a letter from Dr. Whitman to my father. Stickas said, "Camp at the foot of the hill, at the edge of the Grande Ronde River." Stickas had with him his wife and two daughters, and at our evening devotions that night the two girls sang some beautiful hymns, and Stickas himself offered a short prayer. Stickas said, "Prepare your axes for you will need them tomorrow."

— Edward Henry Lenox, 1843

Sunday, October 1 .... Started over the mountains .... Had a beautiful prospect of the Grande Ronde from the top of the mountains. Found [them] covered with evergreen trees which remind me of the scenes of my childhood.

— James Willis Nesmith, 1843

[September] 27th .... As we caught our horses for our aftenoons travel Some Indian as is their habit when they discover Strangers in their country set fire to the grass about a half mile ahiad of us .... when we overtook the fire we had some difficulty in passing it but all got through nearly suffocated with smoke & dust & entered the grand Round vally ....

[September] 28. Concluded to ly still to day and rest ourselves and horses before taking the Blue Mountains....

in this vally are several hudred Indians of the Skyuse [Cayuse] nation now amalgamated with Shehaptin or Pierce nose [Nez Perce] nation 30 or 40 of these people visited us this afternoon & from whoom we traded a little cammerce [camas] thy bringing with them some peas & Squashes of their own raising they seemed to be anxious to see our wagons & cattle they being anxious to trade horses ...

— James Clyman, 1844

The next morning a very dense fog lay over the Grand Ronde. We took to the trail, however, and just as we got to where we started into the Blue Mountains the fog lifted and we found a number of Indians. All of them were men, except one exceedingly handsome girl. She was dressed in buckskin, highly ornamented, and mounted on a proud and beautiful horse. A fine man, past middle age, was her company — father and daughter they appeared .... We took the Mountain trail, which was as bad as Mr. Grant's description, and were soon overtaken by two of the Indians, who had followed to trade me a better horse and get the pistol — which I had fired in compliment to the Indian girl — to boot. They got their bargain, and I got much the worse horse.

We camped that night with the most advanced section of [Richard] Woodcock's company, in a deep valley in the Blue Mountains. The Cayuse chief, Sticcus, and his family are with the first teams of 1844 to cross these mountains. The family conducted worship by singing and prayer in the evening and morning. The singing sounded very sweet in the evening and morning, but it gave me a feeling akin to shame to note that a supposed wild man was the only one who formally recognized God in his daily life.

— John Minto, 1844

We were visited by great numbers of Indians, including men, sqaws, and papooses .... They brought wheat, corn, potatoes, peas, pumpkins, fish, &c which they were anxious to dispose of for clothes, calico, nankins and other articles of wearing apparel . . . some of our party becoming scant of provisions, started for Dr. Whitmans, the missionary establishment on the Walla Walla river. My old friend Aliquot generously proferred his services as pilot for them, which were readly accepted.

. . . The Chief [Aliquot by name — perhaps Cayuse Chief Tiloukaikt] . . . had pitched his tent some three hundred yards to the rear of our camp. In the evening, in strolling about the camp, I came near his tent, and entered with the intention of employing his sqaw in the soling of my moccasins; . . . a conversation had sprung up between the old chief and myself, in which he took occasion to ask me if I were a Christian, as also whether there were many upon the road; to which questions I, of course, answered in the affirmative, supposing that he merely wished to know whether I classed myself with the heathens or Christians. On my return to our camp, some one of our party proposed that we should while away an hour or so, in a game at cards . . . . We had but engaged in our amusement when the old Chief Alequot made his appearence, holding a small stick in his hand; he stood transfixed for a moment, and then advanced to me, raising his hand, which held the stick in the act of chastising me, and gently taking me by the arm, said "Captain — Captain — no good; no good."

You may guess my astonishment, at being thus lectured by a "wild and untutored savage," twenty five hundred miles from a civilized land. I inwardly resolved to abandon card playing forever.

— *Joel Palmer, 1845*

October 12th. Our company separated. Some went to Whitman's Mission to winter. My husband bought beef of the Indians. He traded them a cow and a calf and a new shirt for it.

— *Elizabeth Geer, 1847*

At our first camp in the Grande Ronde Valley [near the town of LaGrande], there came that evening several Cayuse Indians. When they came in sight on their ponies, they displayed a white flag to show that they were friends, but they approached us very slowly. When they came up they made signs of being friendly, and one of them, supposed to be a chief, had a paper with writing on it, which he handed to my father. The Indian supposed it to be a fine report and recommendation. My father being the captain of our company read the paper aloud, which was as follows:

> "Take notice emigrants, you will have to watch this damned Indian. He will steal anything he can get his hands on."

This paper was signed by John Dawson, and caused everyone who heard it to laugh, and the Indians laughed also. The chief had to have the paper back to show someone else how good he was.

— *James D. Miller, 1848*

On the third day from seeing the signal smoke we arrived at the rim of the Grand Ronde valley. Looking down upon this, the most beautiful valley in Oregon, we could see large numbers of Indians riding over the plains.

No choice was left us; friendly or warlike, we had to pass through that valley, and down the hill we started. Reaching the foot we soon learned that the Indians we had seen were a large band of Cayuses and Nez Perces, who, following the custom taught them by Dr. [Marcus] Whitman, had come this far out to meet the immigrants, trade with them and protect them from the Snake Indians. Here for the first time in several months we felt safe . . . .

The smoke which had caused so much apprehension was the Nez Perce signal of aid. It was the firey banner of friendship and succor, sent aloft by these dusky people to proclaim their presence and good will.

— *George B. Currey, 1853*

I wonder if the ground has anything to say? I wonder if the ground is listening to what is said? I wonder if the ground would come alive and what is on it? Though I hear what the ground says. The ground says, It is the Great Spirit that placed me here. The Great Spirit tells me to take care of the Indians, to feed them aright. The Great Spirit appointed the roots to feed the Indians on. The water says the same thing. The Great Spirit directs me, Feed the Indians well. The grass says the same thing, Feed the Indians well. The ground, water and grass say, The Great Spirit has given us our names. We have these names and hold these names. The ground says, The Great Spirit has placed me here to produce all that grows on me, trees and fruit. The same way the ground says, It was from me man was made. The Great Spirit, in placing men on the earth, desired them to take good care of the ground and to do each other no harm.

— *Young Chief, Cayuse, 1855*

Blue Mountains

September 20 — . . . We tried to make the Indians understand that we wanted to go to Walla Walla. That being the only word in common between us, the conversation had to be by signs. An Indian drew a map on the sand; one sign meant river, making a motion of paddling; another the trail, by pointing to a horse.

We understood that we were to keep down the river three sleeps (laying his head on his hand and shutting his eyes three times) thus giving us to understand we were to go by day, and if we whipped up, could cover the ground in two days. There the river went into the mountains, and we were to go over these mountains, and sleep; then another range [Blue Mountains], and sleep; then making a sign of a plain [near Pendleton, Ore.] then two more sleeps, and then Walla Walla. I was quite confident I understood him, if it was by signs. It proved as he said.

— *John Ball, 1832*

29th . . . . Rode over many logs an obstruction that we had not found in our way since we left the states. Here I frequently met old acquaintances, in the trees & flowers & was not a little delighted. Indeed I do not know as I was ever so much affected with any scenery in my life . . . . But this scene was of short duration. Only one day. Before noon we began to descend one of the most terrible mountains [Blue] for steepness & length I have yet seen. I [It] was like winding stairs in its decent & in some places almost perpendicular. We were a long time descending it . . . . Our ride this afternoon exceeded everything we have had yet & what rendered it the more aggravating the path all the way was very stony resembling a newly McAdamized road . . . . While upon this elevation, we had a view of the valley of the Columbia river. It was beautiful. Just as we gained the highest elevation & began to decend, the sun was dipping his disk behind the western horizon. Beyond the valley we could see two distant Mountains Mount Hood & Mount St. Helens. These lofty peaks were of a conical form & separate from each other by a considerable distance.

— *Narcissa Prentiss Whitman, 1836*

From the Grand Round we assended the Blue Mountains our course was S of West and decended into a deep hole for it was down and up again in the midst of a forest of Pine Spruce and Balsom though not like the forrests in the states . . . . the ground is covered with tall grass and weads making the woods beautifull to travel in.

— *Rev. W. H. Gray, 1838*

The timber had to be cut and removed to make way for the wagons. The trees were cut just near enough to the ground to allow the wagons to pass over the stumps and the road through the forest was only cleared out wide enough for a wagon to pass along . . . . The people of this emigration even talked about the possibility of a railroad being built across the plains, and yet there were few of the party that had actual knowledge of what a railroad was . . . .

Oregon Trail Entrance into Blue Mountain Forest (Umatilla County, Oregon)

In passing across the mountains we were overtaken by a snow storm which made the prospect very dismal. I remember wading through mud and snow and suffering from the cold and wet . . . About the stream were quaking asp [aspen] and black haws [Hawthorn]. The fruit of the black haw was in demand, for we had not had any berries for a long time . . . . It was told for a fact that a woman died during the night we stayed there, from the effects of a gorge of black haws. I ate about all I could get my hands on, but experienced no bad results — they were ripe and mellow.

— *Jesse Applegate, 1843*

West Side of Blue Mountains (near Deadman's Gulch, Umatilla County)

29 Sunday Left our camp in the grand Round vally and took up the Blue Mountains which are steep & rough but not so bad as I had anticipated from Previous information . . . the mountain so far is mostly Prairie & fairly covered with g[r]ass . . .

Saw but little sign of any wile animals Except Pheasants which are plenty . . . .

. . . . . the South sides of the ridgis are bare or thinly sit with grass all the rocks & they are plenty shew the effects of fire at some remote period . . . .

Tuesday Oct 1st 1844 A Beautiful morning & fine clear nights I neglected to mention yesterday that this vally was nearly covered with horses when we came down the [west side of the] mountain but no Indians came to our camp . . . . There is no climate finer than this if dry weather constitutes a fine climate & indeed the days remind one of Byrons description of Italy . . . .

. . . we came to a Kyuse farm Krailed [corralled] in with willows and planted with corn beans potatoes &c &c here we left the wagon trail which turns to the right & goes to Dr Whitmans said to be 40 or 50 miles further than the rout we took which goes down the Utilla [Umatilla] . . .

— *James Clyman, 1844*

Umatilla River

[Eastward, July] Friday 24. — We reached the Umatilla River before night opposite which we encamped . . . . This stream takes its rise in the mountains which bound the Columbia Plains to South East & is 80 yds at its mouth & well stocked with furr'd race [beaver].

— *Robert Stuart, 1812*

188

We mooved camp about 6 miles onto the Utilla [Umatilla] River the 30th and lay by all day to wait for the animals to come up. As we were decending the last Mountain I was almost awed into Adoration while looking at the scenery arround me before lay the Plains of Columbia in full view on our right and left was piled in grand and magnificent heights Mountains seperated from us by deep gulfs of 1500 feet deepth . . . . the Mountains on either side seamed to be fluted and were also covered with bunch grass partly dry except in places where the rocks seamed to have been burned in a furnice and broken in piecies and thrown on the sides of the Mountain.

— *Rev. W. H. Gray, 1836*

We are now on the west side of the Blue mountains, crossed them in a day & half . . . . Yesterday & for two or three days past I have felt weak and restless and scarcely able to sit on my horse yesterday in particular. But see how I have been diverted with the scenery & carried out of myself in conversation about home & friends.

— *Narcissa Prentiss Whitman, 1836*

. . . the camp on the Umatella was a very pleasant place . . . the Umatella was a small stream with sandy banks and bottom.

— *Jesse Applegate, 1843*

. . . their was not the amount of one cord of wood & perhaps not a drop of water in the same distance [west of the Umatilla] except what flowed in the Columbia & and other extravagancies.

— *James Clyman, 1844*

[September] Friday 2nd Passed over a ridge of high land, then down the bottom to the crossing of the umatilla, the river has a large channel here but water all stinks, and we crossed on a bed of gravel and pebble stones, for which the stream is famous all along. On the west bank is the United States Agency [named Fort Henrietta, one mile above the town of Echo, Oregon], a very neat looking frame house painted white, it looked cheering, as we had not seen a frame house since we left fort Laramie. There had passed the agency up to this morning of emigrants three thousand six hundred, of wagons seven hundred and eighty, and of stock, ten thousand three hundred. Here we leave the umatilla and strike out on one seeming endless prarie as there is no timber of any kind to be seen in any direction, prarie rolling, soil sand, roads good, plenty of grass . . .

— *David (or John) Dinwiddie, 1853*

Whitman's Mission

. . . we arrived at Fort Walla Walla on October 18, where we found Captain Wyeth, who had been there two or three days.

The fort was built of upright timbers set in the ground. The timbers were some fifteen or eighteen feet high. A small stockade, with stations or bastions at the corners for lookouts. The Hudson Bay Company kept a fort here for the trade. There was a clerk and half a dozen men.

We were received kindly, and for the first time since we left the forks of the Platte on June 1 we tasted bread. It was a very interesting and gratifying sight to look on the Columbia [Fort Walla Walla stands where Walla Walla Creek empties into the Columbia] after our long and tedious journey.

— *John Ball, 1832*

[September 3rd] . . . the pasture here, being good, we allowed our horses an hour's rest to feed at the Walla Walla river, and then traveled on over the plain, until near dark, when on rising a sandy hill, the noble Columbia at once burst upon our view. I could scarcely repress a loud exclamation of delight and pleasure, as I gazed upon the magnificent river, flowing silently and majestically on, and reflected that I had actually crossed the vast American continent and now stood upon a stream that poured its waters directly into the Pacific.

This, then, was the great Oregon [Columbia], the first appearance of which gave Lewis and Clark so many emotions of joy and pleasure, and on this stream our indefatigable countrymen wintered . . . . My reverie was suddenly interrupted by one of the men exclaiming from his position in advance, "there is the fort." [Fort Walla Walla is near present-day Wallula, Ore.]

The next morning we visited Walla-Walla Fort, and were introduced, by Captain W[yeth], to Lieutenant Pierre C. Pambrum [of the Voltigeurs Canadiens], the Superintendent. Wyeth and Mr. Pambrum had met before, and were well acquainted . . . .

The fort . . . stands about a hundred yards, from the river, on the south bank, in a bleak and unprotected situation, surrounded on every side by a great, sandy plain, which supports little vegetation.

— *John K. Townsend, 1834*

Sept 1st off 6¾ Am get to Walla Wallah 9 Am 10 miles The sight of Fort Wallah Wallah was truely gratefull to our eyes to mine at least haveing been five month and 16 days traveling four thousand two hundred miles

"Fort Walla Walla, Washington," by John Mix Stanley, c. 1848

over the most rugged part of our continent. To God belongeth all the praise of our safe arrival Br S [Spalding] came on to W. W. two days after us All safe and Well. Mrs. Spaldings health and strength is improoved beyond all expectation Mrs. Whitman has indured the Journey like a heroine. And shure I am from this esperiment and traveling through the romantic sceneries of the Mountains . . . . We remained at W W Sabbath and Monday receiving the kindest attention from Mr. Pambran the superintendent of the Fort. We concluded it was best for all of us to accompany Mr. P. to Van-Couver As the Nez Persies [Nez Perce] will not meet till about the 15th of Oct and make arrangement for our winter supplies &c . . . . The country just around the Ft is barren and sandy as well as the country along the shores of the Columbia.

— *Rev. W. H. Gray, 1836*

During that whole summer the doctor [Marcus Whitman] was their every-where-present angel of mercy, ministering to the sick, helping the weary, encouraging the wavering, cheering the mothers, mending wagons, setting broken bones, hunting stray oxen, climbing precipices; now on the rear, now in the front, in rivers looking for fords through quicksands, in the desert looking for water, in the mountains looking out passes at noontide or at midnight, as if those people were his own children and those wagons and flocks were his own property.

— *Rev. Henry Harmon Spalding, 1836*

[At Whitman's mission.] When the smoking vegetables, the hissing steak, bread as white as snow, and the newly-churned golden butter graced the breakfast table, and the happy countenances of countrymen and country-women shone around, I could with difficulty believe myself in a country so far from and so unlike my native land in all its features. But during breakfast the pleasant illusion was dispelled by one of the causes which induced it . . . . Our steak was horse-flesh!

— *Thomas J. Farnham, 1839*

[February] There was lately a very serious circumstance took place, with a man named Monger [Asahel Munger], one of the mechanics of the [Whitman] Presbyterian Mission, who considered that he was a great prophet; and said that if he were to burn himself to death, God would raise him up again. To test the truth of what he said, he went into a shop, by himself, where he made a great fire, and then hauled out the coals, and laid down upon them. His wife being in another part of the house, heard him making a great noise, and ran into the room, and found him struggling in the pangs of death. She, with the help of some others, got him out of the fire. He, then saw his dreadful delusion, and prayed to the Lord to forgive him. He lived three days after this, then expired.

— *Rev. Joseph Williams, 1842*

Fri. Feb. 4, 1842 .... We are informed of the death of Mr. Munger. He locked himself in his shop, drove two nails through his hand, & then burnt it to a cinder & nearly roasted himself. His hand was amputated, but he survived only a few days.

— *Mary Richardson Walker, 1842*

At length we arrived at Dr. Whitman's [mission] ... my father found it necessary to get new oxen, ours were so worn out, so we traded our five oxen for two fresh ones ... working our cows to make out a full team.

— *Edward Henry Lenox, 1843*

Friday, October 13th [Dr. Whitman's mission] ... Many of the emigrants here and a few gone on. Most of them are about exchanging their cattle at the fort for cattle at Vancouver, and building canoes to go down the river [Columbia] to Willamette. Some have already built canoes; others have gone down to [Rev. H. K. W.] Perkins Mission [at The Dalles], and intend leaving their cattle till spring, and go down themselves this winter. Little provisions at Whitmans. Some corn at $1.00; potatoes 40¢, beef 6¢ ... some of the packers had robbed the Doctor's house while away.

Sunday, October 15th ... We then determined to sell our animals at the Fort and go down the river in canoes. (the following day) Sold our mules for $12 each, and horses for $10. Many of the emigrants came in to go down the river in canoes, intending to exchange their cattle for others at Vancouver .... Bought a canoe for 1 blanket and 2 shirts; traded it for a larger one and gave a blanket &c to boot, and got things ready to go. Applegate's company sawing boards to build a boat ....

— *John Boardman, 1843*

Worm Fence on Grounds of Whitman Mission

October 23rd . . . I found Dr. Whitman absent on a visit to the Dalles of the Columbia; but had the pleasure to see a fine looking large family of emigrants, men, women, and children, in robust health, all indemnifying themselves for previous scanty fare, in a hearty consumption of potatoes, which are produced here of a remarkably good quality. We were disappointed in our expectations of obtaining corn-meal or flour at this station, the mill belonging to the mission having been lately burn down . . . .

From the South Pass to this place [Walla Walla] is about 1,000 miles; and as it is about the same distance from that place to the Missouri river at the mouth of the Kansas, it may be assumed that 2,000 miles is the necessary land travel in crossing from the United States to the Pacific ocean on this line.

At the time of our arrival, a considerable body of the emigrants under the direction of Mr. [Lindsay] Applegate, a man of considerable resolution and energy, had nearly completed the building of a number of Mackinaw boats, in which they proposed to continue their further voyage down the Columbia.

The other portion of the emigrants had preferred to complete their journey by land along the banks of the Columbia, taking their stock and wagons with them.

— *Brevet-Capt. John C. Frémont, 1843*

At Fort Walla Walla, on the banks of the Columbia river, with our teams about exhausted, we were advised to leave our wagons and animals over winter at that place in the care of Hudson's Bay Co. A portion of the emigrants, including my two brothers' families and my own [family], accepted the proposition, providing we could secure boats in which to descend the river, as it was supposed we might secure them from the Hudson's Bay Co. Under these considerations we made arrangements with the said company for the care of the latter through the winter. We failed in our efforts to obtain boats; having a whipsaw and other tools with us, we hunted logs from the masses of driftwood lodged along the river banks, hewed them out, sawed them into lumber, and built boats, and with our families and the contents of our wagons, commenced the descent of the river. Dr. Whitman procured the service of two Indians to act as pilots to the Dalles.

— *Lindsay Applegate, 1843*

A train of wagons with their once white, now torn, grease and dust stained covers, parked on the bank of the Columbia River, was a novel spectacle . . . . The faithful oxen, now sore-necked, sore footed, and jaded, which had marched week after week, and month after month, drawing those wagons with their loads from the Missouri River to the Columbia, had done their task, and were unhitched for the last time, and I hope, all

recovered from their fatigue and lived to enjoy a long rest on the banks, "where rolls the Oregon and hears no sound save his own dashing [from *Thanatopsis*]".

During the time we remained at Walla Walla, probably two weeks, the men were busy sawing lumber and building small boats. They called them skiffs, and one of average size would carry a family of eight or ten persons. The lumber was sawed by hand with a pit-saw or whip-saw, from timber that had drifted to that place when the river was very high.

To carry out the plan of descending the Columbia River to the Willamette country in those small boats, it was of course necessary to leave the wagons and cattle behind. The cattle and horses were branded with the Hudson Bay Company's brand, "H.B." and the property was understood to be under the protection of that company.

— *Jesse Applegate, 1843*

We reached the [Whitman's] station in the forenoon. For weeks this place had been subject for our talk by day and formed our dreams at night. We expected to see log houses, occupied by Indians and such people as we had seen about the forts. Instead we saw a large white house surrounded with palisades. A short distance from the doctor's [Marcus Whitman's] dwelling was another large adobe house, built by Mr. Gray [Rev. W. H. Gray], but now used by immigrants in the winter, and for a granary in the summer. It was situated near the mill pond, and the grist mill was not far from it.

Between the two houses were the blacksmith shop and the corral . . . . The garden lay between the mill and the house, and a large field was on the opposite side. A good-sized ditch passed in front of the house, connecting with the mill pond, intersecting other ditches all around the farm, for the purpose of irrigating the land. We drove up and halted near this ditch. Captain Shaw was in the house conversing with Mrs. [Narcissa] Whitman . . . .

She [Narcissa Whitman] was a large well formed woman, fair complexioned, with beautiful auburn hair, nose rather large, and large grey eyes. She had on a dark calico dress and gingham sunbonnet. We thought as we shyly looked at her that she was the prettiest woman we had ever seen. She spoke kindly to us as she came up, but like frightened things we ran behind the cart, peeping shyly around at her.

— *Catherine Sager Pringle, 1844*

September 17 . . . . he [Marcus Whitman] related that during his residence in this country, he had been reduced to such necessity for want of food, as to be compelled to slay his horse; stating that within that period, no less than thirty-two horses had been served up at his table.

— *Joel Palmer, 1845*

Two Sisters Peaks, Columbia River and Bluffs (near Wallula, Washington)

Columbia River Bluffs

November 1 . . . . Shoving out from Walla Walla canoe landing . . . our little fleet of boats began the voyage down the great [Columbia,] "River of the West."

. . . I did see some ugly cliffs of rock, black and forbidding in appearance . . . . Neither did the grown-up people seem to be delighted with scenery along the river.

— *Jesse Applegate, 1843*

[October] 4. Had a Quiet nights rest and a Beautifull clear morning Lef our camp on the great river [Columbia River] & proceed down the River passed several Indian villages all on the oposite side nothing seen but rocks [Two Sisters] sand & a shrubby stinted groth of vegetation with here and there Bunch of short grass the north side of the River appears to be closely Bound by a ridge of Black frowning rocks current of the river rapid

The ridge of rocks mentioned in the fore noon closed up on the sauth side in afternoon and gave us an uncommon bad road even in this steril region and we had to travil over sharp rocks or deep sands & sometimes both the rocks being covered deep in sand so that our horses sunk half leg deep in sand & then stepd on unknown sharp rocks at the bottom makeing the way extremely tiresome & bad

— *James Clyman, 1844*

Overland to the Columbia

[After the massacre by Cayuse Indians of Rev. Marcus and Narcissa Prentiss Whitman and other members of the mission in 1847, alarmed emigrants pioneered a new route from the west side of the Blue Mountains to Pendleton, Echo, the Umatilla River, Butter Creek, Ella, Cecil, Willow Creek, the John Day River, and the Deschutes River's entrance into the Columbia River.]

West of the Blues

There are about thirty wagons ahead of us, and the cattle had to be watered out of buckets, a slow process [east of Wells Springs, site in 1847 of a battle with Cayuse Indians].

Saturday September 11 . . . course is nearly due west today [north of Ella, Ore.]. The country is a rolling, dry plain, like that of yesterday . . . see no water and camp [at Cecil]. Here a trading post sells poor flour to-day, and buy more at this high price. A man . . . says he has walked forty-five miles and eaten nothing but a few grains of wheat, without being able to find food anywhere. Another ox is lost to-day, the fourteenth.

— *John Tucker Scott, 1852*

Wed. — Oct. 13. Traveled down three miles to the Indian Agency, the first frame house we have seen since we left the Missouri and they have actually got a stoned-up well. The agent was gone to the Dalles but we left 2 of our wagon's there and sold three cattle to some traders and put all the teams to Stephen's wagon and proceeded. Our loads are light but our cattle are getting powerful weak . . . 70 graves since leaving Fort Boise.

Thur. — Oct. 14 . . . traveled over the same heavy sand about 5 miles more to Alder Creek [Butter]. A sluggish, dirty stream with some willows on its banks . . . . no wood, no water for our cattle.

Frid. — Oct. 15 . . . . Stephen bought an Indian pony and they will take it and go to the Dalles and there meet us. Encamped at a spring of miserable water . . . .

Sat. Oct. 16 Traveled all day over deep sand and dust. Had no water till night.

— *Mrs. C. E. McMillian Adams, 1852*

Sand Hills on Oregon Trail (near Hermiston, Oregon)

Rolling Plains Along John Day River (Gilliam County, Oregon)

Emigrant Trail (West of Ella, Oregon)

Friday [Tuesday] 6th . . . . Traveled over very rolling broken and barren prarie, very little grass, about twelve miles over hilly, but good roads brought us to a valley. Here the water was standing in pools, a heavy rain having fallen recently. Followed down the valley about six miles to the [another] forks of the road, the right hand road leads . . . over the bluffs to John Days River.

[September] Friday 9th Started up a ravine, had a long ascent traveled over very rolling prairie.

— David (or John) Dinwiddie, 1853

The Deschutes River

After making our way through this broken country for three or four days, along this river Deschutes we arrived at a part of it where the banks were not too high to swim our cattle to the other shore, this being the direction of our travel; at this point Indians came to us and said we were within two days travel of the Columbia river, which we rejoiced to hear though not positive of its authenticity; after hearing this our guide [Steven S. Meeks] said we were not more than thirty miles from Waller's Mission, a Methodist establishment [at The Dalles] . . . .

We regarded it unsafe to launch our water tight wagon beds for ferrying ourselves and property across, so resolved upon . . . stretching a rope from bank to bank and suspending a wagon bed beneath to work on rollers. With a rope attached to it from either side of the stream, we were enabled to cross without being exposed to the water.

— Samuel Hancock, 1845

On the evening of the 10th we had opened a road to the top of the [Blue] mountains, which we were to descend to the branch of the De Shutes. The sides of the mountain was covered with a species of laurel bush and so thick, that it was almost impossible to pass through it, and as it was very dry we set it on fire.

. . . . The mouth of the DeShutes is near fifteen miles east of the Dalles . . . . Some of the companies behind us, however, drove over at its mouth by crossing on a bar. Preparatious to ferrying, we unloaded our wagons, and taking them apart, put them aboard some Indian canoes . . . and crossed in safety.

— Joel Palmer, 1845

We arrived at John Day River, which we followed for a distance, camping at a place where we left the river to make a 30 mile drive to the Columbia River. We made this drive and camped . . . about six miles from the Deschutes River. On this last drive or day's journey two of our cattle oxen gave out about 10 miles from the Columbia . . . .

Canyon Near Deschutes River (behind hill, right); Columbia River

The first day's drive from this camp, we got to Tenmile Creek, and camped, and on the following day camped on the Columbia River near where Umatilla House stands in The Dalles .... This was the first house or settler that we found on our route, after leaving Big Blue River, not over 100 miles from Saint Joseph, Missouri, except at ... Forts Laramie, Hall and Boise, all of which had adobe houses occupied by traders.

— *James D. Miller, 1848*

Tuesday 13th Had another hill to ascend from the valley [Deschutes River ford] then had pretty good roads to another creek .... To day dull and smoky ... the country ahead appears to be covered with a dense forest, in the evening got a view of Mount Hood, but was soon obscured by clouds again.

— *David (or John) Dinwiddie, 1853*

Provisions had begun to be scarce, but dried peas and some potatoes were purchased from the Indians, and a small quantity of flour, at fifty cents per pound, was procured from some white traders .... in due time all arrived on the west bank of the DesChutes — some continuing over the Cascade mountains, by the Barlow road, and others passing down the Columbia river, taking the families, wagons and remaining effects in open boats, and driving the cattle along the precipitous banks of the Columbia, and finally all arrived in the Willamette valley, wearied, sunburnt, impoverished and hungry. Winter was fast approaching.

— *George B. Currey, 1853*

The Showy-Phlox (near Cecil, Oregon)

Down the Columbia

I have found the Indian population in the lower country — below the falls of the Columbia, far less than I had expected, or what it was when Lewis and Clarke made their tour. Since the year 1829, probably seven-eighths, if not as Dr. McLoughlin believed, nine-tenths, have been swept away by disease, principally by fever and ague.

The malignancy of this disease may have been increased by predisposing causes, such as intemperance, and the influence of intercourse with sailors ....

This great mortality extended not only from the vicinity of the Cascades to the shores of the Pacific, but far north and south; it is said as far south as California.

The fever and ague were never known in this country before the year of 1829, and Dr. McLoughlin mentioned it as a singular circumstance, that this was the year in which fields were ploughed for the first time. He thought there must have been some connexion between breaking up the soil and the fever.

I informed him that the same fever prevailed in the United States, about the same time, and in places which had not before been subject to the complaint.

— *Rev. Samuel Parker, 1835*

We continued down the Columbia River [from Fort Walla Walla] on a very dangerous road, on the side of the hills, where, if a horse should stumble, he would fall two hundred feet down the river. We traveled through large white sand banks, and passed the falls, where the Indians catch great quantities of fish .... We passed the "Dalles" or Narrows, where the Columbia River is contracted to not more than twenty yards wide. Around this place the Indians are numerous.

Shortly after this we arrived at the Methodist mission, where brother Daniel Lee, brother Perkins, brother Brewer, and their families are stationed .... They were very good to us and supplied us with provisions, free of charge. I was often invited to eat with them, but not to sleep in the house.

— *Rev. Joseph Williams, 1841*

... at Fort Walla Walla we disposed of our animals, procured canoes from the Indians, and having obtained a pilot from them, we cast our frail barks on the waters of the Columbia .... On the first day after leaving the Fort, one of our canoes, in which there were three persons, one of whom was a lady [Mrs. William T. Newby], in passing through a narrow shoot in the Grand Rapids, struck a rock, upset and filled instantly. The lady and her husband succeeded in gaining the rock, which was about three feet across the top, and just

"The Dalls Mission," c. 1849

under the surface of the water. Our pilot succeeded in taking them off in safety, and regained most of the property.

— *Overton Johnson and W. H. Winter, 1843*

Thursday, October 19th. Pleasant. About 12 started [from Fort Walla Walla]; 4 canoes of us, with an Indian pilot. Banks of the river very high, rocky; country sandy. At the falls near the mouth of John's [John Day] River, one of the canoes struck a rock and upset, the lady [Mrs. Newby] and two men clinging to the rocks, and were taken off by the Indian pilot pushing a canoe to them. Some attempted to wade to them but the current too strong; lost some of the things. Friday, October 20th. Pleasant. Drying up their bedding . . .

— *John Boardman, 1843*

Somewhere in this [Cascades] part of the country an effort was made to get a colt for food . . . . We had been without flesh of beast or bird for a long time . . . .

We drew the line, however, at a few of the Waskopum luxuries and dainties, namely, caterpillars, the larvae of yellow jackets and tainted fish eggs.

. . . . Children seated in the boats would enjoy themselves for hours gnawing off the fat coating from the dried salmon skins. An emigrant not hungry was thought to be ill.

— *Jesse Applegate, 1843*

The Dalles to Fort Vancouver

We did well [down the Columbia] till we reached the Dalles, a series of falls and cataracts. Just above the Cascade mountains one of our boats, containing six persons, was caught in one of those terrible whirlpools and upset.

My son, ten years old, my brother Jesse's son, Edward, same age . . . were lost . . . .

Leaving the women and children on shore while we rushed to the rescue, it was only with the greatest effort that we were able to keep our boats from sharing the same fate. William Doake, a young man who could not swim, held on to a feather bed until overtaken and rescued. W. Parker and my son Elisha, then twelve years old . . . rescued themselves by catching hold of a large rock . . . . It was a painful scene beyond description. We dare not go to their assistance without exposing the occupants of the other boats to certain destruction . . . . The whole scene was witnessed by Gen. Fremont and his company of explorers who were camped immediately opposite, and were powerless to render us any assistance. The bodies of the drowned were never recovered.

— *Lindsay Applegate, 1843*

We reached The Dalles, November 1, 1843. Here we hired two Indians with their large Chinook canoe, to take father, mother, and the other seven children in our family, to Oregon City.

— *Edward Henry Lenox, 1843*

Sunday, October 29th. Just five months this day since I left the States, and here [at The Dalles] I am on the banks of the Columbia wind bound, and perhaps occupied just as I would be at home, by cracking nuts . . . .

Monday, 30th October. Clear. Oh! the pleasure of lying by on this river for wind, to feast our eyes on the high peaks and cliffs that adorn the banks of this river on either side. Sublime landscapes, views that a Raphael or Carreggio would have given thousands and endured any fatigue to have seen . . . .

Table: United States to Laramie 680 miles; Laramie to Fort Hall 650; Fort Hall to Boise 259; Fort Boise to Whitmans [Walla Walla] 184; Whitman to Vancouver 220 — 1,993 miles

— John Boardman, 1843

October 20. The next day we moved down the Columbia river and about noon arrived at the Methodist Mission, called The Dalles . . . . We moved about nine miles below and camped and found a great many that we had started with building boats [in the Chenoweth vicinity], or contriving other ways to get down into the Willamette valley . . . . We returned to camp and commenced our flat boat 18 feet by 47 feet long, whip sawing our lumber, etc. We were almost out of provisions . . . we did not finish our boat until about the 11th day of November. We put our cargo aboard, which consisted of 15 families and 18 wagons and luggage. Part of our men drove the cattle down the trail . . . going some of the time up the side of a mountain for four or five hundred feet like stairs, but only wide enough for one ox to walk . . . .

November 26, we again went aboard our boat, and five families that came in last, making in all 20 families. We took aboard a few wagons, boxes with their covers on to shelter against the rain, leaving all our wagons at the Portage. We passed a place called Cape Horn, which is the last perpendicular high spar of the Cascade mountains.

— Rev. Edward Evans Parrish, 1844

[October] Reached Mr [H. K. W.] Perkins missionary station [at The Dalles] in the fore noon now occupid by Mr [Alvan F.] Waller delivered to him a letter taken from the office at west port Mr. Waller apears to be a gentleman but I do not recolect that he thanked me for the care & trouble of bringing the letter but the reverend gentleman must be excused for my appearance certanly did not shew that I could appreceate any civilites not haveing shaved for about 15 day or changed clothes for more than 30 and the Reverend gentleman pricking himself verry much on outward appearances.

. . . if you are scarce of funds you may hire an Indian to guide you over the cascade mountains or as we did guide yourself These mountains are 70 or 80 miles acoss by the way of the Trail verry thickly timber and Extremely steep rocky and rough The columbia on its entrance into the mountains passes through a verry dangerous rapid called the delles whare the river is nearly choked by large masses of sunken rock which raise their black heads in the utmost confusion forming Tremendious whirlpools and are nearly impassable in low water and in fact at all tmes some 50 or 60 miles

Celilo Falls of Columbia River

below is the greate falls which are at all times impassable and whare a portage or two has to be made by all the watercraft passing the river this last fall occurs 80 or 100 miles above vacouver [Fort Vancouver] from this fall the river is clear of obstructions to its mouth for small craft and its navigation would be good for stiam boats Likewise

— *James Clyman, 1844*

After crossing the river we had everything made ready for starting in the direction of Waller's Mission [at The Dalles], which we had reached the following day; here Mr. Waller had wheat, peas and potatoes, which he sold to the half famished emigrants, who were too hungry to cook their food more than half done, before eating it, in consequence of which before morning many of them were very sick, and my most intimate companion on this journey had died from the effects; the others all recovered but I felt the loss of my friend most sensibly.

— *Samuel Hancock, 1845*

September 29. This day we traveled about five miles which brought us to the Dalles, or Methodist Missions.

Here was the end of our road, as no wagons had ever gone below this place. We found some sixty families in waiting for a passage down the river; and . . . but two small boats running to the Cascade falls . . . .

— *Joel Palmer, 1845*

We reached The Dalles, Oregon, on the 14th day of September, 1845, just two days before my seventeenth birthday . . . .

One day shortly after our arrival in The Dalles a man was seen approaching . . . he told us that his wife, and five other mothers had died. The children and the remainder of the party were in camp about a day's travel up the Columbia river. They were dying of starvation . . . .

One woman had died as they were driving down the steep side of a mountain and they dared not stop until the foot of the mountain was reached and the little company in a safe location on account of the Indians . . . . One woman whose death occurred in this party was Mrs. [Rev.] Sam Parker. She left a large family of children . . .

. . . . While here we washed clothing, repacked our goods, and, for the first time in many months, used the flat-irons, thus enjoying a good degree of wholesome comfort.

On Monday, September 20th, a party went out to explore the country, and discover, if possible, any route that could be traversed by wagons across the Cascade mountains. The return of this exploring party convinced us that such an undertaking was utterly impossible, except for the loose stock.

The next plan was to devise some means of conveying the wagons and families down the river, together with the household goods.

Father had lost only one head of stock on the road, and one calf born on the road made the herd just as it was when starting, one hundred head. It would be impossible to take so large a herd down the [Columbia] river so it was decided that father take the family and goods down the river and my husband take the stock over the mountains. The train was now broken into families or groups as the fear of Indians was past. Father chartered two ship yawls that had been towed up the river by the Hudson Bay Company, also three Indian canoes and the Indian owners were hired to assist us in the trip down the river. Our men went to work preparing these for the trip . . . .

My husband and Mrs. Welch's three sons were to drive the stock. After some deliberation it was decided that my brother, Lemuel, should accompany them. That decided my case. I, too, would accompany them . . . . Mother wept but I told them of my fears concerning their frail boats to stem the current of that raging river, for we had seen the Celilo Falls.

— *Sarah Cummins, 1845*

On the day following our departure [October 1] from The Dalles on our perilous journey across the Cascade mountains my father began the work [October 2] of loading all our goods on the improvised boats. The wagons were taken to pieces and loaded a piece at a time first. Then the household goods were placed around our trunks and chests. It has been well said that on such a journey one should take only the bare necessities of life, but in every home there are many treasures . . . . My little chair made of sugar maple wood, a chest of books sent me from Massachusetts when but eight years of age, calicoes bought during the Revolutionary war and paid for at the rate of $75.00 a yard was used to make most of my stock of spare quilts, also many rare bits of needlework . . . and father was careful to see that not one of our keep-sakes was misplaced.

My sheeting, pillow covers, towels and all other household linen was of pure bleached homespun linen and this was all packed in the great walnut-wood sea chest . . . .

These floats were constructed of Indian canoes lashed together. The family and children were placed in the ship yawl, as some of the women were too nervous to attempt riding in the Indian canoes. There was no difficulty in securing the aid of Indian boatmen and on the third day, October 21, 1845, their journey was begun.

. . . . On the third day they reached the Cascades of the Columbia. Here all the goods had to be unloaded and carried around . . . .

After reaching the lower level of the river three ship yawls were found waiting which had been sent by

Beacon Rock, Columbia River (Clark County, Washington)

Doctor McLaughlin from Vancouver to meet any emigrant that might reach that point . . . .

My mother and Mrs. Welch and the children were compelled to walk the five miles or more around the portage. The Indian boatmen assisted the children in this long walk over the rugged ground and before nightfall they were safely around the Cascades.

When the goods and family were safely loaded in the yawls the descent of the lower river was begun and from there on the trip to Fort Vancouver was a delightful pleasure trip. From that point dear father and mother looked with anxious thought and fear toward the snowy summit of old Mount Hood, feeling that their children might even then be forever lost in that wild and dangerous region . . . .

They camped on the sandy beach of the Columbia river at Vancouver for several days while father made a journey by canoe [via Willamette] to Oregon City.

— *Sarah Cummins, 1845*

[Fort Vancouver] . . . enclosed by a sort of wooden wall, made of pickets . . . closely fitted together, twenty feet high, and strongly secured on the inside by buttresses . . . and designed for various purposes — such as [Hudson's Bay Company] offices, apartments for the clerks, and other officers — warehouses for furs, English goods, other commodeties — workshops for different mechanics; carpenters, blacksmiths, coopers, wheelwrights, tinners, &c . . . . There is also a schoolhouse and chapel, and a powder magazine, built of brick and stone.

— *John Dunn, 1845*

Rafting Past Beacon Rock

Columbia River Near the Cascades

October 27. Passed The Dalles Mission where two white families lived with the Indians. It looks like starvation.

October 28. Here are a great many emigrants camped, some making rafts, others going down in boats which have been sent up by speculators.

November 2. We took off our wagon wheels, laid them on the raft, placed the wagon beds on them and started. There are three families of us . . . on twelve logs eighteen inches through and forty feet long. The water runs three inches over our raft.

November 4. Rain all day. Laid by for the water to become calm. We clambered up a steep hillside among the rocks and built a fire and tried to cook and warm ourselves and children, while the wind blew and the waves rolled beneath.

November 7. Put out in rough water. Moved a few miles. The water became so rough that we were forced to land. No one to man the raft but my husband and my oldest boy, sixteen years old . . . . Russell Welch and our youngest boys are driving our cattle over the mountains. Here we are lying, smoking our eyes, burning our clothes and trying to keep warm . . . .

November 8 . . . . We have but one day's provisions ahead of us . . . . Here were some hundreds camped waiting for some boats to come and take them down to Vancouver, Portland or Oregon City.

November 10. Find us still waiting for calm weather. My husband returned at two o'clock. Brought fifty pounds of beef on his back twelve miles . . . . We women and children didn't attempt to get out of the wagons tonight.

November 13. We got the ferryman to shift our load onto their boat and take us down to the falls [Celilo], where we found quite a town of people waiting for their cattle to pull them around the falls. Rain all day.

November 18. My husband is sick. It rains and snows. We start around the falls this morning with our wagons. We have five miles to go. I carry my babe and lead, or rather carry another through snow, mud, and water almost to my knees. It is the worst road a team could possibly travel . . . . My children gave out with cold and fatigue and could not travel, and the boys had to unhitch the oxen and bring them and carry the children on to camp . . . .

Cascade Mountains (Clackamas County, Oregon)

November 20 . . . . I froze or chilled my feet so that I can not wear a shoe, so I have to go around in the cold water in my bare feet.

November 27. Embarked once more on the Columbia on a flatboat. Ran all day, though the waves threatened hard to sink us. Passed Fort Vancouver in the night. Landed a mile below. My husband has never left his bed since he was taken sick.

— *Elizabeth Geer, 1847*

At Cascade falls, our raft arrived one or two days before the stock, as the trail down the river was slow. We found good grass all along our trail. At or below Wind Mountain, [eight miles above Cascade Locks] a few miles above the Cascade falls, we swam our cattle and horses over to the north side of the river and drove them down to or near our camp, close to where our people unloaded from the raft, which had, by the time they arrived there, set very low in the water — so much so that the running gears of the wagons were in the water, the logs getting water-soaked.

We next hitched up our teams and pulled our wagons five miles over the portage. Here, my father contracted . . . to take our wagons and other effects from the lower Cascades to Fort Vancouver in a large bateau, a boat about 40 feet long, 6 feet wide, 3½ feet deep. About all of the traffic on the lower Columbia and Willamette rivers was done by what were then called Hudson's Bay bateaux. One of them would carry 300 or 350 bushels of wheat, or 10 tons weight.

— *James D. Miller, 1848*

Our cattle stampeded [on The Dalles route] when they were yoked up and were being watched by herdsmen. Many ran off in the yoke . . . and once over 400 head were overtaken the next day nearly 40 miles from camp, having travelled this whole distance through alkali plain, without grass or water. We lost so many cattle this way, that many wagons were left in the wilderness. We cut other wagonboxes down to 8 ft. in length, and threw away such articles as we could spare in order to lighten our loads . . . . Some men's hearts died within them, and some of our women sat down by the roadside, a thousand miles from settlements, and cried, saying they had abandoned all hopes of ever reaching the promised land. I saw women with babes but a week old, toiling up mountains in the burning sun, on foot, because our jaded teams were not able to haul them. We went down mountains so steep that we had to let our wagons down with ropes. My wife and I carried our children up muddy mountains in the Cascades, half a mile high, and then carried the loading of our wagons up on our backs by piecemeal, as our cattle were so reduced that they were hardly able to haul up the empty wagon.

— *W. L. Adams, 1848*

206

Barlow Trail

[When Joel Palmer and Samuel Kimborough Barlow (captain of a large company, one that brought part of 3,000 emigrants westward in 1845) arrived at The Dalles on the Columbia River, a long line of wagons was waiting for rafts, canoes, and dugouts to carry the emigrants to Fort Vancouver — the last 100 miles and the most dangerous stretch. There was no road through the Columbia Gorge. The Dalles was the western terminus of wagon trains, and Oregon City and Fort Vancouver could be reached only by water, down the Columbia, until Palmer and Barlow pioneered a trail from the eastern slopes of the Cascade Range, around the south slope of Mount Hood, then west to Oregon City. The Barlow Road opened to emigrants in 1846.]

[September 30] . . . . We then determined to make a trip over the mountains [around the south slopes of Mount Hood] . . . . We finally ascertained that a Mr. [Samuel Kimborough] Barlow and Mr. [H. M.] Nighton had, with the same object, penetrated some twenty or twenty-five miles into the interior, and found it impracticable. Nighton had returned, but Barlow was yet in the mountains endeavoring to force a passage; they had been absent six days, with seven wagons in their train, intending to go as far as they could, and if found to be impracticable, to return and go down the river. We succeeded in persuading fifteen families to accompany us on our trip. On the afternoon of the first of October, . . . we took up our line of march [from The Dalles]; Others in the meantime had joined us, and should we fall in with Barlow, our train would consist of some thirty wagons . . . .

October 3 . . . . Our course led us south over a rolling, grassy plain; portions of the road were very stony. After a travel of . . . [nineteen] miles brought us to Stony Branch, and to scattering yellow pine timber. Here we found Barlow's company of seven wagons. Barlow was absent at the time, having with three others started into the mountain two days before.

— *Joel Palmer, 1845*

Mr. Wm. H. Rector . . . volunteered [October 1] to accompany Mr. [Samuel Kimborough] Barlow and help make the preliminary surveys of the untried route . . . . Armed with an ax, a gun, a few blankets, light provisions, and plenty of resolute will the two pathfinders struck out to strike the first steel blade into the primeval forest of the Cascade Mountains. The remainder of the party [nineteen men and women, "besides children"] was divided into two forces; one, a working party of about ten men and boys, was to cut out the road after the blazers; the other, composed of women and children and two boys to assist, was to follow the road builders . . . .

The east side of the Cascades is but slightly timbered; our teams passed around and under the pine and hemlock trees with ease, but on the west side the trees were thick and the underbrush made every yard or foot even an impassable barrier to our wagons, till ax, saw, or fire demolished or burned the barriers away.

Days and weeks passed and no tidings of the road hunters came. Our men had cut to the head or source of the Little Des Chutes River, close to Mount Hood. The wagons had advanced but twelve miles. We stopped at the long but not very steep hill and waited for the road hunters to return . . . .

. . . a few days after our halt rifle shots heralded the approach of those whom we awaited . . . . "Tallows" were lighted and men, women, and children went with a rush to meet the stalwart pioneers and learn the fate of future movements. Greetings over, the first thing the old gent said was, "Don't give us much to eat; a little coffee must be food and stimulant too." Mr. Rector said: "Speak for yourself, Barlow; I am going to eat whatever my good wife will cook for me . . . ."

In the morning all gathered around to hear the result of the advance expedition. Mr. Rector spoke first and said: "We have found a good route for a road, but it will be a very hazardous journey this time of the year. I dread the possibility of the danger for my wife, so we have concluded to return to The Dalles." Mr. Barlow . . . spoke quickly, "Mr. Rector, you are at liberty to do as you please. If I had any fears of losing any of my company on account of the road, I would not say 'Go' to any of them; but I know we can go on from here and reach the summit of the Cascade . . . . If we can not go on from there we will build a cache for our surplus wagons and baggage and leave two of our trusty young men to guard them. We, ourselves, will follow the trail we have just made, and soon reach the civilization of the Northwest."

It was now late in November. The snow was liable to blockade us at any day, so it was decided to send cattle over the Indian trail at once. [I,] Wm.[,] was to accompany James A. Barlow and John L. Barlow over the mountain as far as the main Sandy road. Here he would procure what supplies he could and return to the hungry men and women in the mountains . . . .

We were two days in going over Mount Hood trail. Leaving the young men on the established road to Foster's, Wm. Barlow returned to camp and assisted in building a safe and snug cache for the goods and a cabin for the men who were to care for all the emigrants' worldly goods that winter . . . . Captain Barlow packed the horses snugly with women, children, and provisions and started over the last and most dangerous part of the route — the coastal side of the Cascades. Then it was that hard times came. Whortleberry swamps confronted us frequently, and many a time all had to wade through them, as the horses mired with the least load upon them. The best time we could make was from three to five miles a day. A snowstorm coming on covered the ground with a foot of snow, leaving nothing for our horses to eat . . . . Mrs. Caplinger and some of the others became much disheartened and bemoaned the fate of "doubly dying" of starvation and cold. Mrs. Gaines, Mr. Barlow's oldest child, laughed at their fears and said, "why, we are in the midst of plenty, — plenty of snow, plenty of wood to melt it, plenty of horse meat, plenty of dog meat if the worst comes." Notwithstanding this courageous spirit it was deemed best to send John M. Bacon and Wm. Barlow on foot into Foster's settlement for more supplies . . . .

We started out with our scanty quota of coffee and four small biscuits. A dull chopping ax was the only tool that could be spared for our purposes. We knew the necessity of haste . . . . We therefore went down Laurel Hill like "shot off of a shovel," and in less time than two hours we had to look back to see the snow. We soon struck the Big Sandy trail and our troubles were over . . . .

In the morning . . . I sang "good-bye" to Bacon, and bounded away to [Philip] Foster's [farm, near Peter Hatch's], eight miles further on, for food and rescue. In three hours I was with my brothers, James and "Dock," and sent them posthaste to Oregon City for men, food, and horses. I remained to rest and recuperate my half-famished condition. The next morning we were ready to retrace our steps and carry the much needed succor. To our surprise we met the emigrants that evening. They had moved steadily on, knowing that the distance was short and that food, raiment, and rest were near at hand. We followed the blazed road and it led us to a safe crossing over the treacherous Sandy. The next day, December 23, 1845, the whole party arrived at Foster's haven. Food was set before us in abundance, but we out heralded Tantalus himself and ate sparingly. The roads were still pretty good, and we felt that there should be no rest for the weary till Oregon City was reached. We accordingly pushed on with most of our party, and arrived at our final destination, Oregon City, December 25, 1845, just eight months and twenty-four days from Fulton County, Illinois.

— *William Barlow, 1845*

On the day of our departure [October 1] I placed my new Spanish saddle that was bought for me in St. Louis, on my strong and trusty young nag, and, with parting tears and good-byes, we dared the wilderness and the desert [via the Barlow Road].

. . . on the second day out from The Dalles [hired man] Marion Poe . . . met a band of straggling Indians. As he attempted to talk to them they deliberately led

Mount Hood, in the Cascades

the pack horse into ambush.... So it was left us to attempt the mountains without food, except beef....

The traveling was slow and toilsome. Heavy fall rains were coming on and the steep [Cascades] slopes were almost impassible for man and beast. On the... [seventh] day we found it impossible to proceed through the dense growth of Mountain Laurel. The cattle ate freely of this shrub and were so poisoned that we dared not eat the meat.

.... Our course seemed to be up a gradual steep slope [of Mount Hood]. As night was coming on it seemed we must all perish, but weak, faint and starving we went on. The stronger men now led the way and left relays to shout back so that we might follow them. My husband and I were the last in the line. The strongest horses had given out before noon and we were compelled to walk and lead our riding nags.... At a few minutes before 10:00 o'clock that night we were walking on firmer ground, the wet snow being about a foot deep. I was so faint and weak that I could scarcely put one foot before the other.... My husband lifted me on the horse but not one step would the poor beast take although I weighed less than eighty pounds at that time .... We were of course the last in line of relays and the welcome sound of "we have found wood," was wafted to our ears. This gave us a renewed energy and by an almost super-human effort we at last reached the assembled group. No sign of a fire was to be seen and most of the men and all the boys were shedding tears. We were told that not a man could be found whose hands had strength to fire a gun, and not a dry thread of clothing for kindling. All were panic stricken and all hope seemed abandoned.

My husband... now made every man present haul off his coat and in the inner lining of Mr. J. Moore's coat a small piece of dry quilted lining was found. This was placed in a handful of whittlings.... With almost super-human effort Mr. Walden succeeded in firing the gun and in an instant the flames burst forth. A great shout of thanksgiving burst forth and each poor suffering traveler crowded as near as possible to the welcome fire.

I was so exhausted and discouraged that I sat down on a hummock and was perfectly indifferent as to the result. But soon as there was sufficient warmth my husband led me to the fire side. No sooner had the warmth penetrated my wet and freezing garments than such excruciating pains seized me that I was wild with pain.... Mr. Walden presented me with a biscuit, one that he had carried since our morning meal, fearing that some such extremity might overtake us. The morsel of food renewed my strength and as the warm woolen blankets were wrapped snugly around me I reclined near the great heap of glowing logs and felt that God in his great mercy would yet guide us safely into the land of our adoption....

.... [Two days later.] My own party had been fourteen days with only nine hardtack biscuits and four small slices of bacon. The Smith boys and all the others in the crowd were also about out of food, and it was decided to make forced marches in the direction of Oregon City....

We kept the stock with us until we reached the grass lands at the head of Sandy river. Each one then decided to go in quest of food as the men were becoming desperate and had lost all fear of wild beasts so that even the sight of a grizzly bear would not have frightened us. Our horses were now so weak that my husband could not ride any one of them only a few rods at a time. My case now developed the last stages of starvation....

We rested until daybreak. The horses had lain all night by the fire and we had great difficulty in getting them up by daybreak.... Husband and I went on as fast as our weary limbs would carry us. Most of the party reached the home of Peter Hatch about 2:00 o'clock on that afternoon. They were given some food and were put to bed....

I now took off my blanket dress and put on my spick and span new dress and corded sunbonnet which I had carried safely on my saddle, and thus arrayed, by my husband's help, I staggered into the door. Mrs. Hatch caught me in her arms and her first words were, "Why my dear woman, I supposed your clothing had been torn off your body long ago."

We were seated by the fire. She bathed our weary limbs, and after we had rested a few moments, seeing our starved, wan look, she apologized for having but one potato baked with salt and a little butter for each. She then entertained us with pleasant conversation and put more potatoes to bake. In less than an hour's time we were served with baked potatoes, meat, butter, and a small slice of bread. We then retired for the night.

We awoke early with ravenous appetites. Mrs. Hatch was aware of this, and, knowing the danger of our condition had wisely stinted our meals. Our breakfast was more substantial. They had beef of excellent quality and on this day we were given four meals, and each one recovered from this nineteen days of want with no serious after effects.

My husband and the others were equally blest but they did not rest contentedly.... and returned to the stock and were blest in finding every one of the animals in better condition and grazing in a friendly herd, horses, oxen and stock cattle. Not a hoof was missing and within a week's time we were surprised to see them all brought safely to the end of our journey.

— *Sarah Cummins, 1845*

The failure of Dr. [Elijah] White's enterprise [searching for a new emigrant trace on the upper reaches of Santiam River, without finding a suitable pass] left the large emigration of 1845, to find their way into the

Willamette Valley by usual means; . . . the supply of boats being wholly inadequate to their speedy conveyance down the Columbia, and the stock of provisions failing at the Dalles, famine, and a malignant disease at the same time raging amongst them, a sense of human misery ensued which scarcely has a parallel in history — the loss of life and property was enormous.

— The Oregon Spectator, Feb. 4, 1847

Sept. 2nd. We started as early as usual and traveled eight miles to Laurel Hill. The road on this hill is something terrible. It is worn down into the soil from five to seven feet, leaving steep banks on both sides, and so narrow that it is almost impossible to walk alongside of the cattle for any distance without leaning against the oxen. The emigrants cut down a small tree about ten inches in diameter and about forty feet long, and the more limbs it has on it, so much the better. This tree they fasten to the rear axle with chains or ropes, top end foremost. This makes an excellent brake for the wagon, especially in going down such hills as this one.

[September 14] After lunch we traveled 2 miles to Tygh Valley. Here is quite a good sized Indian village —— some few whites among them. We crossed the creek in Tyghe valley and ascended a long and very steep hill, one mile to the summit.

— Enoch W. Conyers, 1852

About noon of the tenth day, after leaving the Dalles, we began to see, through the timber, on ahead a vision of an open valley. Peering out, I saw that it was sprinkled over with spreading oaks, while it seemed to be surrounded by a fringe of evergreens reaching up onto those mountains, and on into the blue sky above, I thought, "Yes, this is the Oregon I have been hoping to get to." . . . . Soon we found our way to Howell's Prairie, not far from Salem. We landed there October the 16th, having been on our way over six long months.

— Adriette Applegate Hixon, 1853

Barlow Road; Last Descent East of Mount Hood

Oxen and Children, Oregon Woods

Willamette Valley

I will now tell you something of the people of this country. There are [February 19] about seventy-five to eighty French Canadians settled in this country, principally discharged from the service of the Hudson Bay Company; there are also about fifty Americans settled in and about this country, making, perhaps, one hundred and twenty-five to one hundred and thirty male inhabitants, who are married to Indian women . . . .

We have now a committee at work drafting a constitution and code of laws; have in nomination a governor, an attorney-general, three justices of the peace, etc.; overseers of the poor, road commissioners, etc. We have already chosen a supreme judge with probate powers, a clerk of the court and recorder, a high sheriff, and three constables: so that you see we are in a fair way of starting a rival republic on this side of the mountains, especially as we are constantly receiving recruits . . . .

— Peter H. Burnett, 1842

[October] Distance from Independence to Willamette Falls according to my estimate 1746 miles. Laramy 553 miles; Fort Hall 1107; Walla Walla 1552; Perkins [Mission at The Dalles] 1656; W. [Willamette] Falls 1746.

— Medorem Crawford, 1842

After father had looked about for some three weeks, going as far as the mouth of the Columbia River, with a small company of his fellows, he decided to settle about twenty-two miles out from Oregon City, on the Tualitin plains. He bought a house from two brothers by the name of Kelsey, trading his [three] mules for it . . . .

The fields were not fenced at all, and so father and I went to work making rails and fencing the fields.

— Edward Henry Lenox, 1843

We arrived at Oregon City [it was laid out in 1842] situated at the Falls of the Willamette, the place of our destination. This was the 13th of November, 1843, and it was five months and nineteen days after we left Independence, in Missouri. Here we were able to procure such things as were really necessary to make us comfortable . . . and were happy, after a long and tedious tour, over mountains and deserts, through a wild and savage wilderness, to witness, . . . the home of civilization, to see houses, farms, mills, storehouses, shops, to hear the busy hum of industry, the noise of the workman's hammer, the sound of the woodman's axe, the crash of the falling pines, and to enjoy the warm welcome of country men and friends . . . .

Land of Milk and Honey

Those who intended to cultivate the soil, laid claims, built cabins, and prepared for the coming winter . . . . All found enough to do . . . . Every one seemed satisfied for a time with being permitted to have a home and a plentiful subsistence.

— Overton Johnson and W. H. Winter, 1843

. . . after seven months of tedious traveling, arrived at Willamet Fall, on a branch of the Columbia River. My road lay through a SAVAGE country, a distance of Twenty-three hundred miles, which you are aware makes it necessary to travel in caravans.

I set out from Independence, Jackson County, Missouri, which is the general place of rendezvous for emigrants to this country; April 25th, 1843; in a company of One Thousand; three hundred of which were able men; the remainder were women and children. There was one hundred & twenty wagons, drawn by oxen or mules chiefly oxen of about three yoke to each wagon; they performed the journey admirably, I was myself equipped with two yoke of cattle, to haul my provisions; two Horses & one Mule, to ride by turn, & though my horses and mule were of the best quality, they were not sufficient to carry me the whole distance. We traveled in some confusion, 'till we arrived at Con [Kaw or Kansas] River, a distance of about ninety miles from the Missouri line; We there found it necessary to have some order in traveling, for which purpose we elected Officers, & came under a sort of military discipline, & thus marched very pleasantly through a fertile country, until we arrived at Blue River, a branch of the Con. Here we found our stock was too large to get sufficient sustenance from one campground, therefore we concluded to sepparte & form two divisions, & march a few miles apart. I had the honor of being second in command, of the division in which I traveled.

We struck Big Platte River about 300 miles from the Missouri lines . . . . The whole distance from the Platte River, to the east base of the Blue Mountains Oregon), is entirely unfit for the residence of civilized man, and is inhabited only by wandering tribes of hostile Indians . . . . Just say for me to the young men of old Milton, Don't live & die in sight of your Father's house, but take a trip to Oregon! you can perform the journey . . . . & I am sure you will never regret spending the time.

But, if they should come to settle here, I would advise them to bring a wife along, as ladies are (like the specie) very scarce. And if you have any maiden ladies about dying in despair, just fit up their teeth well, & send them to Oregon.

— *Tallmadge B. Wood, 1844*

I say the man is alive, full grown, and is listening to what I say (without believing), who will yet see the Asiatic commerce traversing the North Pacific Ocean — entering the Oregon River — climbing the western slope of the Rocky Mountains — issuing from its gorges — and spreading its fertilizing streams over our wide-extended Union! The steamboat and the steam-car have not exhausted all their wonders. They have not even yet found their amplest and most appropriate theatres — the tranquill surface of the North Pacific Ocean, and the vast inclined plains which spread east and west from the base of the Rocky Mountains. The magic boat and the flying car are not yet seen upon this ocean and this plain, but they will be seen there; and St. Louis is yet to find herself as near to Canton as she now is to London, with a better and safer route, by land and sea, to China and Japan, than she now has to France and Great Britain.

— *Senator Thomas Hart Benton, 1844*

But we got a hundred and fifty dollars for what oxen we had to sell. Of course, it was all in Oregon currency, which were orders on any of the stores in Oregon City.

— *William Barlow, 1845*

[January] 15 . . . . I now witnessed the catching and branding of a lot of wild cattle about 500 ware drove in to a strong pound and 4 or 5 men well mounted rode in to the pound the animal to be taken being pointed out some one went full speed amongst the herd and threw a rope with a almost dead certainty a round the horns or neck of the animal the cord being made fast to his saddle Bow he stoped his horse and checked the speed of the animal and if his horse was not sufficiantly strong 3, 4 or 5 other men threw their cords on the animal then putting spurs to their horses they draged him out of the pound by main force and hampering his legs with cords they threw him then Butchered or branded him as the case might be

[April] 5 . . . about 9 oclock arived at champoeg here a village is laid out but nothing doing in the way of improvement this place is a dry sandy level a few feet above high water [of Willamette River] and is Twenty five miles above the falls a settlement of about Two Hunded familes of Half breeds and canadian French reside in the vicinity stoped with Mr. Newel [Robert Newell] the proprietor who has been one of the Rocky Mountan trappers and . . . has had the honor of being one of the members of the provisional Legislature for the past year

— *James Clyman, 1845*

Willamet Falls, Oregon, October 27, 1844

I arrived here on the 13th day of the present month, having been on the way 151 days from Independence, Missouri, which was at least one month longer than were the last year's company of emigrants. This was

Fort Vancouver

Champoeg Park, at the Willamette River

owing to the unusual rains that fell during the first two months after our departure from Missouri.

. . . . Even the last year's emigrants, some of whom have not been more than 9 or 10 months on their new farms, have plenty for themselves, and some to spare for their countrymen now on the way. Of bread, beef, fish, and potatoes of a superior kind, we have plenty.

. . . . Standing in the door of my present lodgings I can count sixty-two buildings. They form the present village of the city of Oregon. Timber and lumber lay scattered about for more buildings, say 8 or 10. Several other villages, one or two of them I have seen have some pretensions to future greatness, but are quite small as yet.

— *James Clyman*
Milwaukee Courier, August 13, 1845

This valley of the Willamette certainly presents strong inducements to the emigrants . . . . The valley is perhaps two hundred miles long, and forty wide, with very little exceptionable land within its limits, being abundantly timbered and water so all were soon comfortably settled, the land producing all necessary vegetables, while venison could be procured easily and in abundance, and those who had cattle were constantly increasing their stock.

— *Samuel Hancock, 1845*

After two months work [for Dr. McLoughlin at his saw-mill on the Taualatin River] we learned that we were to receive nothing for our work that fall and we returned to Oregon City where we learned that father, mother, and all our friends with whom we had parted at The Dalles, were safely established in good houses at the foundry works on the Willamette river. Father came right up to see us and took the stock home with him. Mr. Walden rented rooms in Oregon City and we remained there all winter . . . .

The environs of our new home, surrounded by giant fir trees, the healthful sea breezes, the strange sights and sounds were sources of continual thought. The long distance that separated us from our old home in the Mississippi valley, precluded any form of home sickness and our united efforts were wholly set upon the building of a home.

— *Sarah Cummins, 1845*

[Oregon City, Sept. 3] — Some of the Oregon emigrants of 1846, arrived at Oregon City on the 25th of August — also a naval officer, (Lieut. Woodworth, who is connected with the U. S. Navy,) crossed over the Rocky Mountains . . . . He declares that one newspaper left by accident at Fort Hall, contained the news of the final passage of the bill through the Senate, giving Great Britain the required year's notice of the termination of

Oregon City

the joint occupancy of Oregon .... our doubts are now sufficiently expelled to convince us that the 49th degree of parallel will be the definite line ultimately agreed upon both by Great Britain and the United States ....

.... Some fifteen or sixteen emigrants have arrived, having performed the last part of their journey with pack-horses. They state that between 300 and 400 waggons must be near the Dalls at this time, and nothing extraordinary preventing, they will probably arrive at Oregon City about the 25th instant. Mr. Barlow has gone to meet them in order to conduct them safely over his road. They state that between 500 and 600 waggons that were bound to Oregon and California were counted after leaving the states .... It is reported that one family in this company is bringing a hive and swarm of bees to Oregon.

— *Oregon Spectator, 1846*

[Oregon City, Sept. 17] — Emigrants. — Several families with their wagons have arrived in our City, and appear healthy and cheerful. They traveled over Mr. Barlow's road, over which probably most of the emigration will come.

— *Oregon Spectator, 1846*

[Oregon City, Oct. 1] — The public mind has been happily put at rest, in relation to the welfare of Captain Jesse Applegate and party, by the arrival of intelligence, at Fort Vancouver, recently, to the effect, that he had succeeded in discovering a most admirable road for the emigration — one much more direct.

— *Oregon Spectator, 1846*

[Oregon City, Oct. 29] — Mr. Editor. — Sir, by your request, I herewith send you the number of wagons and stock that passed the toll-gate on the Mount Hood road. There were one hundred and forty-five wagons, fifteen hundred and fifty-nine head of horses, mules, and horned cattle all together, and one lot of sheep, the number not recollected, but I think thirteen. Yours, &c.

— *Saml. K. Barlow, Oregon Spectator, 1846*

With three comrades, I left the emigration on the Umatilla river ... and after a variety of adventures ... we arrived in a canoe at Fort Vancouver on the evening of the 23rd of October, 1843. We encamped on the bank of the river about where the government wharf now

216

stands. The greater part of our slender means were expended in the purchase of provisions and hickory shirts, consigning those that had done such long and continuous service, with their inhabitants, to the Columbia. On the morning of the 24th, we started for what was known as the "Willamette" settlement at the Falls . . . .

In 1843, the only settler on the river below the Falls, was an old English sailor by the name of William Johnson . . . . He was a fine specimen of the British tar, and had at an early day abandoned his allegiance to the British lion and taken service on the old frigate Constitution. I have frequently listened to his narrative of the action between Old Ironsides and the Guerriere, on which occasion he served with the boarding party . . . .

. . . the immigration of 1843 arrived safely in the valley during the fall and early part of the winter, and found homes in the then settled neighborhoods. Dr. John McLoughlin, then at the head of the Hudson Bay Company, from his own private resources, rendered the new settlers much valuable aid by furnishing the destitute with food, clothing and seed, waiting for his pay until they had a surplus to dispose of. Dr. John McLoughlin was a public benefactor . . . .

. . . my wife and self . . . [had a] palatial residence, which consisted of a pole cabin fourteen feet square, the interstices between the poles, puncheon floor and a mud chimney, and not a pane of glass or particle of sawed lumber about the institution . . . .

In the year 1843, Fremont, then a Lieutenant in the Engineer Corps, did cross the plains, and brought his party to the Dalles, and visited Vancouver to procure supplies. I saw him on the plains, though he reached the Dalles in the rear of our emigration. His outfit contained all of the conveniences and luxuries that a Government appropriation could procure, while he "roughed it" in a covered carriage, surrounded by servants paid from the public purse. He returned to the States and was afterward rewarded with a Presidential nomination as the "Pathfinder." The path he found was made by the hardy frontiersmen who preceded him to the Pacific . . . .

["Uncle" Jesse Applegate] . . . . I traveled in his company across the plains . . . was at the rendezvous at Fitzhugh's Mill on the 17th day of May, 1843 . . . .

He was the leader in forming our Provisional Government in 1845, as he was of the party of 1846 that escorted the first immigration by the Southern route—an unselfish service in which he periled his life to ruin himself pecuniarily.

— *James Willis Nesmith, 1847*

Emigrant Cabin (Aurora Colony), Willamette Valley, Oregon

Doctor John McLoughlin of Vancouver employed my father to go to Champoeg to repair a grist mill there. He furnished father a bateau with eight Indian oarsmen . . . . We landed near the old Indian landing near where the monument to the provisional government now stands. We stayed there that winter while father worked on the mill. The winter of 1846 was one of the coldest that the oldest settlers of Oregon could remember . . . .

My father's donation land claim [in 1847 near Hubbard] on the Pudding river bottom had forty acres of fine timber on it. We split our cedar timbers for both Ford's and Kiser's houses. We got $10 per thousand for the cedar shingles. People came from all over Mission Bottom and French Prairie to buy shingles of us.

— *Benjamin Franklin Bonney, 1847*

Cabin Kitchen (Aurora Colony)

"Love One Another," Framed Motto (Aurora Colony)

My Dear Sir [James M. Hughes]:
By the late emigrants I received your welcome letter, written last spring [from Liberty, Missouri].

The emigration of last year [1846] have all arrived with the exception of some five families now at Dr. Whitman's, and about the same number at Fort Umqua. . . . That emigration was not so large as the one of the previous year. The emigrants came in by two new routes, one across the Cascade mountains near the Columbia river, and the other a southern route entering the Wallmette valley near the sources of that River, and crossing the head waters of the Sacramento in California, and the Umqua and Klamet rivers in Oregon. Mr. Barlow obtained from the Oregon Legislature a charter for the opening of a wagon road across the Cascade mountains to the Wallamette valley, and allow him to charge certain amounts of toll as a compensation for the labor incurred. This road was in readiness when the first portion of the emigrants arrived, and those who came the old accustomed route by Fort Baise, the Grand Round and the Blue mountains came through Barlow's road, with their wagons, teams, families and loose stock to the Wallamette Falls before the rainy season sets in. Some of these arrived as early at the 15th September . . . .

The southern route was surveyed by Messrs. Jessee Applegate, Moses Harris and others . . . . These gentlemen left the Wallamette Settlements in the latter part of last summer, and reached Fort Hall after the larger portion of the late emigrants had passed. Those they met at that place agreed to try this new route with their wagons, teams and cattle. They continued the old route for the distance of about 40 miles this side of the Fort, when they turned to the left, fell upon Mary's river which they travelled down some three hundred miles over an excellent road. This route passes thro' a portion of California, crosses the head waters of the Sacramento, then falls upon the waters of the Klamet and Umqua rivers.

— *Peter H. Burnett, 1847*

An imigrant will come in during the Autumn, put himself up a log house with a mud & stick chimney, split boards & shingles, break eight or ten or twenty acres of prairie and sow it with wheat. You call upon him the next year & he will have a fine field ripe for the sickle. His large field will be well fenced with newly split fir rails. There will be a patch of corn, another of potatoes, & another of garden vegetables. Outside a large piece will be broken for the present year's sowing. His cattle & horse & hogs will be on the prairie, thriving and increasing without care. A few sheep may be around the house. He has a spring near . . . . The farmer wears buckskin pants. His family has few cooking utensils, few chairs. No additions since they came into the Territory.

— *Rev. George H. Atkinson, 1847*

Mother was at first in despair — no money, nothing to sell, and Oregon City sixteen miles away through an unbroken wilderness . . . . There stood the ever-ready ash hopper [stove] without which no family was equipped for living. They were soon at work leaching the ashes for lye, and the soap kettle was boiling. Each had a bucket of soap, and in the early morning they mounted their horses and holding their bucket of soap in front of them, were off for Oregon City to exchange it for at least Mother's first Oregon dress.

— *Mary Osborn Douthit, 1847*

Fiddle and Jug

November 30. [Portland] Raining. This morning I ran about trying to get a house to get into with my sick husband. At last I found a small, leaky concern with two families already in it . . . you could have stirred us with a stick . . . . My children and I carried up a bed. The distance was nearly a quarter of a mile. Made it down on the floor in the mud. I got some men to carry my husband up through the rain and lay him on it and he was never out of that shed until he was carried out in his coffin. Here lay five of us bedfast at one time and we had no money and what few things we had left that would bring money I had to sell. I had to give ten cents a pound for fresh pork, seventy-five cents a bushel for potatoes and four cents a pound for fish. There are so many of us sick that I can not write any more . . . .

January 15, 1848. My husband is still alive, but very sick. There is no medicine here except at Fort Vancouver, and the people there will not sell one bit — not even a bottle of wine.

January 16. We are still living in the old leaky shed in Portland. It is six miles below Vancouver and up the Willamette twelve miles. Portland has two white houses and one brick and three wood-colored frame buildings and a few log cabins.

January 20. Cool and dry. Soldiers are collecting here from every part of Oregon to go and fight the Indians in middle Oregon in consequence of the massacre at Whitman's mission. There were seventeen men killed at the massacre, but no women or children except Whitman's wife. They killed every white man there except one, and he was an Englishman. They took the young women for wives . . . .

Rifles at Rest

Apple Tree Planted by Hudson's Bay Company (near Aurora, Oregon)

January 31. Rain all day. If I could tell you how we suffer you would not believe it. Our house, or rather a shed joined to a house, leaks all over. The roof descends in such a manner that the rain runs right down into the fire. I have dipped as much as six pails of water off our dirt hearth in one night. Here I sit up night after night with my poor sick husband, all alone, and expecting him every day to die . . . . I have not undressed to lie down for six weeks. Besides our sickness I had a cross little babe to care of. Indeed, I cannot tell you half.

February 1. Rain all day. This day my dear husband, my last remaining friend, died.

February 2. Today we buried my earthly companion. Now I know what none but widows know: that is, how comfortless is a widow's life; especially when left in a strange land without money or friends, and the care of seven children.

— *Elizabeth Geer, 1848*

At Vancouver, we swam our cattle over to the south bank of the Columbia. After crossing all of the stock over, we then hitched up our teams and drove sixteen miles, arriving at Oregon City, the capital of the provisional government of the Territory of Oregon. We arrived here the first week in November, making our trip from Saint Joseph, Missouri, to Oregon City, Oregon, in about six months.

On our arrival at Oregon City, I found everything quite different from what I had expected . . . . Oregon City contained a population of 350 to 400 whites, possibly 500, including halfbreeds and Indians. There were three small churches, Methodist, Congregational and Catholic. The Baptists held their meetings in a school house. There were three stores, a large one of the Hudson's Bay Company . . . . There were also one or two blacksmith shops, a wagon shop, one meat market, possibly one saloon, two flour mills, two sawmills and one weekly newspaper, Oregon Spectator . . . .

My father purchased a house and lot in Linn City, opposite Oregon City, and we moved into it soon after we arrived, and commenced the sale of our boots and shoes, Kentucky jeans and cloth that we brought with us. For fine boots, we got $5 per pair, shoes for men, women and children in proportion. If we had held them for six months, they would have brought us double . . .

Father traded our mules and horses for one acre of land in Clackamas City, a city on paper adjoining the Oregon City town plat . . . . The provisional government had passed a law that every male citizen was entitled to a donation of 640 acres of land.

— *James D. Miller, 1848*

220

The first Oregon Missionaries, Jason and David Lee, with seventy men, journeyed to the Northwest in 1834; and the Rev. Samuel Parker and party went in 1835, accompanied part way by Dr. Marcus Whitman.

In 1836 Dr. Whitman, Dr. H. H. Spalding, and their wives, made the overland journey with a wagon.

Dr. Wm. H. Gray and party went in 1838, Thomas J. Farnam in 1839, Dr. Elijah White and Medorem Crawford in 1842, and other parties at other dates, making the average annual emigration to both Oregon and California probably less than a hundred persons.

In the winter of 1842–3, Dr. Whitman made his celebrated trip, largely on horseback, from Oregon to Washington, D. C., . . . and is credited with stimulating Oregon emigration considerably, the emigrants that year, 1843, numbering about a thousand, mostly families.

Thereafter the yearly cavalcade increased steadily to about 4500 in 1847.

. . . . The highest up [mission] is the Catholic mission, on the Columbia River. Mr. de Smidt [DeSmet], and two other priests, are stationed there. They have baptized a great many; six hundred the first winter . . . .

In this station [Jason Lee's, on the Willamette] . . . French farmers and French Catholics accuse them of being too unfriendly to strangers, and the poor. Brother Babcock told me they were willing to receive me as a man, but not as a preacher, because I had not a recent recommendation from the presiding elder. Truly, I did not look much like a preacher; for after traveling three thousand miles, my old linsey coat looked very shabby. But many of the people about there said, if I had worn as fine a coat as Dr. Babcock, I would have been very well received.

— *Rev. Joseph Williams, 1848*

When we, the American emigrants, came into what the Indians claimed as their own country [Oregon], we were considerable in numbers, and we came, not to establish trade with the Indians, but to take and settle the country exclusively for ourselves. Consequently, we went anywhere we pleased, settled down without any treaty or consultation with the Indians, and occupied our claims without their consent and without compensation . . . . Every succeeding fall they found the white population about doubled, and our settlements continually extending, and rapidly encroaching more and more upon their pasture and camas grounds . . . . They instinctively saw annihilation before them.

— *Peter H. Burnett, 1848*

The rest of our party continued on down to the Willamette Valley and reached Oregon City on June 16, 1854. My father, who was a cooper and millwright, got a job coopering for a Mr. Fellows, while my mother secured work from Governor [George] Abernethy . . . .

A large proportion of this [emigrant] outfit has been consumed by the disastrous journey, and the well-to-do thrifty looking citizen and his family have been worn by the friction of the trip to a tattered band of hungry petitioners — begging his brothers of the earth to give him leave to toil. But if the old home and early life's earnings were consumed by the desert, there was one thing that was not diminished . . . our appetites.

An immigrant's appetite — who can forget or describe it? It was illimitable in its voracity, and then seemed eternal in its cravings . . . . It would attack anything from dried salmon to boiled wheat, and get away with it. It prescribed but one condition to the cook —

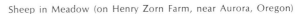

Sheep in Meadow (on Henry Zorn Farm, near Aurora, Oregon)

plenty. The only word it learned from the courtly jargon was muck-a-muck. Hi-yu-muck-a-muck [was] the la-la-ly to which we went to sleep to dream of pots of flesh and kettles of potatoes.

When we reached Oregon in the fall of 1853 a population of something near 40,000 whites had settled in the Willamette, Umpqua and Rogue River valleys. Society was organized socially and politically. A large portion of the people were residing on their donation claims, but there were several towns. Oregon City was just about to become the Lowell of the Pacific. She was soon going to harness the Willamette falls and set up spinning for all creation. Portland had metropolitan dreams, and soon hoped to dictate terms of per cent and profit to the rest of the country. Champoeg was hilarious with hope.

— George B. Currey, 1854

My people are few. They resemble the scattering trees of a storm-swept plain . . . . There was a time when our people covered the land as the waves of a wind-ruffled sea cover its shell-paved floor, but that time long since passed away with the greatness of tribes that are now but a mournful memory . . . .

To us the ashes of our ancestors are sacred and their resting place is hallowed ground. You wander far from the graves of your ancestors and seemingly without regret. Your religion was written on tables of stone by the iron finger of your God so that you could not forget. The Red Man could never comprehend nor remember it. Our religion is the traditions of our ancestors — the dreams of our old men, given them in the solemn hours of night by the Great Spirit; and the visions of our sachems, and is written in the hearts of our people.

Your dead cease to love you and the land of their nativity as soon as they pass the portals of the tomb and wander away beyond the stars. They are soon forgotten and never return. Our dead never forget the beautiful world that gave them being.

Day and night cannot dwell together. The Red Man has ever fled the approach of the White Man, as the morning mist flees before the morning sun . . . .

When the last Red Man shall have perished, and the memory of my tribe shall have become a myth among the white man, these shores will swarm with the invisible dead of my tribe, and when your childrens' children think themselves alone in the field, the store, the shop, or in the silence of the pathless woods, they will not be alone . . . . At night when the streets of your cities and villages are silent and you think them deserted, they will throng with the returning hosts that once filled them and still love this beautiful land. The White Man will never be alone.

Let him be just and deal kindly with my people, for the dead are not powerless. Dead — I say? There is no death. Only a change of worlds.

— Chief Seathl [Sealth], Dwamish, 1855

Grave of Eugenie Mathiot (near Canby, Oregon)

Bibliography

Diaries, Journals, Reminiscenses

Anderson, William M. *Anderson's Narrative of a Ride to the Rocky Mountains.* Edited by A. J. Partoll. Historical Reprints, Sources of Northwest History, No. 27. Montana State University. 1938. Anderson, William M. *The Rocky Mountain Journals of William Marshall Anderson.* Edited by D. L. Morgan and E. T. Harris. 1967. Applegate, Jesse A. *A Day with the Cow Column in 1843.* Edited by J. Schafer. 1934. Applegate, Lindsay. "Notes and Reminiscences of Laying Out and Establishing the Old Emigrant Road into Southern Oregon in the Year 1846," *Oregon Historical Quarterly* 22 (1921): 12-45. Bagley, Clarence B. "Chief Seattle and Angeline," *Washington Historical Quarterly* 22 (1931): 243-75. Ball, John. "Across the Continent Seventy Years Ago," *Oregon Historical Quarterly* 3 (1902): 82-101. Boardman, J. "The Journal of John Boardman. An Overland Journey from Kansas to Oregon in 1843," *Utah Historical Quarterly* 2 (1929): 99-121. Burnett, Peter H. *Recollections & Opinions of an Old Pioneer.* 1880. Burton, Richard F. *City of the Saints.* 1862. Carpenter, Helen M. *Overland Journey.* Entry for June 23rd. (Newberry Microfilm 4-7). Compiled by M. J. Mattes—1945; transcribed by L. Ridge—2-46. Clyman, J. *James Clyman, American Frontiersman, 1792-1881.* Edited by C. L. Camp. 1928. Cummins, Sarah. *Autobiography and Reminiscences.* 1914. Dale, Harrison C., ed. *The Ashley-Smith Explorations and the Discovery of a Central Route to the Pacific 1822-1829.* 1918. DeSmet, Fr. Pierre-Jean. *Life, Letters and Travels,* 4 vols. Edited by H. M. Chittenden. 1905. Dinwiddie, David (or John). *Journal of 1853.* Historical Reprints, Sources of Northwest History, No. 1. Montana State University. Dougherty, L. B. "Experiences of Lewis Bissell Dougherty on the Oregon Trail," edited by E. M. Withers, *Missouri Historical Review* 24 (1929-30): 359-78, 550-67; 25 (1930-31): 102-15, 306-21, 474-89. Douthit, Mary O. *A Souvenir of Western Women.* 1905. Evans, James W. *Journal of a Trip to California.* (MS). Farnham, Thomas J. *Travels in the Great Western Prairies, the Anahuac and Rocky Mountains, and in the Oregon Territory,* vol. 1. 1843. Field, Matthew C. *Prairie and Mountain Sketches.* Edited by K. L. Gregg and J. F. McDermott. Collected by C. and M. R. Porter. 1957. Geer, Elizabeth. "Diary Written on the Oregon Trail in 1847," *Transactions, Oregon Pioneer Association—*(1907): 153-85. Geiger, Vincent, and Bryarly, Wakeman. *Trail to California.* Edited by D. M. Potter. 1945. Hancock, S. *The Narrative of Samuel Hancock (1845-1860).* 1927. Hastings, Lansford W. *Emigrants' Guide to Oregon and California.* 1845. Hines, C. "Diary of Celinda Hines," *Transactions, Oregon Pioneer Association—*(1918): 69-125. Irving, Washington. *Adventures of Captain Bonneville.* 1847. Johnson, Overton, and Winter, William H. *Route Across the Rocky Mountains.* 1846. Ketcham, Rebecca. "From Ithaca to Clatsop Plains," *Oregon Historical Quarterly* 62 (1961): 237-87, 337-402. Kurz, R. F. *Journal of Rudolph Friederich Kurz.* Edited by J. N. B. Hewitt. Translated by M. Jarrell. 1937. Lee, J. "Diary of Rev. Jason Lee," *Oregon Historical Quarterly* 17 (1916): 116-46, 240-66, 397-430. Lenox, Edward H. *Overland to Oregon in 1843.* Edited by R. Whitaker. 1904. Lockley, Fred. "Recollections of Benjamin Franklin Bonney," *Oregon Historical Quarterly* 24 (1923): 36-55. Longsworth, B. N. *The Diary of Basil Nelson Longsworth.* 1927. Lord, Israel, M.D. Journal (incomplete), with excerpts from the Elgin, Ill., *Western Christian.* McComas, E. S. *A Journal of Travel.* Introduction by M. Schmitt. 1954. Marcy, Randolph B. *The Prairie Traveler, A Hand-Book for Overland Expeditions.* 1859. Meeker, Ezra, and Driggs, Howard. *Covered Wagon Centennial and Ox Team Days.* 1932. Miller, James D. "Early Oregon Scenes, A Pioneer Narrative," *Oregon Historical Quarterly* 31 (1930): 55-68, 160-80, 275-84. Minto, John. "Reminiscences of Experiences on the Oregon Trail in 1844," *Oregon Historical Quarterly* 2 (1901): 119-67, 209-54. Missionary Letters, American Board of Commissioners of Foreign Missions, vol. 138, letter 101. Newberry Library, Chicago. (Transcript). Mudge, Z. A. *The Missionary Teacher, A Memoir of Cyrus Shepard.* 1848. Munger, A. "Diary of Asahel Munger and Wife (1839)," *Oregon Historical Quarterly* 8 (1907): 387-415. Nesmith, James W. "Diary Written While Crossing the Plains in 1843," *Transactions, Oregon Pioneer Association—*(1876)—. Newby, W. T. "William T. Newby's Diary of the Emigration of 1843," edited by H. N. J. Winton, *Oregon Historical Quarterly* 40 (1939): 219-42. Palmer, Joel. *Journal of Travels Over the Rocky Mountains 1845-1846.* 1847. Parker, Samuel. *Journal of an Exploring Tour Beyond the Rocky Mountains 1835-7.* 1838. Parkman, Francis. *The California and Oregon Trail.* 1849. Parrish, Edward E. "Crossing the Plains in 1844," *Transactions, Oregon Pioneer Association* 16 (1888): 82-121. Pigman, W. G. *Journal of Walter G. Pigman.* Edited by U. S. Fowkes. 1942. Preuss, Charles. *Exploring with Frémont.* Edited and translated by E. G. and E. K. Gudde. 1958. Pringle, V. K. "Diary of Virgil K. Pringle," *Transactions, Oregon Pioneer Association—*(1920): 281-300. Robidoux, O. M. *Memorial to the Robidoux Brothers.* 1924. Sappington, John, M.D. *The Theory and Treatment of Fevers* (Revised and corrected by F. Stith, M.D.). 1844. Sawyer, Lorenzo. *Way Sketches.* Edited by E. Eberstadt. 1926. Shaw, Reuben Cole. *Across the Plains in Forty-Nine.* 1896. Smith, William E. "The Oregon Trail Through Pottawatomie County," *Kansas State Historical Society Collections* 17 (1928): 435-64. Stansbury, Capt. Howard. *Exploration and Survey of the Valley of the Great Salt Lake of Utah.* 1853. Stewart, Agnes. "The Journey to Oregon—A Pioneer Girl's Diary," edited by C. W. Churchill, *Oregon Historical Quarterly* 29 (1928): 77-98. Stuart, Robert. *The Discovery of the Oregon Trail.* Edited by P. A. Rollins. 1935. Thompson, M. Article in *St. Joseph Gazette,* February 23, 1849. Townsend, John K. *Narrative of a Journey Across the Rocky Mountains to the Columbia River.* 1839. Wells, Eugene T. "The Growth of Independence, Missouri, 1827-1850," *Bulletin of the Missouri Historical Society* 16 (1959): 33-46. Whitman, Narcissa P. *Coming of the White Women, 1836.* Compiled by T. C. Elliott. 1937. Whitman, Narcissa P. "A Journey Across the Plains in 1836: Journal of Mrs. Marcus Whitman," *Transactions, Oregon Pioneer Association—*(1891)—. Williams, Joseph. *Narrative of a Tour from the State of Indiana to the Oregon Territory in the Years 1841-2.* 1843. Wislizenus, F. A., M.D. *A Journey to the Rocky Mountains in the Year 1839.* 1912. Wyeth, Capt. Nathaniel J. *Correspondence and Journals.* 1899.

Books

Bancroft, George. *History of Oregon,* vol. 1. 1886. Clark, Dan E. *The West in American History.* 1937. Dodge, Grenville M. *Biographical Sketch of James Bridger, Mountaineer, Trapper and Guide.* 1905. Drury, Clifford M. *Elkanah and Mary Walker, Pioneers Among the Spokanes.* 1940. Drury, Clifford M., ed. *First White Women Over the Rockies,* 2 vols. 1963. Dunbar, Seymour. *A History of Travel in America,* 4 vols. 1915. Ghent, W. J. *The Road to Oregon, A Chronicle of the Great Emigrant Trail.* 1929. Grinnell, George B. *Pawnee Hero Stories and Folk Tales.* 1889. Hafen, LeRoy R., and Young, Francis M. *Fort Laramie and the Pageant of the West, 1834-1890.* 1938. Henderson, Paul C. *The Landmarks of the Oregon Trail.* 1953. Mattes, M. J., *Great Platte River Road,* 1969. Thwaites, R. G., ed. *Early Western Travels, 1748-1846,* 32 vols. 1904-7.

Federal Documents

Annual Report of the Quartermaster General, of the Operations of the Quartermaster's Department. For the fiscal year ending on the 30th of June, 1850. Frémont, John C. *Report of the Exploring Expedition to the Rocky Mountains in the Year 1842, and to Oregon and North California in the Years 1843-44.* 28th Cong. and sess., Sen. Ex. Doc., No. 174 (Serial, 461), 1845. *Report to the Quartermaster General, of the March of the Regiment of Mounted Riflemen to Oregon from May 18 to Oct. 5, 1849.* (In the form of a journal.) U.S. War Dept. Report, 1849-50. *Report of Smith, Jackson and Sublette (1830) on Reaching South Pass and Prospects of Traveling over Mountains to the Pacific.* 21st Cong., 2nd sess., Sen. Doc., No. 39.

Index